SOUTH ITAL...

CW00643876

LEO ZANELLI
081 341 3655

Other books by the author

PALLADIO'S VILLAS: LIFE IN THE RENAISSANCE COUNTRYSIDE

SOUTH ITALY

A Traveller's Guide

♦ ♦ ♦

PAUL HOLBERTON

JOHN MURRAY

© Paul Holberton 1992

First published in 1992
by John Murray (Publishers) Ltd.,
50 Albemarle Street, London W1X 4BD

The moral right of the author has been asserted

All rights reserved
Unauthorized duplication
contravenes applicable laws

A catalogue record for this book is available from the British Library

ISBN 0-7195-4902-7

Typeset in 10½/12pt Garamond Book by
Rowland Phototypesetting Ltd., Bury St Edmunds, Suffolk
Printed and bound in Great Britain by
Biddles Ltd, Guildford and King's Lynn

Contents

Illustrations

The author and publishers would like to thank the following for permission to reproduce pictures: Plate 12 © Heinz Götze, *Castel del Monte*, Prestel Verlag, Munich, 1991, 3rd edition; Plates 14 & 15 © Patrizia Mastrorilli; Plate 19 by courtesy of the Italian State Tourist Office (E.N.I.T.), London; Plates 24 & 27 © Serge Chirol. All the other photographs were taken by the author.

Ground Plans

In the plans the following conventions have been used: full black indicates a surviving masonry elevation; full white between outlines indicates lost or vestigial masonry; shaded areas indicate a later or irrelevant addition; dotted lines indicate an interior vaulting system.

Acknowledgements

I am grateful to Michael Rose, who wrote the material on the Southern-born composers Piccinni, Paisiello, Mercadante, Giordano and Vinci, and on the castrati Farinelli and Caffarelli.

I am grateful to Italiatour, the Italian specialist tour operator in London (241 Euston Road, London NW1 2BU; tel: 071 383 3886), whose generous loan of a hire car for two weeks made possible my final exploration of Calabria.

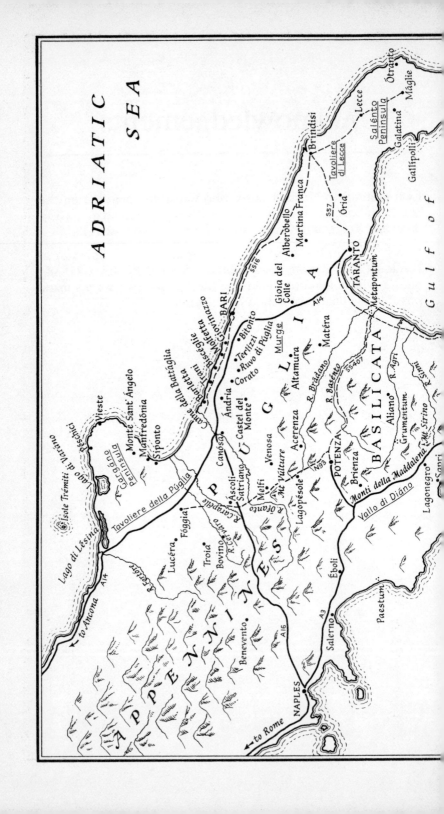

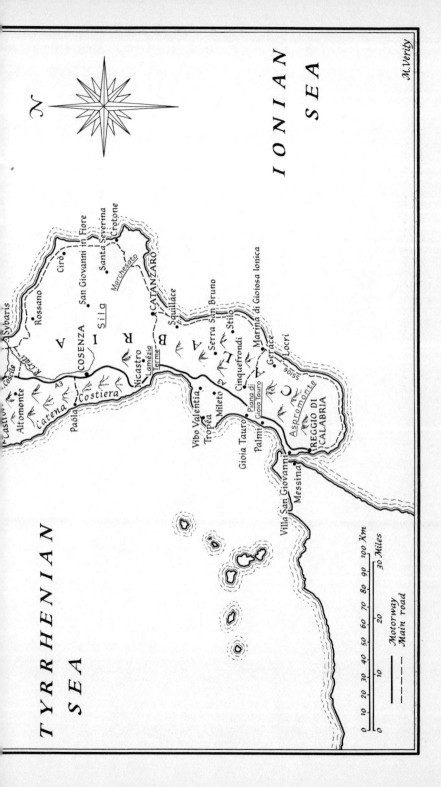

Foreword

Foreigners commonly believe the south of Italy to be all of a piece, but the regions of Campania, that is Naples and its hinterland, of Puglia, that is the heel of Italy, and of Basilicata and Calabria, the instep and toe, are all different. It is true that from the time of the Norman conquest (completed by Roger II of Sicily in 1130) to the Unification of Italy, a mere 700 or more years, these four regions were one state, known as 'the Kingdom' (by contrast to the constitution of the rest of Italy). Undoubtedly the legacy of the Kingdom partly explains the divide that now exists between northern Italians and southern Italians, which is every bit as strong as the divide between English and Scots. But within the south there are again antitheses and antagonisms, large geographic and economic variations, and diversities in values and outlook, even if the heel and the toe are about equal in the degree to which they are unknown.

It is still the case that 'for most travellers . . . the Columns of Hercules are situated at Naples, and, once having arrived there, they return home satisfied', as one Georg Arnold Jacobi wrote in preface to his epistles from Puglia in 1792. Others have regarded the extreme south as belonging properly to Africa rather than Europe. Today people make excursions from the Bay of Naples out to Paestum, but no further. Flying into Italy, you still have to change 'planes to reach BARI or BRINDISI or COSENZA or CATANZARO. By train, the journey from Milan to Rome is four hours; from Rome to REGGIO CALABRIA, the same distance, it is seven, when the train is not late. Few would drive from Milan to Rome without stopping, but after Naples, where does one stop? However, not only the Autostrada del Sole but more, very new roads are opening up all of southern Italy as never before.

Very few package holidays are available from Britain to the 'deep' south, while few will have call to visit on business. Therefore, even though daily prices are a little less than in the north of Italy, it is comparatively expensive to get there, to stay there and to get around. Furthermore, to see any of the sights, you will have to have a car (or a great deal of time). Driving around, unless you want simply to broil your brains on a beach, is essential, because neither heel nor toe have cities worth staying a week in, and the things to see are scattered. But driving is a great joy in the south, if you like the open road. Indeed, unless you simply want the sun, most of the point of going to the south is exploration.

Should one wish to travel about in an exotic, often empty land still largely unconscious of tourism, the south will remain available for a few years yet. It will perhaps have just about caught up with the 20th century by the time we enter the 21st. It offers fresh territory of a kind exceedingly rare in Europe today. (It is almost completely unknown to the British tourist industry. Italian tourism is highly seasonal and beach bound, as is most German; but anyway the spaces are vast. The most discriminating tourists are the French. I have never heard, met or seen an American there or who has been there, with the important exception of bilingual descendants of emigrants.) So, while you can go into any high street travel agent and book a holiday in the Bay of Naples, not even the Italian state agencies of Italiatour and CIT list hotels or villas in Puglia or Calabria (though they offer to prepare you a package or itinerary on request). Gladly instead the tourist industry will send you to Sicily – preferably Taormina – or virtually anywhere in the Mediterranean so long as it is not Puglia or Calabria. But again, just as the new roads have transformed and quickened travelling, so now there are at last hotels and some restaurants. It is fair to say that the main preoccupation of 19th- and early 20th-century travellers, and consequently the recurrent topic of their travel accounts, was finding somewhere tolerable to sleep and something tolerable to eat and drink. Today that is no longer a problem, thanks to the Italians' own tourism and a greater demand for business hotels (virtually all hotels in the south are business hotels).

There are some other good reasons to visit the heel and toe, besides their being remote and unknown. There are sea, sky and beaches everywhere, some of them so photogenic one is amazed they have not been used for brochure copy. Otherwise, the heel and the toe differ. The heel has a more interesting history and many more signs of it: every town has something of note, and it is densely settled. It has particular beauties, such as the GARGANO PENINSULA or the Baroque churches of LECCE, or the unique CASTEL DEL MONTE. The toe is a land of general scenery, some of it dreary, much of it exhilarating, in which only here or there towns or villages have a history or anything to see – usually a castle. However, peculiarly in Basilicata and Calabria, the quality of what there is to see is less important than the pleasure of coming across it in the middle of nowhere. It is a considerable pleasure, especially perhaps for those who are already well travelled.

The history, the monuments – but there is no painting to speak of, except Giovanni Andrea Coppola in Gallipoli or Mattia Preti in Taverna; no Renaissance or Baroque sculpture to compare with the wealth of the rest of Italy, except perhaps the Indian-looking stone-work of lo Zingarello in LECCE; sometimes charming, but no important period architecture. To enjoy the region the traveller has to take a large leap across time to the Middle Ages and antiquity. You have to set out to visit Magna Grecia, and the glittering cities of Sybaris and Taras; Roman Apulia, where Hannibal won CANNAE but could not use it, where Horace was born and Virgil died; Byzantine Calabria, where the 'eastern Romans' held on despite the penetration of the Lombards and the incursions of the Saracens until the Normans came. From the early 11th century to the later 13th, South Italy was a crucible of history. In the early 11th century the Byzantines of the Macedonian Renaissance reconquered 'all Italy as far as Rome', but began to lose it to the Normans almost immediately; the Hauteville family first marshalled the other Normans, then brutally subjugated their stolen territory into statehood, then gave it away to the German emperor through defect of male seed. In the early 13th century northern Puglia became the homeland of the Swabian Frederick II 'stupor mundi' and the holdout of his son Manfred, who lost it to Charles of Anjou whose ambitions were checked by the Sicilian Vespers in 1282. End of story: Charles made Naples his capital; thereafter the rest of the south of Italy became provincial and marginal, reduced to poverty and depopulation by the dire combination of an absentee and unenlightened government inheriting an effectively centralised feudal base.

It must be repeated that the heel and the toe are different. After Unification in 1861, eventually Puglia recovered and is now prosperous: Puglia, unlike Basilicata and much of Calabria, is not naturally poor. In the 18th century, when the Kingdom was at its nadir, no traveller failed to observe how very fertile Puglia nevertheless was, which roused especially German Protestants to indignation at the appalling government. The French who came would more charitably attribute its poverty to lack of water. Both those deficiencies have since been remedied, by the Acquedotto Pugliese, built between the Wars, which pipes water from the Appennines both to the northern prairie and to the flat, rocky orchards of southern Puglia, and by full integration into the economic and political system of federal Italy, which still may not conform to Nordic ideals but is more than viable. Puglia, as the director of the Chamber of Commerce in BARI crisply informed me, is currently a net exporter both to the rest of the world and to the rest of Italy. Again unlike Calabria, it is not a land of Mafia, which in its primary stage flourishes only where the economic opportunities are limited. BARI is truly a Milan of the south, except – as the adage has it – they have lakes and we have the sea; but if the city gains by brine it loses by lack of Attic salt.

Not so Calabria and Basilicata. Here the poverty remains not simply one of people but of place, not the dregs of a buoyant society but the contaminant. Agriculture can be profitable in the Sila and in the fertile plains, from which malaria was at last eliminated by American DDT after the Second World War; nevertheless, the peninsula remains weak in the secondary and tertiary sectors – industry, which can be an eyesore in Puglia, is hardly present at all. Even in a modern city like COSENZA, economically the richest in Calabria, there do not seem to be properly businessmen, only commercial travellers; no variety of shops, only shops selling cheap shoes. And if the virtual serfdom and the brigandage rife in the 18th and 19th centuries have vanished together with the donkeys and the hoes, a recidivist mentality haunts Basilicata and Calabria; Calabria even more than Sicily is the cradle of the Mafia (here called 'ndrangheta). All the money seems to be government money (which is why the row over the division of administration between the rival capitals of REGGIO DI CALABRIA and CATANZARO was so bitter) and it seems as if it is poured away leaving nothing altered except the worsening environment; this land once of monasteries and castles threatens to become a land of quarries and concrete, still more so than in Greece.

It is worth emphasizing once again that things really have changed. One indication is precisely the nature of the Mafia crime that is taken as a sign of the area's backwardness. Actually the Mafia today no more resembles the Mafia of a hundred or even fifty years ago than, for instance, does the Catholic Church. In the same way it may seem to have become still more absurd and inhuman, but that is because its practice and conditions have updated, not retrogressed. Anyway, given Northern Ireland, civil violence is not a yardstick for the British to use. Again, the myth of the primitive peasant which such writers as Norman Douglas and Carlo Levi inflated has been blown away by cars, television and refrigerators – leaving, unfortunately perhaps, people who, instead of making the sign against the evil eye or chasing a solitary scrawny chicken in Bruegelian uproar round the village for the pot of the visiting *signore*, eat pizzas like the rest of us.

This is not a book about the Problem of the Mezzogiorno; it is written for the 'passionate sightseer' in Berenson's phrase, with particular emphasis on the medieval history and monuments, which animate me. It is divided into two parts, the heel and the toe. In the first part, I set off from Trajan's Arch in BENEVENTO, roughly following the old via Appia Trajana across the north Puglia plain and down the Adriatic coast as if to take ship for Greece; since BENEVENTO was the capital of the region in the high Middle Ages, it also provides a fitting overture to South Italy's medieval history. In the second part, my starting point is Eboli, where 'Christ stopped' in Carlo Levi's book of that name. Eboli is a quite undistinguished town in southern Campania, the gateway not to a road but to a desert where men are 'not men but beasts, beasts of burden', as Carlo Levi put it. To be clear, he was writing about Basilicata, the smallest and poorest province of Italy where it is still today difficult to communicate or to sympathize; everybody seems to be wall-eyed. Calabria is larger and more varied and its people much more genial. Though they are few and scattered, Calabria has some magnificent monuments, besides castles: the cathedral at GERACE is one of the most beautiful churches in the world.

One does not need to come to the south from the north, nor, coming down the Italian peninsula, to go via Naples, although it remains the usual route from Rome. While travelling roughly southwards from my two different starting points, I have been forced sometimes to move crablike to east or west, or even to backtrack. (There are inconveniences in any arrangement of the material, but none that cannot be redeemed by the index.) I hope this book will help to give some colour to otherwise ghostly names: I have tried to write about them in such a way that the reader can both use the book while travelling and read it when not. I have tried not to say South Italy is more wonderful than it is, but I would be happy to have led anyone to the wonders it has.

Cross references within the text are indicated by SMALL CAPITALS.

ITINERARY ONE

THE HEEL

On the via Appia (Benevento and Capua)

Nowadays in Benevento one can sit in a café and contemplate the Rome side of Trajan's Arch: they have pedestrianized the street leading down to it and chained off the surrounding tarmac, although the local youth still like to park their motorcycles against it. The Arch is impressive: such a dense and grand programme of sculpture, comprising so many deeply carved life-size figures (cleaned and well preserved), is a rarity anywhere. Further down the via Appia, there will be no other Roman antiquity to match it. It has never been buried; incorporated into the city walls in the Middle Ages, it was known as the Golden Gate, a perennial reminder to South Italians, medieval and modern, that they are pygmies beside their ancestors. Since it was built, only one man in this vicinity has measured himself shoulder to shoulder with Trajan, and that is the Emperor Frederick II Hohenstaufen, whose Gate at Capua originally rose almost twice the height of the Arch at Benevento, and again carried accomplished life-size figures, if not so many.

Both Frederick's Gate at Capua and Trajan's Arch at Roman Beneventum stood over the 'queen of the long roads' as Domitian's client poet Statius called it in the 1st century AD, the via Appia that led from Rome down to Naples and then crossed the ankle of Italy to the southern Adriatic ports, in particular Brundisium (BRINDISI). It was built as far as Capua on the initiative of Appius Claudius when he was censor in 312 BC, an essential first step towards the Roman conquest of Magna Grecia. At Capua the road was carried on six arches over the river Volturno – until the bridge was destroyed in the Second World War. Frederick's Gate guarded the northern side of the intact bridge. The same Appius Claudius, old and blind, harangued the Senate not to accept terms during the war with Pyrrhus in 279 and urged the Romans to pursue the conquest of the whole of Apulia; it was a speech later learnt by Roman schoolboys. After the conquest the via Appia was extended to Roman Tarentum (Greek Taras, modern TARANTO) and Brundisium, and from 148 BC onwards it was continued on the other side of the water from

Dyrracchium (Durazzo) across Macedonia to the straits of the
Bosphorus, as the via Egnatia. This was the land route between
Rome and Constantinople, not only during antiquity but throughout
the high Middle Ages and the period of the Crusades.

Originally, from Capua and Beneventum the via Appia crossed to
Venusium (VENOSA) and Tarentum, the greatest city of Magna Grecia,
and thence across to Brundisium, but as Brundisium became the
more important port a more direct, northern route was preferred,
notably by Horace in the journey he describes in *Satires* (Book 1,5).
Though Venusium was his birthplace, he preferred to travel through
little places staying at rustic inns in the mountains until he reached
Canusium (CANOSA), Rubi (RUVO), Barium (BARI) and down the coast
to Brundisium. A still more northerly route, faster because it had
fewer mountainous stages, was relaid by Trajan in the first decade of
the 2nd century AD and is known as the via Appia Trajana. The Appia
Trajana entered Apulia at TROIA (Roman Aecae) and thence crossed
the plain to Herdoniae, now an archaeological site, then to CANOSA;
there was also a branch past Luceria (LUCERA) to Sipontum (SIPONTO,
re-founded in the 13th century as Manfredonia). Yet another road
through the Appennines existed, one which Horace's contemporary
the Greek geographer Strabo cursorily describes, and which probably already in Lombard times had become the usual way, travelling
along the valley of the Cervaro and leaving the mountains at BOVINO
(Roman Vibinum), not far south of TROIA. It remained the preferred
route until the 20th century; the railway comes down this valley as
well. But the motorway A16 Naples-Canosa passes further to the
south again, nearer the old via Appia, in fact along the route Horace
probably took, down the valley of the Calaggio, which becomes the
Carapelle and emerges on to the plain beneath Ascoli Satriano
(Ausculum), a key fortress since antiquity.

Trajan's Arch was a symbolic gateway to the east, commemorating his rebuilding of the road and incidentally his victories against
the Dacians in modern Romania. Frederick II's Gate at Capua, on the
other hand, guarded a frontier: the duchy of Capua was the northernmost part of the Kingdom that had been forged by Roger II in the
years following AD 1127, and the road continued further north to
Montecassino and into papal territory. During the intervening millennium the Empire had been dismembered, although it had never
at any definable moment fallen: rather it had been repeatedly diluted
by successive waves of tribes descending from the north, each one
of which Romanized less and knew less how to keep what it had

taken. The worst of the barbarians, still worse than Attila and the Huns, had been the Ostrogoths led by Totila, whose figure is traumatically engraved in the popular history of several medieval Italian cities. Even though Totila was eventually defeated in 552 by Justinian's general Narses, Narses decided not to fight the Lombards but to allow them to take possession among the ruins. Paradoxically the Lombards seem to have been some of the feeblest of the barbarians, though they were numerous, and altered the language, customs and cities of Italy more profoundly than any others. Large, lumbering cowherds – though they turned to agriculture on arrival in Italy – the Lombards were usually disunited, and their king in the north, residing in Pavia, seldom received homage from the 'duchies' of Spoleto and Benevento in the south. In the south the Lombards fought and sometimes defeated but never overcame the Byzantines, and they were equally ineffectual against raiding Saracens. In the north their rule was destroyed by Charlemagne, who defeated king Desiderius in 774, but Desiderius's kingdom did not include the 'duchy' of Benevento, which, under the successor of the energetic Arech II (758–787), continued in existence until the 11th century.

In Benevento Arech II built the church of Santa Sofia (Holy Wisdom), still standing, and founded the adjacent monastery, famous until the Norman period for the *beneventana* script of its scriptorium. The dedication to Holy Wisdom seems deliberately to have echoed Justinian's great Hagia Sophia in Constantinople, for in the same sort of way Arech's church was to be a national sanctuary. Architecturally it is not related to Hagia Sophia, but it imitates the central plan of the imperial church of San Vitale in Ravenna, though it is smaller. There is an alternative idea that its peculiar plan – star-shaped, with sixteen internal columns forming a concentric decagon and hexagon, over which rose the dome – reproduced the kingly tent, and particularly from the outside (obfuscated by later building) the ten gables of its roof would have resembled canvas pleated over so many poles. But that is to dismiss almost altogether any continuity from the Roman past. By the same token Frederick's octagonal castle at CASTEL DEL MONTE would reflect only recent Islamic fashion, without reference to the imperial tradition which he consciously perpetuated elsewhere. The point can be argued. But there is an undeniable continuity in the vaulting system of Santa Sofia, which is late Roman, though crude and cramped. So, too, in the rest of southern Italy it was never forgotten how to build a dome. Near Trajan's Arch the church of Sant'Ilario a Port'Aurea, a small, two-bay

building of the late 7th or early 8th century, has a nave of consecu-
tive square compartments each surmounted by a dome, and is a type
that recurs in Puglia. Recently the isolated church at Seppannibale
has been recognized as another of the same; also the church of San
Salvatore on MONTE SANT'ANGELO, which was a Lombard shrine.

The great number of churches and monasteries in the city and in
the Lombard duchy of Benevento include the abbey of Montecassino, founded by St Benedict (and still possessing at least his
tomb), re-founded by the Lombards, to become in the 11th century a
hearth of Church renewal. A counterflowing Byzantine contribution
to this 'Gregorian' reform should not be overlooked, for example
through the spiritual leadership of a figure such as St Nilus from
ROSSANO. In the general European revival of the 11th century, southern Italy was particularly awake: Amalfi, Naples and Salerno had
emerged as independent trading cities almost before the high
Middle Ages were over. A comparable ebullience on the Adriatic
coast was accompanied by the newly strengthened rule of the
Byzantines, which prevented a city such as BARI achieving autonomy.
But first the Saracen threat – intermittently devastating in southern
Italy throughout the 8th, 9th and 10th centuries – had to be met and
turned, a task the Byzantines were pursuing with an expedition to
Sicily when they were first attacked on the mainland by a brigade of
Normans. Eventually the Normans, exploiting that well-timed in-
road, drove out both powers both from the island and from the
mainland, and from the bridgehead of the Greeks' western interests
Puglia was swung rapidly round to become the platform for the
Latins' eastern ambition: Robert Guiscard had led an abortive Norman expedition into the Balkans as early as 1079, nearly 20 years
before the first Crusade. In circumstances very different from their
distant cousins' conquest of England (not least because Sicily was
conquered in the pope's name from the heathen), the Hauteville
family transformed a march into a kingdom, which for a moment
under Roger II was the greatest in Europe.

Inheriting Roger II's kingdom at the end of the 12th century,
Frederick II was bound by a vassaldom to the pope which rubbed up
inflammably against the imperial status he held from Germany. In
1229 the unspeakable paradox was achieved of Frederick wearing
his crown as king of Jerusalem in Jerusalem beneath the Dome of the
Rock in a state of excommunication declared by the pope for the
very fault of his not having gone on Crusade as he had sworn to do.
The Gate at Capua, preventing any attempt to cross the Volturno,

was erected by Frederick after his return, in a campaign of fortification undertaken after Gregory IX had fomented rebellion during his absence in the Holy Land. While he lived, Frederick fought the pope successfully, though the success he wanted was not to fight at all. At the same time the Gate at Capua is a manifesto of the efficient, bureaucratic, pyramidal statehood that Frederick developed from its Norman foundation, and which was the most advanced in medieval Europe. Unfortunately he failed to determine its posthumous ownership. He both developed the Kingdom progressively and as a result lastingly destroyed its future capacity.

Only stumps of the Gate's towers and fragments of its sculpture survive, but there is a 13th-century chronicler's report of the admiration it excited: 'This is the bridge on which . . . Frederick built two towers of marvellous size, strength and beauty, expending 20,000 ounces of pure gold, and there had carved his effigy for eternal and immortal memory, extending its arms and raising two fingers, the mouth seeming to thunder the following verses of furious threat . . . "How miserable I make those whose fortune I know how to change!"' That was written above the emperor. Below him, round a huge female bust, were the words 'Thanks to Caesar's imperial rule I, the concord of the Kingdom, am made'. Beneath and to either side of Concordia, two male busts announced: 'Let them enter safely who seek to live purely' and 'Let the faithless fear to be turned away or thrust into prison'. These verses announce totalitarian tyranny. The first suggests that the emperor is master of changeable Fortune, otherwise regarded in the Middle Ages as mistress of men's state. The third and fourth, with their biblical echoes, declare his spiritual as well as secular authority. Roger II had founded his kingdom on an equation of God's peace with the crown's decree, and so in his famous law codes Frederick equated heretics and traitors; here the 'pure' and the 'faithless' may as well be spiritual as secular offenders.

The elimination of discord and impurity struck above all at the cities, which were subsequently agents of the Renaissance in the rest of Europe but had been rendered inactive here. The Communes with whom Frederick battled hard in the north survived, while urban autonomy and enterprise were crushed in the south. Nevertheless the Italian Renaissance, though germinated by the Communes, had seeds here – both in so far as it depended on emulation of classical antiquity and more broadly. The head of *Concord*, which survives from the Gate in the civic museum at Capua, is a close copy of an Augustan Roman *Juno* (in a style itself influenced by Classical Greece, therefore binding in both aspects of Apulia's past); the male busts are an early instance of the revival of the Roman 'clipeate' or round-niche bust. In the history of Western art, the sculpture of Frederick's reign in southern Italy is a crucial link between the classicizing figures of Reims cathedral (about 1220) and of Bamberg (about 1230) and those of Nicola Pisano (active from about 1260), who is known to have trained in Puglia. In the history of Western political evolution, it is significant that the Communes attempted to found their states on the very same ideal of Concord. Concordia appears again, for example, as an allegorical figure in Ambrogio Lorenzetti's *Good Government* fresco in Siena, a century later. Frederick's imperial iconography soon fell away after his death in 1250, but his reign was nothing if not catalytic.

After the death of Frederick's son Manfred in 1266 outside the walls of Benevento, in battle against the usurper Charles of Anjou, the south of Italy soon became a much less important region in European history. The imperial dimension was removed, the pope who had so frequently journeyed southwards was on his way to Avignon, and the Kingdom itself was broken up by the Sicilian Vespers. By losing Sicily and by residing by preference in Naples, Charles initiated the provincialisation of both toe and heel; in addition petty war between Sicily and Calabria dragged on for a century. The decline of the provinces happened only gradually: Charles's son Charles II and his successor good king Robert travelled and dispensed patronage in all parts of the Kingdom – from BARLETTA to ROSSANO – but with the reign of Joanna I the crown's central power ebbed and was to prove irrecoverable. Until the end of the Anjou dynasty the Kingdom lay under the pall of the horrible, unsolved murder in 1348 of the young Andrew shortly after his marriage to Joanna, a marriage intended to heal the dissensions of Charles II's many children and children's children. A monomaniac Angevin ruler uniting the territory of South Italy, Hungary and Yugoslavia might have achieved incalculable wonders. But no.

It should be explained that Robert, his successor, was Charles II's third son, the second son having been Louis, saintly bishop of Toulouse, and the first Charles-Martel, who died in 1296 but not childless: his son Carobert ruled Hungary while Robert ruled Naples, two wise kings in harmony until their deaths in 1342 and 1343. Carobert had two sons, Louis, who inherited Hungary, and Andrew, who should have ruled Naples as Joanna's consort; Joanna was the daughter of Robert's early deceased son Charles, duke of Calabria. Charles II's other sons Philip and John were the founders respectively of the rival lines of Taranto and Durazzo; Philip's grandson Louis married Joanna after Andrew's murder, and John's son Charles married Joanna's younger sister Maria, but for all the incestuous matchmaking the internecine jostling was ceaseless. Furthermore, Charles II's four daughters had carried dowries that alienated further parcels of the royal demesne to scheming husbands. John of Durazzo's grandson, Charles of Durazzo's nephew, became Joanna's successor Charles III, founder of the 'second house of Anjou', an unstable edifice.

After gaining the Kingdom in 1443 even Alfonso of Aragon the Magnanimous could scarcely attempt to unprise the hold of the barons ensconced on its territory and in its justice and finances, and his heirs were unable to secure the crown against them when they chose to combine with a foreign power. Occupancy of the throne was decided on the broader field of European politics, by the defeat of king Francis I of France by emperor Charles V of Spain and Germany. From Charles's victory in 1529 until the advent of Napoleon, the Spanish viceroyalty remained unchallenged by the French. During that time it was able successfully to stymie the barons' nuisance, but abjectly avoided attempting any control over their treatment of their own feudal subjects – townspeople as well as peasants – despite numerous uprisings.

From the time of Joanna I the rulers of the Kingdom budged more seldom from Naples, while the unregenerate barons became ever more overlording lords and unaccountable counts – except in so far as they, too, became absentee, gaming away their distant castles at tables in Naples during the later Spanish viceroyalty. Corsairs depopulated the coasts, arable land went to pasturage, and brigands depredated, while cancerous Naples became the largest city in Italy, having already reached perhaps 200,000 during the Renaissance, phenomenal for that time. Politically there was plenty of ferment, but it was always repressed and nothing was changed or initiated. Not quite nothing, perhaps: but the fair Baroque of a city like LECCE is an exception proving the rule, since those churches were mostly built with the money and piety of its market-town burghers, a social stratum generally thin in the Kingdom. Otherwise the impotence and indiscrimination of the crown were compounded by the indifference and deliberate inertia of the barons: certainly the aristocratic ideal of public service in return for privilege did not inspire them.

Their perennial lack of responsibility and cohesion, in Benedetto Croce's famous indictment of 1925, left a nation dispossessed of nationhood, a land without a history; after the Norman conquest, the only significant history it had was other people's history, not its own. Croce's point of view can be challenged, but it is mostly the other people's history that other people go to South Italy to see.

1

Capitanata

Bovino

In the 18th century, and probably for a long time earlier, the usual road into Puglia was the present SS 90, on the track of a Roman road which ran between the via Appia Trajana to the north and the original via Appia to the south. It passes through the Valle di Bovino, a bosky valley giving good cover for the brigands that frequently infested it. Descending, you have crossed a watershed: the river is the Cervaro, which flows to the east across the TAVOLIERE to the flats of Manfredonia. Above on the right the city of Bovino (Vibinum) was an important settlement in both Roman and medieval times; its main square is probably the old forum and its cathedral dates to the late 10th century. Coming out of the valley, travellers crossed the river at the Ponte di Bovino on to what is now the SS 161, heading for ancient Herdoniae or later Orta Nova, where there was civilization in the shape of a Jesuit settlement.

Today Bovino is satisfyingly remote, to the outer world unknown and by it undisturbed; it was the quieter when I arrived because the entire town seemed to be attending a funeral in the cathedral. Wandering around I eventually found two housewives gossiping on their doorsteps whom I asked the whereabouts of the church of San Pietro, but was told by the elder of them that she did not know, it was in another part of town. The younger woman was more willing to provide directions, but finished with: 'It's easier to arrive there than explain.' Fortunately, San Pietro is only one of hundreds of small Romanesque churches in South Italy.

At the cathedral the funeral had finished: I moved in as they poured out. The church was reconstructed after an earthquake in 1930, and as a result looks a little too clean. Nevertheless the great thick rendered walls and diminutive clerestory windows, the short rows of columns framed by heavy piers, the block-like details and box-like, uneasy space, usher you immediately into the Ottonian era, recalling German churches of the same date. Otto I the Great led armies into this region during his quarrels with the Byzantine emperors which were eventually resolved, in 972, by the marriage of his son Otto II with Theophania the sister of Basil II the Bulgar-slayer. Here at Bovino in 969 he was beseiging the Byzantine garrison guarding the pass into Puglia, when an embassy from Constantinople arrived offering negotiations. Afterwards the cathedral was undertaken, probably by the first bishop of the city, John, who is mentioned in 971. Since in the peace Otto gave up both his own and his Lombard allies' claims to the region, and Byzantine power was firmly reconsolidated during the following half century, John was presumably a Byzantine appointment – made in response, however, to an earlier bull of pope John XIII (965–72) on the matter of bishops specifically in Bovino and nearby Ascoli Satriano. Though schism of the Eastern and Western Churches was not to come until 1054, political and religious rivalry were already inextricable. On the other hand architectural style is no guide to political allegiance, since the church is 'Frankish' and its decoration Lombard.

The nave, beneath a wooden roof, leads up to a 'triumphal arch', a form familiar also in Anglo-Saxon churches; its piers have two sets of imposts, one to support the arch, the lower set once fitting into a screen or iconostasis which would have sealed off the choir or transept. The arch gives on to the crossing, a square beneath a dome that has vanished, though little arches across the angles of the square attest to it. Originally the crossing would have given on to an apse only, but the church was extended eastwards as early as the 12th century. The crossing is open on either side to spaces that can just as well be called *porticus* (as in Anglo-Saxon churches) as pastophories (as in Byzantine). The plan as a whole makes a neat oblong, within which the nave and transept describe a T; this scheme recurs throughout Puglia.

The original 10th- or 11th-century stucco window-grates are now detached and hung on the wall. Stucco was a favourite Lombard material, though the tradition goes back to Roman imperial building. Its chances of survival are not high, though examples exist in northern Italy. On these grilles, the fleshiness of the foliage and other motifs anticipates the plastic sense that characterizes the work of Acceptus, the early master, active around 1040, with whom Pugliese Romanesque sculpture begins. Elsewhere, and in South Italy outside the 'school of Acceptus', masons were carving the kind of flat, cut-out figures that can be seen here in the imposts on the east side of the crossing, supposed to have been transferred here when the façade was rebuilt. The façade is dated 1231 and signed by 'Zanus Gallicus', or Jean the Frenchman, but, Frenchman or not, he adapted the prevailing northern-Puglian pattern, found again at TROIA and FOGGIA, of a central rose window framed by colonettes.

Behind – or through – the cathedral the little church of San Marco has a consecration date of 1197; it was built to house the relics of a local St Mark – not the Evangelist – discovered in the cathedral by the incumbent bishop Robert in 1090. The story is perhaps not entirely untrue, since in some places in Puglia, notably the church at RUVO, burials under the church go back virtually to Roman times; I dare say Robert's evidence for the identification was rather scant, but the bishops had great authority in the community, and the sanctity seems to have been mutually reinforcing. The public buildings in the square have a collection of inscriptions and so on from the Roman city, and the 'Palazzo Ducale' incorporates a round tower that may be taken as Norman. Normans, under Drogo, second son of Tancred d'Hauteville, took the city in 1045: they established themselves first in the mountains (see below), then they took over the plain and seaboard.

Melfi and Venosa; Lagopesole

South of BOVINO a string of fortresses overlooks the plain from the easternmost peaks of the Appennines. The castle at Deliceto preserves a square Norman tower, Sant'Agata di Puglia has another castle and an even better view. At the exit of the valley of the Carapelle, Ascoli Satriano, Roman Ausculum, has a third peak-top castle, enclosing nothing visibly old, though the town is frequently mentioned in chronicles, and was of strategic importance for Pyrrhus (279 BC), Hannibal (217–09), during the Social War (91–89 BC), then for the Lombards, for the Arabs based in BARI (AD 861), the Byzantines, and the Normans, who took it in 1041; later it was held by powerful barons, notably the ubiquitous Orsini. On the same southern side, further up the Carapelle, Candela no longer has a fortress but has a pretty bit of old town, and nearby Rocchetta Sant'Antonio has both a ruined Norman castle and a 16th-century baronial lair. Across the present border with Campania, Lacedonia was once Roman Aquilonia (nearby modern Aquilonia is misplaced), through which the via Appia Antica passed before veering east-south-east towards Venusium (Venosa), crossing the Ofanto, Puglia's greatest river. On the far side, along what once was a winding, viewless way through hostile hills (there is now a swift tunnel-and-viaduct road), one reaches the fortress of Melfi in modern Basilicata.

In the year 1042 William Iron-arm, eldest son of Tancred d'Hauteville, became the accepted leader of a group of Normans who had a number of times defeated Byzantine troops sent against them and now securely occupied these mountain fortresses. By license of Weimar V of Salerno he took the title of count. While the Byzantines, for various external and internal reasons, weakened, the power of the Normans grew: meanwhile William was succeeded by his brother Drogo (count 1046–51), and Drogo by Humphrey (1051–7). With the failure of Byzantine authority the Holy Roman emperor and the pope were drawn into the vacuum, but Humphrey – with the aid of his stepbrother Robert known as the crafty ('Guiscard'), Tancred's eldest son by his second marriage – succeeded in destroying the concert of powers organized to extirpate him at the battle of Civitate in 1053.

Robert Guiscard, succeeding Humphrey, completed the conquest of Puglia and Calabria and in 1071 captured the seat of the Byzantine governor at BARI. Yet even as the Norman county became a duchy and then a kingdom, Melfi remained its heart. Up from Melfi at Venosa, Drogo had endowed the monastery in which he and his successors were to be buried, much as Edward the Confessor would endow Westminster up from London or Roger II would endow Cefalù across from Palermo. So it was at Melfi that in 1129 Roger II of Sicily held great court and received the submission he had forced from the mainland barons. One hundred years later, in 1231, Frederick II, heir to the Norman crown, promulgated at Melfi his Constitutions, codifying, systematizing and unifying his southern kingdom as a state.

The town's castle is sited in classic fashion on a mound, overseeing the hilltop town like the horn on the doge's cap. The road winds spirally up to the castle which is essentially circular, protected by a ditch with a drawbridge on the one side that is not sheer. It is splendid from a distance, but its central block no longer has much character, and most of it is not Norman but early Angevin, and the remainder 16th- or even 18th-century. At the time of writing it has not yet emerged from a prolonged restoration, though the museum it houses is open. One tower holds a sarcophagus (from a tomb on the via Appia) particularly magnificent for its size and state of preservation; it has an effigy of the deceased on the lid and a row of robust deities beneath. The museum contains some fine armour of the Greek Classical period from tombs discovered and excavated only during the last 25 years. The region was well populated in ancient times because the soil around the nearby extinct volcano of the Vulture has always been fertile; but it has also suffered repeatedly from earthquakes.

Down the hill from the castle the town is quiet, with old, narrow streets and very few shops; the hub of modern life, such as it is in the small towns of Basilicata, is in the new town in the valley. The central piazza beside the cathedral is frequently almost deserted. Of the Norman cathedral built from 1155 under William the Bad only the bell-tower has defied earthquake, with its griffins of inlaid black stone facing out over the road from the west. Though retaining the Norman plan, the church is entirely 18th-century, not unpleasing, though it is dark and its furniture heavy.

Over the next hill, the town of Rapolla also has a cathedral, or rather two, old and new, new being 13th-century. The new cathedral confronts a level square; steep alleys lead down the side of a ravine to the old cathedral. Evidently the settlement was once half troglodyte, like so many in the region, and round about there are cave churches, notably Santa Margherita, which has frescos. The new cathedral has a sculpted portal and immured in its flank reliefs patently copied from icons, inscribed with the names of the artist and patron, Sarolo and bishop Richard, who were busy also with the tower in the year 1209. The old cathedral has a unique plan: in outline it is an ordinary longitudinal nave-and-aisled, seven-bay, apsed church but at the second and sixth bays it has two small domes over the nave. Abutting the domes are transverse barrel-vaults, interrupting the sequence of groined vaults over the aisles, and creating two transepts, east and west. It might be compared to the church of Santi Nicolò e Cataldo, LECCE, of 1180, which has a similar dome and transept in the middle of the nave – one, however, not two – and also pointed arches. But this building is squat while Lecce is tall, and looks older (such gently pointed arches are indigenous and not necessarily, like Lecce's, French-influenced).

The Vulture is the name both of the volcano and of the district it dominates. On its southern side there are two lakes and the forest of Monticchio, with a cable-car to the top, and, to complete the excursion, an abbey at San Michele. Off the swift main road continu-

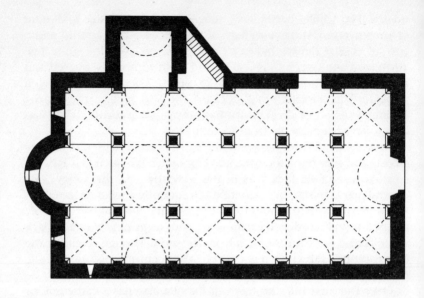

Old Cathedral, Rapolla

ing to POTENZA, Atella has a medieval old town. At Santa Maria di
Pierno, truly in the middle of nowhere, Sarolo built the church
between 1189 and 1197, before working at Rapolla. Though its
interior and east end were re-done in the 16th century, it is still
mostly his structure.

Further south, rising enticingly on its own hill with superb views
up and down the valley, is the castle of Lagopesole, one of the most
important surviving castles of Frederick II. His rebuilding on the site
is known to have begun in 1242 and evidently came to a halt on his
death in 1250, since the brackets in the north range patently carved
by his sculptors were not used for vaulting. The castle is rectangular,
with four corner towers and two more in the middle of the long
sides, a design typical for Frederick although pre-existing structures
forced it out of symmetry. However, during the long restoration
(not yet finished in 1991) it has emerged that the wall dividing the
two courts was inserted after Frederick's time, so the idea that he
simply extended the Norman castle with a second court must be
discarded. It is also no longer so easy to explain why his massive
square keep in the smaller court is obliquely sited; the reason given
used to be that it was necessitated by a previous structure. This keep

is well preserved and above the portal has fine carved heads, one of the hallmarks of Frederick's court sculpture, animated and classi-cizing. As at CASTEL DEL MONTE, the portal is well above ground, having been reached by a wooden staircase, and the inner walls were once revetted with marble. The rest of the castle consists of rather botched later rebuilding; though the tower was there, the chapel inside it is also later than Frederick. (Frederick seems never to have included a chapel in his secular buildings – which, though it does not prove he was an atheist as his papal enemies alleged or that he was in spirit a man of science as posterity has liked to believe, is unusual among medieval rulers.) For all its defensiveness, the castle is described in documents as a *domus solationis*, therefore a 'hunting-lodge' rather than a link in Frederick's ring of strategic fortresses. About Lagopesole there is a watershed, and the Bradano rises, flowing into the Ionian sea.

Down the valley from Rapolla, to the east, lies Venosa, Roman Venusium, famous as the birthplace of Horace, born Quintus Horatius Flaccus in 65 BC. In his metrical *Letters* and *Satires* Horace is comparatively forthcoming about his origins, describing his father's concern for his education and his own schoolboy troubles; allegorically in *Odes* III, he relates that as a boy he slept on Mt Vulture, and by doves was covered with fresh myrtle and laurel, while all were amazed that he was unharmed by bears or serpents, '*non sine dis animosus infans*'. It was a populous town, requiring an aqueduct (remains of which are visible near Ripacandida), and was an important station on the via Appia Antica from Beneventum to Tarentum. Roman fragments are visible in various parts of the modern town, and in particular by the Norman abbey of La Trinità on its north-eastern edge, where parts of the Roman city and an Early Christian baptistry have been excavated. A new church for the abbey undertaken in the 12th century but never completed (see below) was built entirely with blocks taken from the nearby amphi-theatre. In the modern town the castle with its ample, swelling towers and the cathedral were rebuilt from 1470 following an earthquake, and subsequently altered. A statue of Horace was first erected in the late 19th century.

At Venosa Norman Douglas had cause to rail, still in 1915, at the vicious officialdom under which the country lay, policed by men 'whose only intelligible expression is one of malice striving to break through a crust of congenital cretinism'. With them he contrasted the worthiness of the peasants who in their clogs went out from the

town each morning and returned each evening, and whose hovels in
the town smelt appallingly; also the 'Scotch' gravity of the 'decent'
people, though these were few, in fact there was 'no large citizen
class, properly so called' in Venosa. He had confronted the well
known 'Mezzogiorno' society of proprietors and peasants only, in
which the land capitalists, the owners of large estates (*latifondi*)
worked by an agricultural proletariat, struggled, sometimes successfully, sometimes not, to prevent the encroachment of small-
holders. Today no such problem is apparent. Venosa has no slums; it
has successfully geared into the market economy and product
society of the rest of Italy.

The abbey of La Trinità consists of two buildings, one later,
unfinished, to the west of the previous church, which was restored
when the new one was abandoned. The older church, where lay the
brothers William Iron-arm, Drogo, Humphrey and Robert Guiscard
himself, though he died in Corfu, was, it now seems, a surviving Early
Christian (5th/6th-century) basilica, and a report that it was
founded in 942 by Gisulf of Salerno is false. It may itself have
occupied the site of a temple. It had an open transept and a single
apse with openings on to a semicircular ambulatory. Later a crypt
was dug beneath, and the supports of the church were remade when
the abbey was taken over by the Hospitallers of St John at the end of
the 13th century: their work largely determined its present character, though restorations continue (1991). At the west end a guest-
house for the abbey was constructed probably at some time during
the Norman period. Inside, all the Norman tombs have disappeared
except that of Alberada, first wife of Robert Guiscard, mother of
Bohemund; she outlived both former husband and son, dying in
1122.

Outside again, for the new church is roofless, the sight of so many
grey tufa piers and walls, rising uniformly to arcade height, is
melancholy and bizarre, and is rendered still more bizarre by the
incongruous inscriptions or reliefs that punctuate the walls, some of
them upside down – they are Roman workings on the stolen blocks,
some of them relating to favourites in the games. The new church
was to have an entirely French or Anglo-Norman chevet, with
chapels radiating from an ambulatory and two eastern staircase
towers flanking the crossing – a unique import into southern
Norman territory. Since Robert Guiscard had introduced monks
from Evrould-en-Ouche in Normandy in 1066, it is natural to
suppose that they undertook the new church, but its fabric un-

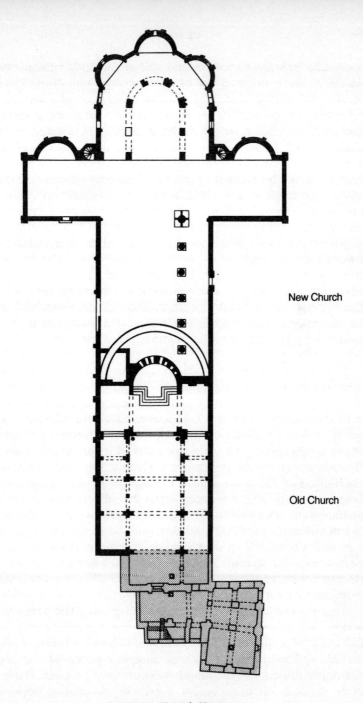

New Church

Old Church

Santissima Trinità, Venosa

doubtedly belongs to the second half of the 12th century; work seems to have dragged on before the new church was finally abandoned at the end of the 13th century. In particular the massive columns laid only for one arcade of the nave cannot be earlier than the later 12th century. In the choir the capitals are of different kinds: some indeed seem to be 11th-century, recalling the style of Romuald at CANOSA, and inside the old church there is a large capital, now used as a holy water stoup, which closely reflects one of the animal capitals from the late 11th-century abbey of Sant'Andrea in BRINDISI. It is possible then that some work had been initiated in Robert Guiscard's time or just after his death in 1085, and that the imported plan was laid out within the time of abbot Berengar, who ruled for twenty-eight years after his arrival in 1066. Otherwise the borrowing at the end of the 12th century of a type of design both alien and obsolete is peculiar – even if it was thereafter used again in the 13th century at nearby Acerenza and was influential perhaps at La Roccelletta near SQUILLACE in Calabria. The road past the abbey leads over a low pass into the TAVOLIERE.

The Tavoliere

Why the plains of northern Puglia were called the Tavoliere was a question which baffled older travellers – was it the table-like flatness of the landscape, or the table suitability of its produce? In ancient times northern Puglia was known as Daunia. The modern name is a corruption of the term *tabulae censuariae* in which land in the emperor's ownership was recorded, as this all once was. Daunia was an important grain-producing region, though not the equal of Sicily, North Africa or Egypt, and it was to ensure his supplies that Hannibal was down here, being shadowed by the Roman army he would defeat at CANNAE. Daunia enjoyed particular prosperity in the late Roman period, especially in the 6th century when it remained free from the turmoil afflicting northern Italy.

After the Lombard invasions Daunia reverted mostly to forest and scrub, and from early modern times was used for the winter pasturage of the herds and flocks that in summer returned north to the Abruzzi mountains. Although its arable potential was recognised, the crown and the landowners preferred a comfortable fee and comparatively easy control of a sparse and migrant population to the complications of capitalist development and the increased liabilities of settlement. However, as early as the 17th century the Jesuits at their settlement at Orta Nova introduced managed tilling, and when their order was suppressed in the 18th century the Bourbons, in a typically tentative initiative, continued the experimental farm. Johann Hermann von Riedesel, Prussian diplomat and a friend in Rome of Winckelmann, stopped there in 1767 and reported the prodigious height and full maturity of the corn already on 5 June – I think it may relieve the modern visitor to know that the enormity of the fruit and other crops in Puglia is frequently reported from before the days of agro-chemistry. Even after Unification things changed slowly, and it is only in this century and with mechanization that the great fertility of the land has been exploited, turning FOGGIA into one of Italy's pasta capitals. For all that, the area is hardly less deserted now than it was then, an empty, rolling, yellow prairie under a vaulting sky.

In medieval times, Frederick II had a hunting lodge at Orta Nova. In 1259, soon after his recovery of his father's kingdom, Manfred led a court of 1,400 to hunt in the forest now marked only by the sanctuary of the Madonna Incoronata. However, Puglia was already known for its cattle: when Manfred set to building Manfredonia, 'the cattle of Puglia', it was said, 'really had some work to do'. Eighteenth-century travellers were impressed by the robust and massive oxen, and also found 'buffalo' or *bufalo*, from which, or rather from the *bufala*, comes the milk to make true *mozzarella* cheese. These animals like marsh – in his *Old Calabria* (1915) Norman Douglas has a fine photograph of one wallowing – and since the land has been reclaimed it has been impossible to find 'buffalo' in Puglia; *mozzarella di bufala* these days comes from southern Campania.

Orta Nova was new in relation to the earlier settlement of Ordona, itself succeeding ancient Herdoniae, of which the site remains just west of Ordona. Possibly Horace stopped here on his journey in *Satires* I, 5; he cannot give the name, he says, because it would not fit into his metre, but the town he means will be instantly known for its terrible water and excellent bread. The experienced traveller, he says, will buy extra bread in *** and take it with him to Canosa, where the bread is like stone. Which town he meant is greatly disputed: the scholiast to the *Satires* gives Aequus Tuticus, which is in Campania and completely the wrong direction; modern scholarship would locate it where no town is known – but if it is not known now would it have been known instantly to Horace's listeners? It must have been a place of some prominence, even if Horace wandered off the most direct route to get there. Neither Herdoniae (——∪—) nor Ausculum (—∪—) will go into a hexameter; Herdoniae is perhaps the better candidate because one can believe the bread was good and the water from its cisterns or from the sluggish river bad. Why by contrast the bread should be so bad in Canosa I do not know, though at least one 18th-century traveller, with his Horace in his hand, found it still to be. Formerly the water in Puglia seems generally to have been abominable (an English 18th-century traveller, Swinburne, reported having to keep the tadpoles out with his teeth) but its supply has now been transformed by the piped water of the Acquedotto Pugliese, which relays water from artificial lakes in the Appennines.

Ancient Herdoniae was situated by a bridge (which remains) over the river Carapelle, serving as an *entrepôt*, in a position rather like that of modern FOGGIA. From the bridge the line of the road is straight to a surviving gate, with stumps of towers, and the perimeter of the old walls can be circumambulated. Inside the town, streets and houses have been laid bare in plan, together with the forum, a circular market-hall, two temples and a basilica, an amphitheatre and baths. Cemeteries outside the town have yielded valuable material now in various Pugliese museums. In the last 25 years and more Herdoniae has been excavated fruitfully by a Belgian team, who have published seven volumes of the series *Ordona*, not to mention several articles reporting their seasons.

I first drove (or rather was driven) through the Tavoliere one Sunday in a car provided by the Foggia Chamber of Commerce, before whom I had posed as a journalist. The driver was employed as a liaison officer and had spent three years learning English in Hull, where he had found a wife. He was pleased that produce from Foggia province was good enough to make its way to Marks and Spencer, while regretting, as do many Italians, that the English cannot tell edible fruit from perfect-looking. He told me more than I could understand about the mills of Foggia and a very good formulation of the difference between the English and the Italians: the Italians, he said, like to disturb people and to be disturbed, as the English do not. That seems to me to encapsulate both the obvious evidence of any railway carriage and a profound difference in mentality. He said it was beautiful living here, beautiful weather and scenery, wide open space, not too many people, first-class roads – he loved to drive, and he had a very nice Lancia. We went on to drive all round the Gargano peninsula. His wife, he said, had completely Italianized: she spent all her time with her in-laws. Anyway, she did not come.

A place like FOGGIA is undoubtedly prosperous, but not so very prosperous, and it is agricultural and still securely provincial, therefore calm. Out on the prairie, occasionally relieving the fenceless fields, are farm-houses or *masserie*, which traditionally take the form of plain, square enclosures consisting of a low range and a high-walled yard. These isolated, white, cubic islands on the open plain are typically Pugliese and at the same time romantically suggestive of North Africa. Occasionally, too, the sails of corn are stitched by green river-banks, or are gently ruptured by rising outcrops, such as the ridge on which TROIA stands. To the south circle the Appennines, though the Carapelle flows down a broad valley, guarded by the strongpoint of Ascoli Satriano. To the east, Cerignola was an ancient and medieval settlement but nothing earlier survived the earthquake of 1731.

Troia

Troia, set above the plain on a gently rising ridge, is a small country town that kindly has been left with its history. Roman Aecae, Troia's predecessor, was a leading town of northern Daunia, the first town on the via Appia Trajana after it left the Appennines. It succumbed at some point during the high Middle Ages and was refounded in 1018 by the Byzantine *catepan* or provincial governor Boioannes. Though a mile and a half from Roman Aecae, it still straddled the via Trajana; in fact the Roman road is still its main street. It shortly became the chief city of Capitanata, as northern Puglia came to be called, seemingly by derivation from the word *catepanos*, until its repeated recalcitrance incurred its lasting destruction in 1230 by Frederick II. He fostered Foggia instead, which remained the administrative capital under the Kingdom and still is, while even today Troia has hardly outgrown the circuit of its former walls. On its old, only street the important Romanesque cathedral stands unprepossessingly, unscenically. Only just a year or two ago, having visited the cathedral, you would have emerged to find only one bar, and nothing to eat in it; but it now attracts enough tourists to have brought into being a *pizzeria* by the lower end of the town. Quite remarkably in modern Italy, the doors of the church remain open even during noontide.

The energetic Boioannes founded the town after he had defeated the rebel Melos of BARI and his Norman mercenaries at the second battle of CANNAE in 1018. It was to be one of a ring of new or rebuilt fortresses in this newly reconquered region with which he intended to ward off 'Frankish' infiltration and aggression. That soon arrived in the person of emperor Henry II, who beseiged the city for three months in 1022, some sources say successfully, others say not. At any rate it held him up most effectively, and he retreated to BENEVENTO, then Montecassino, then Rome, his effective control vanishing with him. However, subsequent catepans had decreasing success when contending with the Normans. The second bishop of Troia, Angel, was drowned in the Ofanto in 1040 in one of several local defeats inflicted by Norman bands, by now ensconced in the Appennines. After the battle of Civitate in 1053 Troia became an isolated strongpoint, and was taken into the hand of Robert Guiscard in 1059.

After the death of Robert Guiscard in 1085, under the feeble grip of Roger Borsa (duke 1085–1111) and the strengthless one of his minor heir, William, the city, led by its bishops, again achieved virtual autonomy. During the early 12th century there was near anarchy in the Norman duchy, and the pope, himself often driven from Rome, became the region's major mediator: the truces or 'landpeaces' declared from assemblies in Troia called by successive popes, by Urban II in 1093 and, during William's dukedom, by Paschal II in 1115, Calixtus II in 1120 and Honorius II in 1127, well illustrate the city's position in the land. By a privilege granted by Alexander II in 1066, its bishopric was a direct papal appointment, and so the town acquired its future Guelf allegiance. On the south doors of the cathedral these early bishops can be found listed, by the ninth of their number; their effigies tell little, but their names illustrate the Latinizing shift: Orian, Angel, John and Stephen are followed by William, Gerald, Hubert, Walter and William II. Though the Norman duchy of Apulia was not yet a kingdom and was only just a state, the governing classes by this time were virtually all Norman – not Lombard and not Greek, even though Robert Guiscard had thought it best to put aside his first Norman wife to marry a Lombard, Sichelgaita.

On duke William's death in 1127 Troia, under its remarkable bishop William II, stood out for independence in a league of dukes, counts and barons united with pope Honorius II's support against the claims on the mainland of Roger of Sicily. The moment is vividly commemorated on the southern bronze doors just mentioned, installed by bishop William II 'liberator of his country', as its inscription calls him: it proudly records that 'in the year when William, 3rd Norman duke of Salerno, died by "common" death, the Trojan people, in order to preserve their liberty, demolished the citadel and protected their city with a rampart and walls'. However, in 1133, as Roger of Sicily finally enforced his claim on the vacant duchy, the citizens were forced to watch their elected magistrates hanged, to break down their new walls, to rebuild the castle for Roger and to flee into the countryside as he burnt their houses. The cathedral, however, he thought not to touch, even with such subversive bronze doors; it retained, too, the library, vessels, vestments and furnishings which bishop William had lavished upon it.

Troia usually figured in the subsequent revolts from which the Norman state was never secure, but the harsh punishments inflicted in return eventually broke it – as they broke all the cities of southern Italy. The career of its later bishop Walter II of Palear was much less closely linked to his see than was William II's: it was consequent chiefly on Henry VI having made him his chancellor, a position he continued to occupy after Henry's death, also becoming archbishop of Palermo. During Frederick's minority Walter was supposed, by virtue of his ecclesiastical tenure, to have been the pope's agent in Sicily, but it suited him better to ally himself with the odious Markward of Anweiler. When the pope reproached him, he replied in session that if St Peter, with orders from Christ himself, were to have commanded him he would not obey, even though he knew he would be damned in hell for it. He saw little of Troia, based in Palermo, though he remained its bishop until 1212. He eventually died friendless, though still nominally chancellor, in Venice. The next bishop of Troia, though more orthodox, was hardly more successful, preaching rebellion against Frederick while he was on crusade in Jerusalem, and spreading the rumour that he was dead. Even when he returned in 1229 and had taken FOGGIA, the Trojans resisted, killing the messengers who told them he was not an imposter. Frederick could not take the city till 1230, and then he razed it, cut off noses, chopped people up and threw the bits to dogs.

These vicissitudes can for the most part be traced in the fabric of the cathedral, though no other part is quite so eloquent as Bishop William II's bronze doors. Of the church on the site in Boioannes's time little visible remains, but probes have revealed it to be there. In common with the cathedral at SIPONTO, the adjoining diocese to the east, it had for decoration round its walls blind arches on half-columns and in their heads blind or open lozenge and circle windows. The motif is often said to derive from Pisa cathedral, but the early dating of Siponto suggests that Pisa, begun only in 1063, borrowed from the south; or both borrowed from the eastern Mediterranean. The present cathedral was built in two stages: the nave was added as an extension on the side of the original church some time after 1093 (repeating its decoration), and the original church was replaced probably in the later 12th century by a higher, broader and longer transept. As a consequence, the new church has a north-south orientation. The new nave was carried through by bishop William II, who by 1119 had a structure in which he could insert the western bronze doors. An inscription in the transept wall recalls his good work: 'The blest bishop lord William II made this house for the Lord and the Blessed Mary, and for you, the faithful, blest Trojans'. In 1027 this considerable publicist then added the southern bronze doors.

The contractor for both sets of doors, those of 1119 and those of 1127, was Oderisius of Benevento, who also made bronze doors for the cathedral in Capua and in BENEVENTO, but these are lost. A Lombard, he worked in the Byzantine tradition, as represented by the 1076 doors of the shrine of MONTE SANT'ANGELO, which were made in Constantinople; he used the same format and techniques but on the south doors his figures are definitely weaker and cruder, more like a sketch than a fair copy. The main doors have been repaired, in 1573 and in 1691, as the inscriptions tell: probably, when the later panels were incorporated, the disposition of those preserved was altered as well, or perhaps a third door was cannibalized, for the two rows of four great bronze lion's heads holding knockers are both magnificent and absurd – what with two more serpent knockers between them, too: they are much more than is needed for knocking, and those on the upper row are too high to reach. Above these, the portraits of Oderisius and of Bishop William, damaged and difficult to see, are likely to have been originally at eye-level. The better preserved southern doors are lesser works of art, though unusually loquacious: no such knockers, and the image of bishop William II beside 'the city of Troy' is entirely conventional.

The cathedral façade was adorned with its profusion of sculpture under later, more anonymous bishops. Probably the large rose-window belongs to the second half of the 13th century, after

Frederick had relented just before his death and allowed its clergy to return to Troia, so long as they were not native of the place; however, the bishopric remained vacant until 1266. Of the same date or still later is the sculpture round the slightly uncomfortable arch of the window, those parts of it that were not replaced in the restorations of 1858–60: it consists of a bestiary in the spirit of French gargoyles, some of the finest work of its kind in Puglia, though there is comparable sculpture on the façade of Bari cathedral as well as on nearby, rival, Foggia cathedral. But the coupled columns beside the great window, by which they are dwarfed, and the commensurate arches beside them, now reduced to half-arches, probably belong to the lower façade of bishop William II's church. The sculpture of the cornice is to be dated somewhere along the century and half separating those two elements. The date of the east end is not obvious, either: if it is 12th-century, it is grander than anything contemporary in all Puglia of that date, with almost French Gothic proportions. Nevertheless the figures of the Evangelists up in the vault of the crossing and, outside, the fine decorated east end window appear untouched by Gothic influence.

In the nave, the marble pulpit displays a bold, broad relief of devouring lions; it is dated 1169 by an inscription respectfully acknowledging king William II. Although lions devouring are extremely common in Puglia, one of these looks to have been derived from a classical design, perhaps a sarcophagus; the use of classical motifs accelerated in William II's reign. Then presumably a new screen or choir furniture, now lost, were installed by Walter of Palear's successor, and that was the source of two stray capitals, one here in the Museo Diocesano, the second in the Cloisters, New York (and there is a third similar in the museum in BRINDISI), which show close affinity with capitals of around 1220 at Reims. An odd and perplexing parallel to the French Gothic influence on the sculpture of Frederick II, the town's enemy.

The church of San Basilio is also worth visiting: having entered its little square, you have only to ask anyone through the several open doors to discover who may have the key. Inside – if the custodian is cooking, the visit must be brief – the unadorned stone of the nave and aisles dates to some time before 1087; the rendered upper parts are more recent, and the church originally had wooden roofs. The nave leads up to a dome before an apse, a standard South Italian plan; the projecting arms of the transept and the tower (rebuilt) over one of them are more unusual. The sill which runs all round the outside of the building is an elegant motif, surely Byzantine rather than Latin, providing a socle for the slender colonnettes on bases that decorate the apse: these, though they may resemble the shafts running up to an eave of little arches common in early Romanesque churches all over Italy and further afield, are nevertheless not quite comparable, because they are more than buttresses or wall patterns, they are the vestige of an 'applied' order not forgotten. Such handling recalls SIPONTO cathedral, where pre-eminently the classical tradition survives in the 11th century neither dead nor ponderously revived, but transmitted, though transmuted, direct from antiquity.

Lucera

Lucera has been a fortress since the beginning of history, though its history as a strategic base effectively came to an end in 1300, when Charles II of Anjou massacred the last of its Saracen inhabitants. Its enormous castle stands on an outcrop commanding the plain from north through west round to south; on the eastern side, where the fortification is concentrated, there is a ditch instead of a drop. The castle was the site of the Roman town, Luceria, though no very conclusive remains have emerged from the excavations; it lies now some way outside the modern town, refounded by Charles II, though the suburbs have crept up towards its adjacent, eastern side. The castle is being refurbished as an amenity, though progress on the car-park has been halted by fresh archaeological finds.

Roman Luceria, the leading city of the region in Early Christian times, was destroyed in 663 by emperor Constans II during his unsuccessful attempt to hold northern Puglia and the prized shrine of MONTE SANT'ANGELO from the Lombards. There remains its substantial amphitheatre, to the east of the modern town: most of its masonry has gone, but the two entrance arches, with inscriptions from the time of Augustus, have been reconstructed. Reconquered by the Byzantines at the end of the 10th century, it was undoubtedly refortified, and so again by the Normans, but the earlier stages of the present castle date from the time of Frederick II. In 1224 he here planted Muslims who had been giving him trouble in Sicily, endowing them with privileges: he gave them 1000 oxen from the imperial demesnes with which to farm; they were not taxed; they were permitted to keep a harem and to worship in the mosques they built. The indignant bishop and many of the Lucerines removed themselves outside the city for fear of contamination. When relations between Frederick and the pope became embittered, Lucera was often cited.

Lucera and its Saracens proved to be the backbone, not so much of Frederick's, but of his son Manfred's power. On Frederick's death Manfred had at first secured the state against rebellious cities, including not only TROIA but FOGGIA, for his brother Conrad IV, who while he lived set out to possess all his father's empire. When he arrived from Germany, landing at Siponto, he behaved as fiercely and viciously as his grandfather Henry VI, alienating Manfred; he then died in 1254 as suddenly and prematurely as Henry VI. Thereafter Manfred was ready to seek his own fortune. In his will Conrad left the Kingdom to his son Conradin under the protection of the pope; promising obedience to the pope, Manfred took on the regency. Relations soon broke down. Innocent IV sent troops into Capitanata. The papal legate was in Troia; Foggia was uncertain; even the captains in charge of Lucera had gone over to the pope. According to the story, Manfred arrived at Lucera with only three companions. He begged entry from the Saracens on guard, who replied that their officers had the keys. One of Manfred's men suggested entering by a conduit or sewer, which the Saracens would not permit, but instead broke down the gate. The fair Manfred harangued them from a window of the now derelict palace, and Capitanata was won. Defeating an army sent by pope Alexander IV, he managed to take over the whole kingdom, and after spreading the rumour that Conradin was dead had himself crowned in Palermo. But he returned to hold court principally, like his father, in Foggia and Lucera, also BARLETTA.

While the popes accused Frederick of many oriental vices – and he had a harem at least, run by eunuchs in Arab fashion – they fulminated in particular against the Saracens of Lucera, because they were so powerful a military force. Reputedly there were 10,000 of them. Lucera held out even after Manfred's death in the battle of Benevento, and when its Saracens surrendered it was not, they said, to Charles of Anjou but to the will of Allah. On the arrival of Conradin Lucera was not alone in rising against Charles but Charles moved first against it, before coming to meet Conradin at Tagliacozzo; subsequently he punished the Saracens and Lucera, which once again resisted even after the leader was dead. Charles I, however, kept the fortress and amplified it, and it was Charles II who finally extirpated the Saracens.

It was left to decay and the keep was almost completely destroyed in 1790 when it was used as a quarry for the new town hall of the nearby town, but it is recorded in drawings by the 18th-century French traveller Desprez, and its original elevation on the base that survives can be reconstructed. The two upper storeys of the square keep rose sheer above two lower storeys in the form of a truncated pyramid, with sloping walls. The restored remains of one corner, and of one great vault, can still be seen. However, it would appear that this outer carapace was added by Charles I to an originally vertical keep. Frederick's castle was constructed, like those of Syracuse, Catania, Augusta and others, on a grid of concentric squares: thus 9 units constituted the central courtyard and 16 the rooms around it, making 25 in all. Bridges across the top corners of the square central courtyard transformed it partially into an oc-

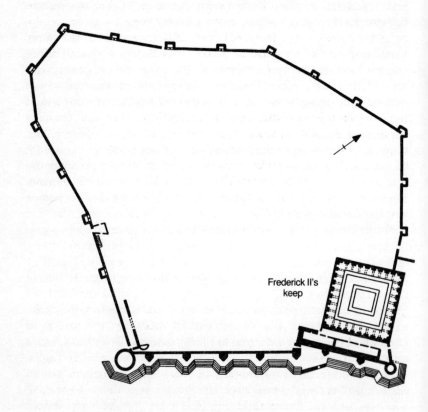

Frederick II's
keep

Castle, Lucera

tagon, a suggestive anticipation of the later CASTEL DEL MONTE. It is recorded that Frederick kept there two antique bronze statues he had picked up in a raid on papal territory; there are other instances, in Sicily, of his setting antique spoils over royal portals.

The outer fortifications, 900 metres in perimeter, date from the time of Charles I, who made this one of his most important strong-points in the years 1269–83, installing a treasury and a mint (though possibly Frederick had one there already). On the town side the walls are particularly massive and of stone, with an enormous barbican; round the rest of the site they are mere curtain walls of brick, punctuated by towers. Various excavations in the enormous open bailey have revealed remnants of houses dating from Charles I's time and of a church built by Charles II.

Charles II also virtually refounded the town. In 1239 Frederick had admitted, in one of his replies to papal charges, that the cathedral was ruins, and in his will he ordered its restoration as an act of penitence. However, the present church dates from Charles II's time, being finished by 1317. It is an entirely French church, with no gesture to Pugliese tradition, in a severe and practical Gothic. The Church's triumph is manifest in the marble altar, brought here in 1406, formerly the royal dining table in Castel Fiorentino, where Frederick died. San Francesco is a con-temporary Franciscan-Gothic church. Not far away is the Museo Civico Giuseppe Fiorelli, which has exhibits from all periods of Lucera: there are significant finds of the Roman republican period and a fine 1st-century AD mosaic; there are one or two notable pieces of sculpture from Frederick's time, including a possible portrait head; there is also a complete furnished *salon* from the 18th century.

Foggia

Foggia is an ugly sister among Italian capitals, loved by no-one, visited by few. Beautiful it will never be, but it has its charms. In the evening, the *serata* or evening promenade that flows down its broad streets is even more genial than most, and less crushed and frenetic, though the numbers are enormous. The city's prosperity is solid, since it is plumb in the middle of the Tavoliere and at the junction of the road and rail routes to Naples, Ancona and BARI. It is the main market town for the abundant produce of the Tavoliere, and in

addition, though it has little industry, it has mills and other process-
ing installations that have flourished: the mills grind not only local
grain but imported North American wheat, which is then exported
as couscous to Algeria.

Though it sprawls into complicated dual-carriageway ring roads
and many new blocks of flats, the centre of modern Foggia is simple:
a road leads from the station past the Cicolella hotel to the head of
the *villa comunale* or municipal garden, from which the rest of the
shopping streets radiate. The Cicolella, a dated post-war building,
featuring shiny stained bentwood in its gloomy lobby, also has the
foremost restaurant of the town; there is, too, a Cicolella cinema and
another Cicolella restaurant in the business fair complex. Signor
Cicolella is a former President of the Chamber of Commerce. The
specialities of the Cicolella restaurant are, like everything in Puglia,
local – local shapes of pasta in local sauces. The ingredients – fish,
meat, vegetables – are excellent, but the meat courses are favoured
heavy. The leading rival to the Cicolella restaurant, the Pietra di
Francia (actually the name of a local marble), is situated on the
ground floor of a block of flats out in the suburbs. Yet another
restaurant had excellent food, but its ambience consisted of a video
screen covering one wall. In the older town the few restaurants tend
towards slum – grandmother at the door in dirty apron over
indistinguishable floral dress and television inside.

Foggia was bombed in the Second World War and the old town is
only intermittently old. Somewhere in it is the cathedral – to find it
takes a surprising amount of wandering about, since the centre of
the town has shifted, and its level streets give no vantage-point.
Where Foggia is was formerly marsh: one day in 1073 a peasant saw
flames over the water, beneath which he discovered a chest holding
an icon of the Madonna, to which the cathedral is dedicated (Santa
Maria Icona Vetere). The town has no Roman precedent, unless you
count nearby Arpi, which had perished before Foggia was founded:
it grew up as an upstart rival to TROIA, whose mantle it stole.
Frederick II instituted it as the capital of Capitanata, and built an
imperial residence here – in which, however, he seldom resided,
but travelled through his kingdom incessantly, even in times of
peace. He seems to have favoured Foggia partly because of the good
hunting in its nearby forests. The remains of the palace amount to no
more than an arch and an inscription, from which it emerges that it
was begun in 1223 as a royal and imperial office and that Bartolomeo
da Foggia was its '*proto*' (master-mason). Inside – that is to say inside

the building in which the arch is immured – the civic museum displays remains taken from Arpi and Herdoniae, and some religious pictures.

The cathedral is one of several churches or sanctuaries that were founded in the middle of nowhere in Puglia in the Middle Ages on the occasion of a miraculous discovery of a Madonna. No-one had a direct vision of the Mother of God, as became usual only after the Baroque revolution in art: there were instead – sometimes following on a dream – bright lights or other effects and an image. The original church of 1073 onwards was replaced by the present one under William II, during a building history extending from 1172 or 1179 to the 1230s and later, but the whole upper part and interior of the church were renewed in a gloomy Baroque style after an earthquake in 1731. The earthquake also spilled the urn containing Frederick II's heart (his body, when he died in 1250 just north at Castel Fiorentino, was shipped to Palermo cathedral). Of the medieval building, deliberately imitating and emulating TROIA cathedral in design, style and ornament, there remain only the external walls of the nave – with their impressively abundant sculpture – the crypt, and the north door into the crypt (access to which is via the curial offices and youth club).

Much of the sculpture, and particularly the north door, is attributed inevitably to Bartolomeo da Foggia, *proto* of the imperial palace, though comparison to the solitary remaining eagles flanking the palace arch is hardly conclusive. However, there is circumstantial support in the definite similarity between the capitals of Foggia crypt, rebuilt following an earthquake in 1223, and those of the pulpit at Ravello signed by Nicola di Bartolomeo da Foggia and dated 1272. Son is likely to have followed father as head of the cathedral workshop (as is documented in BARLETTA). Father would have carved the sculpture over the north door and supervised the decoration of the cornice, and son would have initiated a new phase of building, reconstructing (on a pattern like Troia's) the old east end to which a nave had just been added. Only his crypt survives, with foliage capitals clearly of Gothic stamp. What rose above it is not known, but the intriguing hypothesis has been advanced of an octagonal choir, paralleling Ancona cathedral and directly anticipating the crossing of Siena cathedral. Undoubtedly there was a common current linking masons in Tuscany and South Italy in the second half of the 13th century, even though Nicola's 1272 Ravello pulpit is old-fashioned beside the 1260 and 1265 pulpits of Nicola

Pisano in Pisa and Siena (still, an octagonal pulpit recorded in TRANI might have anticipated those more closely).

The father, Bartolomeo's, sculpture on the north door has awkwardnesses in overall design and a tame figure style, despite its animated subjects, quite close to the Byzantine mosaics of Monreale. Unfortunately the most interesting and central figure, of a horseman – a recurrent badge of Frederick's *imperium* – is largely destroyed. Above the imperial horseman is the figure of Christ; below, Samson wrestles with the lion like good with evil, and the remains of an inscription suggest the bishop to be Majoranus, who dreamt of the angel at MONTE SANT'ANGELO.

Foggia was the birthplace in 1867 of Umberto Giordano, one of the most successful opera composers of the late 19th-century *verismo* school. Following the trail blazed by Puccini and Mascagni, Giordano had his moment of glory with *Andrea Chenier* in 1896 and *Fedora* in 1898, both with 'star' arias that figured regularly on the new gramophone records of Caruso, Gigli and the rest. Like Mascagni, however, he outlived his period, and when he died in 1948 he had not written an opera for 19 years.

North of Foggia

North of Foggia the Tavoliere narrows into a broad valley between the Appennines encroaching from the west and the sudden heights of the Gargano peninsula to the east. In the middle of the valley is San Severo, well placed on old and modern routes of communication and in the midst of fertile land (vineyards in particular; it exports both red and white wine). However, though it has an old town and a couple of churches of ancient foundation, San Severo never had early importance because it was too exposed: it was never a castle or walled town but during the Middle Ages an appanage of the Benedictine monastery of Torremaggiore, set on an eminence to the east. A rare document signed by the abbot in 1116 sets out the constitutions by which its tenants were to be bound, rating how much they should pay in kind or work by the number and quality of animals they possessed; if they wanted to leave, they could leave, so long as they paid or left their goods behind. In the 15th century the nascent town became the seat of the governor of Capitanata and the county of the Molise; at the end of the 16th century it received a bishop and the counts of Torremaggiore moved down and became the princes of Sansevero (*sic*). The town has an adulterated Baroque cathedral and an older church, San Severino, which preserves a 12th-century façade and portal.

Torremaggiore is now hardly half the size of San Severo, and many of the former strongpoints of the region further into the mountains are altogether deserted – notably Civitate to the north-east on the river Fortore, Dragonara to the east further upstream and Castel Fiorentino to the south-east, all ruins. The modern road and the *autostrada* keep close to the coast and then come down the floor of the valley, but the old road north (the present SS 16 *ter*) passed through Torremaggiore, crossed the Fortore at Civitate (by the site of Roman Teanum; there are some scant remains of the Roman bridge), reached Serracaprioli, where the imposing hulk of the castle still looms over the town, then over the pass at Chieuti and down to Campomarino and Termoli in the Molise. However, although the Fortore was the northern boundary of both Roman and high medieval Apulia, it had little strategic significance after the Norman consolidation and the absorption of the Molise into the Kingdom. Termoli cathedral belongs to the group TROIA, FOGGIA, SIPONTO. Castel Fiorentino, where Frederick II died in 1250, was used by him more as a *domus delicie* or *solationis*, a place to go and falcon, than as a fortress.

Immediately before the Norman occupation, which became ineradicable after their defeat of pope Leo IX at Civitate in 1053, the economy of the valley and mouth of the Fortore, extending across to the lagoons of Lesina and Varano, and with close connections to the Tremiti islands a few miles off the coast, seems to have flourished; but it began to decline soon after, witness also the troubles of the monastery on the TREMITI and Manfred's eventual removal of the inhabitants of Civitate to MANFREDONIA on the other coast of the Gargano in 1263. At Ripalta beside the Fortore a few miles inshore, a former dependent priory, and port, of the Tremiti monastery remains, transferred in the early 13th century to the Cistercians, who rebuilt the church. Around the year AD 1000, the area might have had a future like Venice's: Lesina on its homonymous lagoon, founded by refugees from Roman Luceria like Venice from Altinum, grew rich – like Venice in those same distant times – on its fishing (especially eels), and there were similar possibilities of trade. Here, however, the lagoon was more treacherous, shifting waters undermining or flooding settlement and obstructing seafaring; the old Roman city of Uria on the neighbouring lagoon of Varano disappeared altogether. The comparative stability of the present lagoons is a construct of very recent and extensive engineering.

And then there came the Normans. By around 1050 their lesions had virtually destroyed the Lombard and Byzantine bodies politic: the people were crying out, princes were alarmed, unruly rapine raged rife. The Normans were equated to Saracens, only worse. Hitherto the state powers had ambiguously sought to preserve peace partly by legitimating Norman captains in the lordship of lands at their mercy, but now that policy's failure precipitated a general alliance against them of the Holy Roman emperor Henry III, the East Roman emperor Constantine IX Monomachus, and the Church. The Church was moved inexorably to the forefront, because it, too, had become their victim, and because it had already involved its authority by calling a 'landpeace' which had not been respected, and because there was no-one else to raise the banner. So after recognition that his cousin Henry III had too many other troubles to come himself, the tall, charismatic pope Leo IX moved with an army first to Benevento, which had declared itself his subject (and so vanished the Lombard duchy), and then over to Puglia (not by the usual route since it was held by the Normans) hoping to meet up with a Byzantine force in Capitanata. He was in correspondence with Constantine IX, and Argyrus, newly appointed the Byzantine 'duke of Italy', had just before landed at Bari. Unfortunately the link was never made, some say because the Normans had already met and defeated Argyrus; Argyrus probably had few resources, given that his instructions from Constantinople were to persuade the Normans to come and win Byzantine gold by fighting the Saracens in the east. Perhaps they might have done if Leo had prevailed. But Leo, alone though still with a larger army and an elite corps of 700 Germans as tall as him, gave or took battle beneath Civitate, and was defeated and captured. The Normans took him back to Benevento and there held him for a year: their victory was rendered irreversible by the epistolary quarrel that broke out between Rome and Constantinople during that time (ironically, it was largely a consequence of their recent *rapprochement*) and is known as the Great Schism. Inheriting the mantle of his elder brother Humphrey in 1057 Robert Guiscard completed the conquest of Byzantine Apulia and Calabria by 1071.

The Tremiti islands

The Isole Tremiti are three extremely pretty lumps of white calcareous rock set in an azure sea and cloudless sky, about 15 miles
north of the GARGANO PENINSULA. In season they can be visited daily and
within a day by jet-foil from Termoli (45 minutes) or, less hastily, by
boat from several ports such as Vasto, north of Termoli, or Peschici,
Vieste or MANFREDONIA on the Gargano (this last an extremely
leisurely voyage); or by helicopter from Foggia. In summer there are
several places to stay on the islands, which, however, have few
beaches; the numerous grottos and other phenomena of karst
erosion attract anglers and subacquists: the fishing is good, and the
port of San Nicola still breathes salt, paint and tar.

The Tremiti have a history, and the abbey church of Santa Maria a
Mare on the island of San Nicola is an important 11th-century
monument. There is a legend that the Greek hero Diomedes, who
fought at Troy and sailed on the Argo, is buried here, and, con-
veniently, there is a large rock with a hole under it in the midst of a
Greco-Roman necropolis behind the abbey that now bears his name.
On San Domino, across the water, neolithic remains have been
found. Diomedes has also given his name to a breed of petrels that
frequents the islands, *diomedee*. Historically, Augustus hither exiled
his grand-daughter Julia for an adultery with which, it is speculated,
Ovid was involved, and was hence exiled to the Black Sea; Julia here
lived out her own silent *Tristia* for 20 years. Again Paul the Deacon,
the Lombard historian, is reported briefly to have been exiled here
by Charlemagne in 786, when perhaps there was already a monastery. Much later, the Napoleonic regime made the island a penal
colony, and so it remained officially until 1926 – unofficially, for
Mussolini's internal exiles, until the end of the Second World War.

From 1006 there is record of the Benedictine abbey on San
Nicola, set on the islands' only defensible height; it already owned
substantial assets on the mainland, especially on the mouth of the
Fortore and round Lesina and Varano, and its church was consecrated in 1045. There is another legend, illustrating Pugliese faith in
the sacral past of their home stone, that the abbey's hermit founder
was directed to the tomb of Diomedes by an apparition of the Virgin
Mary, and built the church with the treasure it contained. However,
one may doubt that the abbey was an otherworldly retreat devoted
entirely to prayer. It was too much of a fortress in too important a
position at the mouth of the northern Adriatic. There are several

reports in the second half of the 11th century of abbots more
piratical than pious, although the accusations seem to have ema-
nated primarily from Montecassino, which claimed rights over the
abbey fiercely resisted by the monks. Abbot Desiderius of Montecassino managed in 1060 to arraign and depose for ill conduct
abbot Adam, who was replaced by Trasimund, who blinded three
monks and cut out the tongue of a fourth; he, too, was replaced by
another who also had to be replaced, but returned anyway. Such
troubles continued, and in 1226 the abbey was found ruined, its
farms abandoned, the monks 'wandering in the secular on account
of the evil of the abbot, so they said, and the lack of necessities'. Pope
Gregory IX acted by sending in the Cistercians in 1237: they
substituted a vaulted, Gothic choir for the old east end of the church
and further built up the fortifications, but were massacred by Slav
pirates in 1334. In 1409 the ruined abbey was given to Lateran
canons, who were supported rather from the north than from
Naples, as their portal of 1473 indicates: it is by Andrea Alessi from
Durazzo (working under Venetian influence) and Nicolo di
Giovanni Cocari of Florence. The enormously long swags hanging
over the portal recall those of Desiderio da Settignano's monument
to Carlo Marsuppini in Santa Croce in Florence; one was partly shot
away by the British attacking what was then a possession of Joseph
Bonaparte in 1807. The abbey had also survived a Turkish three-day
seige in 1567, escaping unscathed from a raid that devastated
Ancona and Pescara and directly contributed to the effort against
the Turks crowned by the victory of Lepanto in 1571.

The abbey church of 1045 has an unusual plan: though it has a
basilical shape, its nave was formerly twice divided by transverse
arcades into a double narthex, a central square nave and a two-bay
choir. Though the Cistercians replaced the choir, the earlier supports have been excavated and their location is now indicated by
white circles. Though the arcades of the choir match the two
transverse arcades to the west, it does not seem necessary, in fact it
seems impossible, to suppose that there was a gallery over the apses
matching the gallery along the façade. It is perhaps peculiar that the
church was divided into five aisles at the east end, but it is not so
much more extraordinary than descending from a nave to the forest
of columns typical of a crypt; the extra columns may have been felt
as an enrichment. Judging by the surviving responds the choir may
have been lower than the great open space of the nave and the
galleried narthex before it – but nothing is certain since the upper

parts are entirely rebuilt. Peculiar though it is, there are parallels for the plan in the entirely square church of SIPONTO, in the excavated remains of the pre-Norman cathedral at BARI or perhaps in the lost Byzantine church at TROIA or even OTRANTO. Though a rare survival in the north, the church's great bare piers, blind arches and capital-less shafts have close parallels in the Greco-Norman architecture of Calabria, for example the Patirion at ROSSANO or GERACE cathedral.

Further, there remains a fine mosaic floor, datable to the 11th

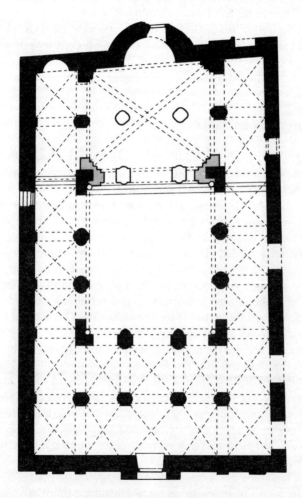

Santa Maria, Isola San Nicola (Tremiti)

century by its parallels to mosaics in the northern Adriatic (Pomposa, Aquileia); but it has in common with them above all its late antique technique (*opus tessellatum*) and vocabulary. A great griffin dominates the central nave (with satellite fish and local, Diomedid petrels), but there are several other surviving beasts in the aisles and round the altar as well; all show an understanding of modelling, admittedly rather shorthand, but which in the Latinized 12th century will have vanished altogether (see OTRANTO). Stripped in restoration, the church retains only two pieces of furniture: one is a great painted Cross of unusual shape, dated to the 13th century, though its inscriptions and style (or the models it copies) are still Greek; on the back the Lamb of God; the other an early 15th-century polyptych of painted wooden statues, imported from the Friuli hinterland of Venice. Very few foreigners come here.

The Gargano peninsula

Offering no large safe harbour, and rising a sheer 1500 ft above sea-level (its peak touching 3000 ft), the Gargano peninsula has never been extensively settled and most of its interior is now a forestry reserve. Around its coast it has only fishing villages or *stazioni balneari* – although Vieste has a cathedral and most other spots have a medieval or older history – until you reach MONTE SANT'ANGELO above the wide bay of Manfredonia at the point where it rejoins the Italian boot. Its spectacularly beautiful coastline is very largely unspoilt, though not deserted; though comparatively unknown abroad, in high summer it is crowded with Italians, not only on the coast but also on the paths of its dense forests. The 'lakes' (*laghi*) of Lesina and Varano are in fact lagoons.

Numerous are the freaks of nature on the Gargano: its karst rock was easily perforated into caves and swallow-holes inland and into grottos and groins by the sea on the coast. Inland there are three huge caverns, for instance, constituting the Grotta di Montenero; the Dolina Pozzatina is an oval crater 2000 ft long punched 300 ft deep, sheer to a flat floor, the Grava di Campolato is a swallow-hole that drops 300 ft in a steep vertical cone and then continues for more than half a mile as a cave. Several other less spectacular recesses have served for prehistoric habitation. Around the coast, especially south from Vieste as far as Mattinata, there are numerous 'blue grottos' as well as 'devil's arches' such as the Architiello at San

Felice and 'needles' such as the Pizzomunno on the beach at Vieste or the upstanding molar of the Faraglione at Mattinata. These can be visited by boat or, on land, by car or on foot; because the cliffs rise so high so rapidly, the views are superb, whether from the coast road or from the many high points inland. From Rignano Garganico on the south-west of the massif, 'the balcony of Puglia', you can look south and see CASTEL DEL MONTE.

In earlier times the peninsula supported a number of Benedictine monasteries, most of which have vanished or become towns. Few were independent but were subject mostly to Santa Maria on the Tremiti islands or to Montecassino. One which has left ruins is the abbey at Pulsano, near Monte Sant'Angelo, which is supposed to have been founded by the 6th-century *dux* Tullianus who was buried in Siponto cathedral; it flourished again in the 12th century, the date of the substantial ruins, but then, like many of the others, declined. Overlooking the Lago di Varano by San Nicola di Varano there is another 11th-century monastery church with the remains of various later frescos; above Peschici the remains of Santa Maria di Calena, once a great monastery, now farm buildings. (The church dates from two different periods, the two bays of the east end to the 12th century, the two of the west to the early 11th or even before. These latter, typically Pugliese, have domes over the nave and quadrant, or half barrel, vaults over the aisles.) San Giovanni in Lamis, now San Matteo, is one to have survived, becoming Cistercian in 1211 and now Franciscan, still rising sheer on a rock over the modern town of San Marco in Lamis. Another monastery became, already under Frederick II, the town of San Giovanni Rotondo; this was always a staging-post on the pilgrims' route to Monte Sant' Angelo, and then became another Lourdes as the dwelling and tomb of Padre Pio (1887–1968), a religious zealot with stigmata and a popular following. Avoid.

Tokens of their medieval past render many of these beach resorts particularly attractive, though Lesina lost its past in the lagoon mud. Behind it the village of Poggio Imperiale is a fake, founded not by an emperor but by one prince Placido Imperiale in the 19th century, but Apricena further inland was a favourite hunting lodge of Frederick II, before it was 'quaked in 1627. The ruins above are those of Castelpagano, one of the towns where Frederick re-settled turbulent Sicilian Muslims, long since deserted. Sannicandro Garganico has a large castle, predominantly 15th-century. Torre Mileto naturally has a tower. On the eastern side of the Lago di

Varano Carpino has a 12th-century church and castle, and Ischitella has Anjou associations, while round the hill Rodi Garganico (Garganic Rhodes) has ancient Greek ones. Several other towns round this part of the coast, like Rodi, sit on the point beside a long wide beach. San Menaio has a corsair tower; inland, Vico del Gargano has the remains of one of Frederick's castles; and there is something more like a folly on the promontory of Monte Pucci just before Peschici. While the castle of Peschici teeters on a high cliff, the old town conserves some authentic grey buildings amidst modern whitewash and new development outside the walls. There follow several other popular beaches and beach resorts, and the archaeological site of Roman and medieval Merinum, down to Vieste.

It was probably shortly after doge Orseolo stopped off here on the Venetian expedition of 1003 to raise the Saracen seige of BARI that Vieste cathedral was built. Though it has been transformed by later superfetation, some of the evocatively crude capitals of its original nave colonnade survive, interesting for their modelling – recalling Lombard stucco-work, like Bovino's – and for their vocabulary (including the dragon or serpent with wings and a stunted curly tail that recurs and recurs in the 11th century). Islamic influence is detected, though of a generic kind that affected the formal vocabulary of the whole Mediterranean in the 9th and 10th centuries. The castle beside the church was built by Frederick II but refurbished several times later: it was needed, since the town was sacked many times by Saracens, Turks or pirates, memorably in 1554 by the terrible Dragut, who cut off thousands of heads. Medieval streets lead to the church and castle, out on the point, but the settlement's origins are much older, not only Roman and Greek (Apeneste) but pre-Greek.

Below Vieste the cliffs are sharper, the bays smaller, the towers fewer, the settlements modern (Testa del Gargano, Pugnochiuso, Baia delle Zagare) until you come to Mattinata, a large bay and valley beneath Monte Sant'Angelo.

Monte Sant'Angelo, Siponto and Manfredonia

The role of angels in the high Middle Ages was an important one. Charlemagne in the *Chanson de Roland* is constantly being fed advice by angels, though often in dreams from which he fails to wake. Carolingian and Ottonian churches contained chapels dedicated to the angel Michael through whom communication to the deity might be more direct. Though his cult was originally Mediterranean, St Michael became so important among the Lombards and Franks, because, it is suggested, he was a suitable substitute for the pagan god Wodin.

The shrine to St Michael on the Gargano peninsula is dated by tradition to the angel's first appearance to Bishop Majoranus in AD 490 (followed by two further epiphanies in 492 and 493). However, recent scholarship favours a date still earlier in the century, when Monte Sant'Angelo would have been one among many cave sanctuaries in Puglia and elsewhere. In the middle of the 7th century the Lombards ousted the Byzantines, and the former bishopric of the port of Siponto, which included Monte Sant'Angelo, was merged into the see of Benevento. Under the Lombards the shrine took on not only local but international importance. The breadth of the angel's appeal is attested by 166 inscriptions dating from the 7th, 8th and 9th centuries that have been found on the shrine's steeped walls, of which four are in Anglo-Saxon runes, the only such known in all Italy. In the 9th century the shrine survived the threat of raiding Saracens, ejected from BARI by the Holy Roman emperor Louis II, who did not fail to visit in 871. Subsequent emperors, notably Otto I who came in 967, continued their interest in the shrine, and all northerners bound east would pass by. There is no reason to doubt the story that Melos of Bari, fomenting revolt against the Byzantines, here in 1016 recruited a group of 40 Normans returning from the Holy Land – the first Normans to fight in southern Italy.

In 1023 the re-conquering Byzantine catepan Boioannes reestablished Siponto, and within it the shrine, as an independent bishopric. The first new bishop was Leo (1023–50), who adorned both his new church at Siponto (in 1039) and the shrine (in 1041) with pulpits carved by Acceptus (for whom see CANOSA). Fragments of both pulpits bearing these dates have been discovered in excavations, and at Monte Sant'Angelo the bishop's throne, which at least in part resembles Acceptus's work, is still *in situ*. Its inscription: 'This seat differs in number from the seat at Siponto; the right and prestige of the seat of the former are also those of the Mount' refers to the quarrels that arose between Monte Sant'Angelo and Siponto soon after bishop Leo's death and raged despite more than one papal ruling even after the destruction of Siponto by earthquake in 1223.

The bishop tended to wish to remain based in Siponto, but the Montesantangelans wanted him up with them, especially to officiate at the important feasts; the pope, however, ruled consistently for the *status quo*, so that the kind of compromise had arisen whereby the bishop on Maundy Thursday consecrated the holy oil in Siponto, then went up to Monte Sant'Angelo to say mass for the pilgrims, then came down again to Siponto. It should be appreciated that Monte Sant'Angelo and Siponto are some 12 miles apart, and Monte Sant'Angelo is on a cliff 800 metres above sea-level. He would have had to spend the whole day on the road.

It proved difficult to find a suitable successor to bishop Leo, as Siponto and the shrine became embroiled in the turmoil following the battle of Civitate. Eventually Gerald, a northerner from Monte-cassino, was appointed bishop; in 1071 he returned to Montecassino for the consecration of abbot Desiderius's splendid new church, newly decorated by Byzantine mosaicists, and endowed with bronze doors made in Constantinople at the expense of the Amalfitan merchant Pantaleone. Surely Gerald and Pantaleone had a word, for another pair of bronze doors was installed thanks to Pantaleone in 1076 at Monte Sant'Angelo, and these survive (see below). Robert Guiscard is said to have provided the portals in which Pantaleone's doors are set, and under the Normans, Swabians and Angevins this southern equivalent to Mont St Michel continued to flourish. It is still one of the major pilgrimage sites of Italy (though fuelled, I suspect, by the greater appeal of Padre Pio in San Giovanni Rotondo); the stalls around the shrine selling trinkets have more colours than Kodak Gold.

Do not visit on a weekend, unless you like to be crushed by pilgrims. Once you have toiled up the vertiginous road to the surprisingly large town (nearly 20,000 inhabitants), and threaded your way among the suburbs garlanding the temples of St Michael's hill, and made your way down the main street with the tourist traps, you come to an octagonal bell-tower of 1274 marking the entrance to the sanctuary. The tower was endowed by Charles I of Anjou, but its design repeats the turrets of CASTEL DEL MONTE, with which it shares almost exactly the same dimensions. One then passes through a portal partly of 1395 but also of the 1860s; the 1395 tympanum was carved by Simeone di Monte Sant'Angelo. The 87 steps down to the cave were also renewed 100 years ago; but on the way down there is an extremely 'medieval' object of devotion, namely rusty reproductions of the instruments of the Passion, which may prepare you for the sickening odour of sanctity that clouds the cave itself. At the bottom of the stairs the corridor leading to the bronze doors and the cave was built under Charles I; there are rich tombs of the 14th century. Inside the cave there are all sorts of crude sculptures one is tempted to date by putting a century on the apparent mental age of their makers; the furnishings are bulbous coloured marble of the 17th century. On the left of the glass case containing the cult statue, with which the name of the sculptor Andrea Sansovino is associated – but this is absurd – is the bishop's throne mentioned above. It has a relief of St Michael after a Byzantine model.

Pantaleone's doors at Monte Sant'Angelo are the best preserved in Europe of the bronze doors with which churches were so commonly adorned in the Middle Ages, because, being set deep down at the entrance to St Michael's cave, they are unweathered, and also because the instructions Pantaleone left that the doors should be cleaned every year seem never quite to have fallen into abeyance in this remote holy place to which pilgrims have never ceased to flock. On the doors, Pantaleone's numerous inscriptions are prominent: 'This work was completed in the royal city of Constantinople with the aid of the lord Pantaleone who ordered the doors to be made in the year 1076'; 'I ask and adjure you, the rectors of St Michael's shrine, that once a year you have these doors cleaned as we have made them now for display so that they are always bright and shining'; 'I ask you all [who] come here to pray that you should first inspect such a beautiful work and so entering, beseech the Lord on your knees for the soul of Pantaleone who was the author of this work'; 'O supreme prince Michael we who come to pray beseech your grace that you hear our prayers for the soul of the author of this so that, together with us, he who by the sanctity of your name was led to decorate these may enjoy eternal delight'. Most unusually the doors have retained their inlaid colours, the silver damascening used for the flesh, the blue *niello* and a red mastic infilling the incised lines delineating the figures (so often these have fallen out or oxidised to black). The Constantinopolitan origin of the work is demonstrated by the fluent draughtsmanship, suggesting movement and vigour in a manner that it would take pedestrian Western Romanesque another three generations to approximate.

On the doors various earlier apparitions of St Michael (alone or in company) culminate in the three to bishop Majoranus: left from the top, the Archangel defeats the rebel angels; he slaughters the Assyrians (II Kings 19.35); he visits Abraham; he transports Habakkuk to Daniel in the lion's den; he climbs Jacob's ladder; he inspires Nathan to call on David to repent (II Samuel 12.1); he appears to Joshua; he wrestles with Jacob; he keeps the Jews cool in the fiery furnace; he restrains Abraham from sacrificing Isaac; he announces the birth of St John to Zacharias; he expels Adam and Eve from Paradise. Right from the top, he announces to the shepherds; he warns Joseph of the Massacre of the Innocents; he admonishes the Holy Women at the Sepulchre; he frees St Peter; he stirs the Pool of Bethesda; he appears to St Martin; he crowns the martyrs Cecilia and Valerian; he appears to St Majoranus for the first time (in the year 490); again (492); a third time (493).

Opposite the sanctuary are two churches, San Pietro and Santa Maria Maggiore, and the so called Tomba di Rotari. This last was supposed to be the tomb of a 7th-century Lombard king, Rothar; the idea arose on the basis of an inscription read over-enthusiastically in the 19th century which in fact commemorates one Rodelgrimi of the early 12th century. The building is on a square plan rising through two squat fenestrated storeys to a dome; were it not for the inscription it would be difficult to date and it is not certain what it was for. However, in its excavated state it can be seen to have been built over an earlier construction housing burial chambers, and it has a *Harrowing of Hell* carved on the lintel, so it is unlikely to have been a baptistery; everything suggests a mausoleum. Its construction is as inexpert as its form is anomalous, although the desire to build a high dome over two or three storeys is also found in Greco-Norman monasteries in Calabria, for instance Santa Maria di Tridetti.

Of San Pietro, a small Romanesque church, there remains only the shell. Santa Maria Maggiore is intact, interesting as an example of the type of TROIA, FOGGIA and Siponto cathedrals, its façade patterned with blind arches inset with lozenges. However, its portal is dated 1198, already with a gable – otherwise a typically 13th-century form – crowning its loaded sequence of arches. Inside, the vaults have been redone, though the plan and supports are said to date to about 1170. Scattered through the town there are old things, including the tiny 8th-/9th-century twin-domed San Salvatore in the medieval district or *rione* Junno. There is a folklore museum, and further afield is the castle, offering panoramic views on a suitable day.

In 1177 William II constituted the so called Honour of Monte Sant'Angelo, essentially the whole Gargano peninsula, as the 'counter-dowry' of his English bride, Joanna, third daughter of Henry II. After William's death its revenues were seized by Tancred of Lecce and Joanna's interest in it ceased after 1191, when her brother Richard I carried her off to Palestine. Thereafter the Gargano suffered tribulations: in 1223 an earthquake that destroyed Siponto, in 1239 a raid by the Venetians taking advantage of the interdict under which the Kingdom lay. However, the port of Siponto had vital importance for Manfred, the centre of whose restricted power had become Lucera, and therefore, once he had won his kingdom, he refounded the city a little to the north-east as Manfredonia, in March 1260, on an hour and a day decided for him by two astrologers. Tracts of the 13th-century walls and the refortified castle remain, amid municipal gardens; however, the town was utterly destroyed by the Turks when they took it in 1620. To the north-east no visitor today will fail to observe the enormous oil refinery. Manfredonia has several restaurants serving fresh fish, in modest *trattorie* within the grid-streeted old town or in more modern places in the concrete buildings, many of them hotels, along or off the 'Lido di Siponto' south-west of the town.

Of Siponto there remain not only the 'Lido' but also two churches, now isolated but both immediately beside the road to Foggia. San Leonardo, further inland, was a priory probably always outside the town; it was given in 1127 to Augustinian canons, who built the surviving church. The church is typically Pugliese in the domical roofing of its nave and quadrant vaults of the aisles. It transpires that in 1234 these Augustinians were richly endowed, owning ten other churches in Capitanata and a few more outside; so they might well then have afforded the elaborate sculptured portal on the main, side entrance to the church. By this date local sculptors were incorporating religious figuration, though not with any great elegance: Christ in glory in the tympanum, the three Magi on the right-hand capitals. On the left it looks like Balaam and his ass, but a more plausible iconography must be St Michael inspiring a mounted pilgrim. One window has a notable carved stone.*transenna* or grille. But alas the canons, lacking a prior, were ruined by the anarchy and war following the death of Frederick II and in 1261 pope Alexander IV gave their buildings to the Teutonic Knights. Hence the dedication to St Leonard, who was frequently invoked against the Saracens: here in a relief on the north flank he appears holding a chain, and in other Teutonic churches dedicated to him 'chains and other instruments of servitude' were hung up as *ex-votos* by former prisoners.

The outbuildings surrounding the church date to the time of the Knights.

Santa Maria Maggiore, now prettily set amid pines and popular for weddings, was the former cathedral of Siponto. Though it has been divergently and rather desperately dated in the past, it seems clear enough today that, fundamentally, this is the church bishop Leo built in the second quarter of the 11th century soon after the see had once again become independent from Benevento. It is not a basilica but square, though it does not resemble the standard medieval Byzantine *quincunx* church, both because it is built in stone and because its interior must have been more spacious. It is a single hall divided only by columns or piers rather than by walls, though the large thick masonry piers are not original: they date from after the 1223 earthquake that brought down all the upper parts. Four great central piers pass through the floor into the crypt, muscling among the network of smaller supports. They should be associated perhaps with a date of 1556 recorded on one of the vaults, but recall the rather similar piers at OTRANTO and might be of the same age, granted that the crypt is itself a later insertion into the church. That is odd, but it is proven by the observation that two of its walls have a second, internal layer of masonry and that its vaults rise a little higher than the bases of the half-columns of the blind arches in the upper church: the floor was raised when the crypt was created. Once again when that was cannot be settled: it may have been as early as 1117, when a consecration is recorded, or after damage sustained in the revolt put down by William I in 1156, or after the earthquake of 1123. So of bishop Leo's church only the walls and their decoration remain (or more exactly the decoration of the internal walls and of the west and south external walls), but they had significant echo in the region (TROIA, FOGGIA, Termoli); and the Sipontine arch and lozenge seems even to recur in Pisa cathedral, built by the Greek-sounding Buschetto from 1063.

The church was built on the site of a still earlier cathedral, which has been excavated beside it to the north – a modest basilica with a mosaic floor. With little doubt the site was never abandoned, for Leo's church preserved the urn of Emilius Tullianus, Byzantine *dux*, who died in 590. The old church probably determined the orientation of Leo's original building, which was originally entered from its northern side, where the old basilica lies, and had a southern apse. The present west entrance with its imposing portal was cut through the wall, and a second, eastern apse provided opposite, in the 13th

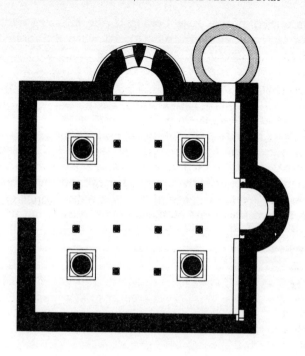

Cathedral, Siponto (crypt level)

century. That did not involve too much disruption to the original decoration since the central arch of the five blind arches to each side was always broader than the others. The blind arches are complemented by an elegant moulding, which runs all the way round the building, linking the imposts of the arches and vaulting the lozenges set into their heads. This moulding-strip, merging into the abaci over the capitals when it meets the imposts, imparts a refined liveliness to the building – refined, because the decoration is otherwise restrained, the capitals and the mouldings spare, only the rows of nondescript foliage round the heads of the arches providing any richness (though most of the capitals of the external arches were later more richly re-carved). Such refinement demands the presumption of established skills, that is to say Byzantine skills, whether the masons were native Pugliese or not: blind arches and so on are common enough in Western Romanesque, but between this and Romanesque there is the same difference as that between Byzantine and Western mosaics, or between living tradition and foreign imitation. Its quality proves it to belong to the masonry tradition of Armenia and especially Syria, where particularly the applied classical orders were developed into a style of relief decoration articulating the whole surface of the building. Siponto is a unique surviving example of sophisticated – not vernacular – Byzantine architecture of the early 11th century.

South of Manfredonia there have been salt-flats at least since Roman times, and they are still extensively farmed (the overhead belt that runs all the way down to BARLETTA conveys the salt to the port there). Also there used to be an acreage of marsh, successfully drained from the later 19th century. The salt must have nourished the vanished Greek city of Salpi, and the remote ruins of Roman Salapia. The coastal resort of Margherita di Savoia and the inland towns of Trinitapoli and San Ferdinando di Puglia are all modern developments.

2

Terra di Bari

Canosa

South of the Cervaro and the Carapelle, which the Romans crossed at Herdoniae, the next river flowing into the gulf of Manfredonia from the Appennines is the Ofanto. The Ofanto they crossed at Canosa, a large and important Roman town in a nodal position on the via Appia Trajana; below the bridge it was once navigable. Today Canosa overlooks the junction of the A14 *autostrada* descending from Ancona and the A16 crossing from Naples. Nevertheless it was already going to sleep in the lower Middle Ages, when first under Norman rule BARI wrested its ancient bishopric away from it, then under Frederick II it was overtaken economically by BARLETTA; Cerignola on the other side of the river is nowadays the more important market town. It still has hardly woken, and at the railway station a spaghetti Western filmcrew seems more likely to arrive than a train.

Numerous Roman tombs are to be seen outside the town, most of them along the old course of the via Trajana between the town and the Ofanto where the Roman bridge still stands, though repaired – also an arch of the 2nd century AD. Within the town in vacant lots there are further Roman remains of no very clear definition, including the *hypogeum* Lagrasta, which in the 19th century yielded a considerable booty now in the museums of Naples and TARANTO. In Canosa's own archaeological museum the collection is more modest. However, the most important ruins are Early Christian. Though certainly prominent earlier (Horace stopped here), Canosa reached its zenith in the 4th, 5th and 6th centuries AD. Virtually unshaken by the invasion and disorder to which Rome and northern Italy fell prey, it was the administrative capital of all 'Apulia and Calabria' (by Calabria was then meant the bottom of the heel, not the toe) and achieved ecclesiastical hegemony under St Sabinus (bishop 514–66), friend of St Benedict, a celebrated builder and saint whose posthumous cult was durable and widespread. He may well have built the dodecagonal baptistery of San Giovanni, which has been rather grossly restored with a dome too heavy and too low. Its closest parallel may be found in the baptistery adjoining the Lateran in Rome. In his *Life* it is reported adjacent to two basilicas, one of which at least has been located by soundings. An inscription bearing his name was found in the ruins of San Leucio, to the south of the town, probably referring to his repair of the 5th-century building.

San Leucio was once very large, on a double tetraconch (2 × 4-apsed) plan found in Italy in only one other example, San Lorenzo in Milan, but more common in Syria. Ultimately it may derive from the Constantinian 'Golden Octagon' in Antioch. The plan is generated by three concentric squares: one open, of four piers supporting the central dome; the second of walls pierced by passages and by an apse in the centre of each side; the third an ambulatory around the second, with its own matching apses. Some of the columns of the inner apses have been re-erected. The altar was in the western inner apse, which probably in the 6th century under Sabinus received its mosaic floor with a peacock. The remaining mosaic floor, geometric but of high quality, is dated to the 5th century. The capitals with female heads expressing baroque pathos derive from an earlier Hellenistic temple on the site, re-used in the Christian church. The dedication to St Leucius, first bishop of Brindisi, cannot have been original, but must date from the end of the 7th century when, his relics having been brought to TRANI, probably Canosa got a piece of them, too. Although at the end of the 6th century Canosa had fallen to the Lombards, and its clergy had fled, the Lombards Christianized and the clergy were soon back. By the end of the 8th century the town was once again 'quite prosperous' though it could not achieve its former pre-eminence. The end of the 8th century is the date favoured for the little ruined church of Santa Sofia in the countryside to the east, on the site of an older catacomb. Various rusty and battered yellow signs indicate the roads to take to these monuments from the main piazza and *villa comunale* beside the cathedral.

The cathedral, which had been standing for some time before its rededication to St Sabinus by pope Paschal II in 1101, is not on the site of the Early Christian cathedral, that much is certain; but a church on this site was chosen as the new deposit of the relics of St Sabinus at the end of the 8th century. To what degree did it dictate the form of the present church, or, as archaeologists have only asked more recently, is there any good reason why the present church is not the very same as that built in the 8th century? It is true that some

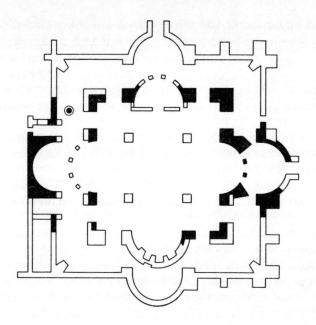

San Leucio, Canosa

of the capitals in the transepts – those that are not spoils – are 11th-century; on the other hand the masonry technique that is exposed above the tomb of Bohemund beside the south transept – strips of brick sandwiched between courses of stone – is typical of much earlier building. Or perhaps it dates more exactly to the mid 9th century, after the Saracens had sacked the town, but failed to take the citadel, the former acropolis and the later Norman and Angevin castle, of which the base walls and one tower incorporating antique masonry remain.

The first three bays of the church are an extension of the early 19th century, although the old portal was transferred to the modern façade. The bays of the original building have coloured-marble columns set forward of the piers to support, or seem to support, the domical vaults; similar columns, rather dwarfed by the massive piers against which they lean, decorate the transepts. The church has five domes in the form of a T, a plan which may recall Holy Apostles in Constantinople, later adopted for St Mark's in Venice; the 'pre-St Mark's' reported in Venice may have been similar, but Holy Apostles and St Mark's have their domes in a Greek cross, not a T. A better

parallel might be the late 8th-century Lombard cathedral of BENE-
VENTO. Many questions besetting the building might have been
settled by the form of the crypt, but it was restored in 1567; formerly
– but not necessarily originally – the deep crypt was on two levels,
with an upper chapel and a larger one below where the body of St
Sabinus rested.

In the later 19th century there was a move to dismember the
church's two outstanding pieces of 11th-century furniture, but by
that time the ice of indifference to the high Middle Ages was melting,
and they were saved. On the left-hand side of the nave Acceptus's
great pulpit is no longer in its original position and is isolated, but
intact. It is signed: 'On the orders of my lord Guitbert the venerable
priest, I the sinner archdeacon Acceptus made this work'. Who
Guitbert may have been is not known, or why he should have been
Acceptus's lord. Thus the pulpit has no date, but is generally
regarded as the first surviving work of the sculptor who carved
pulpits (now extant only in fragments) for MONTE SANT'ANGELO and
SIPONTO dated 1039 and 1041. In a very beautiful, dull grey marble of
a kind not found later (it was quarried probably from a Roman
building), it is a restrained and composed piece; its ornament,
fundamentally Lombard in vocabulary, stylistically retains the fleshiness of Lombard stuccowork but has great sharpness and precision,
thanks to the marble medium and perhaps also to influence from
metalwork. Undoubtedly something of bronze in a treasury – as
likely as not another eagle, probably inlaid with gilt or enamel,
which Acceptus's surface patterns imitate – lies behind the eagle
supporting the lectern. Such eagles rapidly enter the Pugliese
repertoire and suggest Acceptus's influence (he is likely enough also
to have worked in Bari cathedral). Certainly no other named
sculptor of any accomplishment was active in Europe at this date.
However, Acceptus was not in any appropriate sense the 'father' of
Pugliese Romanesque sculpture, since a much wider range of
models and patterns – drawn from antique, Byzantine, Islamic and
even oriental sources – rapidly swamped the tenuous Lombard
inheritance on which he had begun to build. This subsequent
eclecticism is evident in the two diverse parts of the bishop's throne
in the choir.

The throne is inscribed rather obscurely in the upper part:
'Bishop, in order to possess an eternal chair after this one, let the
inner truth correspond to the outer word. That which you hold [a
candle?], give in hope; brandish the light so that as you provide light

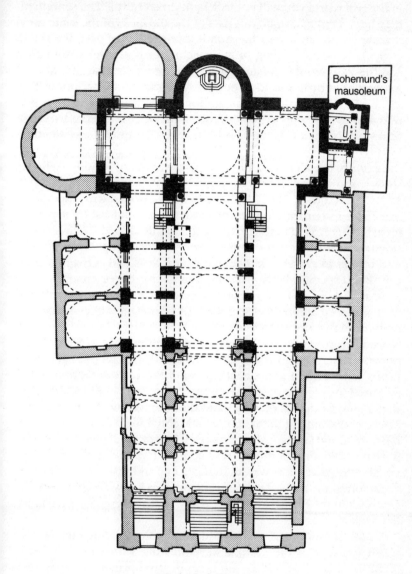

Bohemund's
mausoleum

Cathedral, Canosa

in the real world you will not lack light [in eternity].' The sentiment may be Acceptus's, since this part of the throne is of the same grey marble and is similar to the pulpit; but the lower part, the relief eagles, the beams ending in moustache heads, the relief sphinxes and the wonderful elephants on which the whole rests, are not by Acceptus but by Romuald, as emerges from another inscription: 'For Bishop Urso Romuald was the author to this'. Bishop Urso was the one who tried to oppose abbot Elias on the occasion of the arrival of relics of St Nicholas at BARI; he ruled from 1079 until his assassination in 1089. While the style of the lower part is not so far from Acceptus, the taste is: the elephants in particular, which are wilfully stylized, show a move away from his simple-looking sobriety towards the exotic and fantastic. The elephants are caparisoned with superficial ornament rather than carved or modelled as animals; their plastic form has decreased as their decoration has increased. Their inspiration from exotic objects is beyond doubt, reflecting Puglia's medieval role as an *entrepôt* between east and west, and perhaps, too, at this date a specifically Norman fascination for the oriental.

Something very like the probable models for Romuald's elephants have survived among the so called 'Charlemagne's chesspieces' of ivory from the former treasury of the French kings' burial church of St Denis north of Paris. These were evidently made in South Italy, possibly Salerno, and it has been hazarded that abbot Suger of St Denis (later regent and signal patron of the earliest Gothic style) acquired the pieces when travelling in South Italy in 1123, although they come from different sets and do not make up a whole game. There is also among them an unmistakably Indian ivory, a wonderfully grand and fantastically animated figure of an elephant and rider; it is not known whether it was acquired at the same time, but considering that chess was an Indian game and that the St Denis set are amongst the earliest western chesspieces known (older than the Lewis set in the British Museum), some Indian exemplar there must have been.

Round the dome of a small square marble building outside the south transept of the church the following words may be read: 'Beneath this covering lies the great-hearted prince of Syria, than whom none greater will ever be born. Byzantium, four times defeated, and Persia, the largest country in the world, long felt the strength and cunning of Bohemund. On the battlefield with every ten men he conquered a thousand-strong battalion, as the city of Antioch knows, too.' On its bronze doors another inscription runs:

'Why the world shouts (*boat mundus*), of what great worth was Bohemund (*Boamundus*), Byzantium is witness, Syria tells the tale. He laid seige to the former, the latter he protected from her enemy; therefore the Greeks rejoice at Syria's present loss. May what to Greek brings joy, to Syrian brings grief (both rightly), to you, Bohemund, bring true salvation. Bohemund outdid the wealth of kings and the works of the powerful, and in his own right earned his name: he was a roll of thunder over the world. Since the world lay at his feet, I cannot call him a man, though I will not call him a god. While he lived he strove to die for Christ, and on his death deserved to receive life. This therefore may Christ's mercy grant him, that he fights in heaven as God's own faithful athlete. As you enter look at the doors; see what is written; pray that Bohemund may be granted to heaven and there given a place.' Entering, having seen the doors, you will find the room bare, save for a single slab inscribed 'Boamundus'.

Bohemund, prince of Antioch, was the only son of Robert Guiscard by his first marriage to Alberada, the daughter of a Norman baron, who brought a dowry of 200 knights, extremely useful to the landless, penniless adventurer newly arrived from Normandy about 1050. However, when the death of his second elder brother Humphrey in 1057 had left him leader of the Hauteville clan, Robert divorced Alberada for a much better match, Sichelgaita, daughter of Gisulf, prince of Salerno. His sons by Sichelgaita became his heirs, although Bohemund was brought up by him, served with him, and became his military second-in-command on his expedition in search of the Byzantine empire in 1080. It was Bohemund he left in command of his army when he was forced to return to quell the revolt that had broken out in his absence, although it was his eldest son by Sichelgaita, Roger Borsa, who he had left in Italy as his regent and heir presumptive. When he died in 1085 all he had conquered passed to Roger, with no provision at all for Bohemund, although one chronicler reports that he had planned to make Bohemund Byzantine emperor, while he himself took over the Muslim world. Bohemund's epitaph quite rightly states that he made his own name, without a birthright.

Bohemund's subsequent action incidentally demonstrates the fragility of the early Norman state. As he never would have been able to do after Roger II had established the Kingdom, he made war on Roger Borsa, allying with other untamed barons and also abusing the aspirations of the towns to force territory and concessions, from which he then made war again. He took several towns in southern Puglia from Roger, and suborned the leading city of COSENZA in Calabria by swearing to the citizens that he would never erect a citadel there. Meanwhile Roger Borsa had been forced to make the same concession to the inhabitants of BARI, incited of course by Bohemund to revolt; the half-brothers then swapped ownership of the two towns, each freeing the other's hands. By 1095 Bohemund ruled all southern Puglia (he is often known incorrectly as the prince of Taranto), and was well placed by 1096 to play an increasingly important part in the First Crusade, not only because it sailed from the Pugliese seaboard and he could raise a significant body of men but also because he knew and had fought the emperor Alexius Comnene under his father.

Throughout the journey to Constantinople and after arrival there Bohemund showed greater discipline and clarity of purpose than the other leaders of the Crusade, and he persuaded them to swear fealty to Alexius before setting out for Syria. However, once arrived at Antioch he seems to have known he had found what he was looking for. It was Bohemund who against what looked like rapidly lengthening odds, took from the Muslims the enormous, impregnable and fabulously rich city of Antioch, and defeated the forces sent to relieve it. He then held on to it and pressed his claim for it, fulfilling his crusading vow by a perfunctory visit to Jerusalem, which he had left to others to capture and sack. He shook off his obligation to the Byzantine emperor on the grounds that the emperor had not fulfilled his own obligation as lord to aid his vassal in his need, nor had even dared to come across hostile territory to receive the city from him. In 1099 Bohemund was entitled prince of Antioch by the Pisan patriarch of Jerusalem Daimbert (partly in order to further his own similar, though less successful ambitions). By that time Bohemund enjoyed an immense reputation as a soldier among Franks, Greeks and Muslims (by whom he was known as 'the little god of the Christians', an epithet to which his epitaph probably alludes). His capture in 1100 in a skirmish with the Turks did little to diminish his reputation: his enormous ransom of 100,000 gold pieces only suggested his worth, and in addition a legend became widely known in the west that the emir's daughter had fallen in love with him and therefore sought baptism. However, on his release in 1103 his campaigning was less successful, and, threatened both by the Byzantines and by the Turks, he was forced to return to the west to recruit more knights, landing at BARI early in 1105.

Bohemund's mission to raise a new army was successful, despite the ignominious failure of a second expedition sent to Jerusalem in 1101. He was widely and enthusiastically fêted on the tour he undertook across most of Europe, a new expedition under his sole leadership was accredited by the pope, and he received from king Philip of France the hand of his daughter, Constance. However, Alexius had prepared for his coming, and when he attempted in 1107 to retread the route down the via Egnatia he had once taken with his father, he met many more difficulties. He sat down before Durazzo, but failed to take it, and was forced a year later to make a humiliating peace with Alexius and abandon the expedition. He never saw Antioch again, although his son Bohemund II, only two when his father died in Puglia in 1111, eventually inherited it. His mother Alberada, who lived on until 1122, is known to have arranged the tomb, but its shape and form surely reflect Bohemund's wishes and travels. Precedents for the monument have been found in Cairo, Samarra or Buchara (the mausoleum of Saminid Ismail, dated 907); however, these, too, derive from the mausolea of late antiquity, and surely, if it is not an imitation of the Holy Sepulchre, Bohemund's tomb is likely to reflect something now vanished in Antioch.

The tomb has a square plan (slightly cropped by the wall of the church) over which a small octagonal drum raises a round dome. Its ornament and capitals are local, not orientalizing. The fragmentary adjacent portico seems to have been part of the same construction. The bronze doors of the tomb are signed (lower right): 'Of St Sabinus of Canosa Roger of the bells of Melfi made these doors and the candlestick'. The three discs on the left-hand valve (door) have patterns pastiching Kufic; the right-hand valve has two more Arabizing discs, and two panels of figures in the same technique as the doors of MONTE SANT'ANGELO, although here the silver for the flesh parts and the niello have fallen out. In style the figures are like those of Monte Sant'Angelo, but the modelling is fussier and less confident. Also two separately cast relief figures have fallen out, one from each door. The two figures worshipping the lost Christ on the right-hand door have been identified as Bohemund and Roger Borsa, and the three standing figures below them as Bohemund II, king William I and Bohemund's nephew and lieutenant, Tancred, but there is no evidence for it, and Bohemund II, aged 13 when Alberada died, is an impossibility. It is apparent that the two valves do not match: one or both of them were taken from elsewhere, although the inscription referring to St Sabinus must date from after the rededication of 1101.

Cannae

It is not too easy to tread Hannibal's footsteps on the field where the Carthaginian invader, carrying the Second Punic War to the enemy, achieved his greatest victory against Rome in 216 BC. The best thing to do, perhaps, is to stand on the hill where an unfriendly brick building and the tattered strands of fences – and some remains – indicate an archaeological site (one which has, in fact, nothing to do with the battle), and survey to the north-west the basin of the Ofanto still empty before you. Having advanced up the main street of the site, you will find a column, erected in 1937, on a suitable eminence. There is nothing to see. Probably you will still feel the wind that, in August, blew dust into the Romans' faces; although it is known that the Romans crossed the river to join battle, the course of the Ofanto through the plain has since altered. Another factor in the difficulty of locating the battlefield is the number of other battles that were fought hereabouts: one during the Social War of 89 BC, another between rival Lombards in AD 841 and between Lombards and Saracens in 871, and one more in 1018, an important battle in which the Byzantine catepan Boioannes defeated the rebel Melos of Bari, using against Melos's Normans his own Cossacks. The discovery of mutilated human remains is therefore not conclusive.

Precisely the merit of Hannibal's victory was its achievement against a numerically superior army on a featureless, open plain. Many schoolboys have learnt how he set his weaker centre a little forward of the wings, in order to absorb and encourage the impetus of the Roman advance on which his own stronger wings closed, besetting its flank and rear. The Romans were slaughtered, and only the commanding consul, M. Terentius Varro, and seventy men escaped – no-one knows quite how, says Livy. Like many others before and after, Georg Arnold Jacobi visiting in 1792 felt 'fluttering' about him 'the spirits of all those thousands of men who were massacred for having followed a Hannibal or a Varro', even though he might have been standing miles away. He and others tended to forget, when they took their Livy in hand, that the Augustan historian, for all the vividness of his description, was not a witness to the battle, fought two hundred years earlier. In Jacobi's day one was shown the fountain where the other consul, L. Emilius Paullus, the one whose turn to command it was not that day, the patrician who was sensible and unpopular unlike Varro who was plebeian and who lost the battle by his rashness, had a drink before making the dying speech Livy reports. According to Livy, Varro was deliberately provoked by Hannibal to join battle, Hannibal sending his cavalry against his infantry to infuriate and frustrate them in rather the same way that the Turkish cavalry tried to infuriate the heavily armoured knights of the Latin dominions in the Levant, who, when they broke rank, lost; therefore experienced commanders such as Bohemund insisted they must be patient despite the darts and insults thrown at them. Hannibal was later accused of knowing how to win a victory but not how to use one, but that is a simple view of his formidable problem, to make the Romans fight when they only needed to wait for him to go away. He had been two years on Italian soil before the Romans 'gave' him at Cannae the decisive encounter he needed; even so, it was not enough, and his army of occupation was eventually worn down to an ineffectual, small force, constantly on the move, able only to harry as the cities and strongpoints one by one returned to Roman control. He retreated back to Africa in 206 BC.

Cannae (now known as Canne della Battaglia) was a small town or suburb between Canosa and Barletta. In ancient times it was a grain depot, and it was in order to secure his supplies that Hannibal was here in August 216 BC; both cisterns and pits for the storage of grain have been identified in the site. Its archaeology is not only Roman but medieval, and its most significant remains, besides the fortifications of many periods, are the Early Christian basilicas that have been laid bare.

Barletta

Barletta is a grubby and scabby town, for the most part. Its petrol refinery and its newly restored castle are clean and shiny, but its old town is filthy and porous with crime and decay, its cathedral is derelict, and the new town is without qualities or quality. Barletta is the most northern of a series of similar cities occupying the long, straight, flat seaboard down to BARI: Barletta, TRANI, BISCEGLIE, MOLFETTA, GIOVINAZZO. They have a standard pattern, to which Barletta also conforms: old town, gone to slum, by the old harbour (which has been subsumed at Barletta into the modern industrial port); in the old town the cathedral and beside it a castle; new town surrounding the landward face of the old town, its own inland extension curtailed by the railway line (usually the road from the station to the old town is a central axis). The new town has generally low whitewashed buildings along straight, grid-plan streets, among which the acreage of one large block is given to the *villa comunale*, the hub of the city at any rate during the *serata*. On the other side of the railway line but the hither side of the recently completed *raccordo* ('expressway') there are post-war blocks of flats, and beyond the *raccordo* industry and trading estates.

Barletta does not lack monuments, besides the castle and the cathedral already mentioned. Outside the church of San Sepolcro, situated once just within the walls and now just on the edge of the old town, there stands the formerly mutilated but now whole 'colossus' of the emperor Valerian I (364–75), an interesting survival no doubt but not an important work of art: his armour is broadly modelled and the face, though similar in its characterization to the colossal head of Constantine in Rome, has very little presence, besides being much less colossal, only twice life-size. The statue was cast up on the beach in the 13th century, in the early 14th century those became bells that were his legs and arms, and the present limbs, with the cross the arm upholds, were attached in the late 15th century. From that time it has stood here, regarded as a suitable mascot for the town's market-place. Between the statue and the castle the kind of robbery known as *scippo*, the grabbing of a handbag or camera by a footpad or motorcyclist – a South Italian speciality – is extremely common.

The church of San Sepolcro is so dedicated because it belonged to the canons of the Holy Sepulchre in Jerusalem, although in the early 14th century it became an ordinary parish church. Barletta is first mentioned as a pilgrimage port in 1002, and by the 13th century had establishments run by the Hospitallers of Jerusalem, the Templars, the Teutonic Knights and the Knights of St Lazarus. San Sepolcro is first documented in 1138 (though the document refers back to 1062) and probably always had its present plan; it was never round, unlike most other churches of the same dedication. The present church was built during the course of the 12th century, originally with an octagonal crossing-tower (later replaced and then altogether demolished) and with a wooden roof over the nave, which was not completed until the early 13th century. Its interior proportions and prominent cornice may be compared with RUVO cathedral. The Holy Sepulchre cannons having been undone by the fall of Jerusalem, the church then fell into disrepair. In the early 14th century king Robert provided funds to vault the nave, strengthening

the street-facing flank with blind arches and roofing it in Pugliese
fashion with a series of stone-tiled pyramids. The curious gallery in
the first bay of the nave and its outjutting broken apse belong to the
early 13th century; it was a chapel and perhaps also a committee
room, and gave out on to a portico of which only the arch springers
remain over the western door.

The Museo De Nittis nearby in the via Cavour houses archaeology, odds and ends, an enormous collection of the paintings of
Giuseppe ('Peppino') De Nittis, and a bust of Frederick II more than
life-size. Although the inscription and base were added in the 19th
century, and the bust has only a vague provenance, its identification
can be confirmed by comparison to Frederick's coins, which show
the same toga and brooch, laurel round the head (now missing) and
fillet descending the back of the neck, in a patent revival of ancient
imperial iconography. Unfortunately part of the lip is broken, dis-
torting the expression. It has been suggested that the bust was
originally the upper part of an equestrian statue. What is perhaps
most remarkable is the energetic turn of the elongated neck, which
is completely unclassical but directly anticipates, for instance, the
prophets carved by Giovanni Pisano for Siena cathedral or Pisa
baptistery. (The bust may have been moved to the castle).

Peppino De Nittis (1846–84), whose work occupies several
rooms, is perhaps best known as a friend of Degas. Born in Barletta of
a Risorgimento revolutionary, he reached Paris aged 21 and managed immediately to settle. He painted accomplished and fresh
works in which, like the contemporary Impressionists, he seems to
want us to believe that the 1870s were one long picnic. In 1874 he
exhibited with the 'Independents, Realists and Impressionists' in
Nadar's studio. In 1877 he took up the use of pastels, intending to
demonstrate 'modern qualities' in this 18th-century, but conveni-
ently rapid medium, influencing the like-minded Degas in the same
direction. In 1884 he died of a stroke, aged 38. He was well liked,
successful and skilful – it can rapidly be seen how well he can turn a
vase of flowers or an elegant breakfast dish, or put the chill or heat in
a landscape – and is now perhaps underrated. There are works
here from all periods of his life, recalling Meissonier on the one hand
and anticipating Bonnard on the other.

Entering the old town, passing several ill-kept *palazzi*, one arrives
down the via Duomo at the cathedral, which has been fenced off for
several years. Here in 1162 the *proto* of the cathedral, Simiacca, was
together working with his son Luca; in the nave an inscription

commemorates the donation of the price of two columns in August 1153, when Ascalon fell to Latin seige – indicating directly how Barletta's prosperity depended on the Crusade movement. The collapse of the Latin kingdom of Jerusalem would have delayed consecration until 1267, although most of the sculpture – there are several reliefs set in the stonework as well as guardian animals over the portals – must date to the late 12th century. In the early 14th century at the time when provision was also made for San Sepolcro, the old east end was demolished and a larger French Gothic choir was added to the Pugliese Romanesque nave.

Down the via S. Andrea, the church of Sant'Andrea has a rich Romanesque portal, or rather two, one begun and not carried through, the second one, including the signed tympanum, finishing off. Inside the church, if access can be gained, one can see a painting by Giovanni Bellini's rival Alvise Vivarini, retaining some of its intensity despite the gloom and the dust. Not far away is the Cantina della Disfida: the 'disfida' or challenge which took place in 1503 became in the 19th century a symbol of the town. During the war for the Kingdom between Louis XII and Ferdinand II of Aragon, eventually won by Ferdinand, a captured French captain, La Motte, declared the Italians to be worthless soldiers. A combat was arranged, 13 Italians led by Ettore Fieramosca against 13 Frenchmen, who were all either killed or captured without much trouble by the South Italians. An extravagantly decorated palace, the Della Marra, is late 16th-century.

The castle is Norman, Swabian, Angevin and Hapsburg. Its massive bastions, each housing, beneath a vast dome pierced at the top to let out the smoke, circular platforms from which cannon could fire from slits through 320°, were built between 1532 and 1537 by Charles V. He also built a hangar for the repair of the cannon, and the great ramp and curving stair that carried horses, other wheeled vehicles and cannon from the square central courtyard up on to the ramparts. He considerably rebuilt and thickened the walls, but on the right of the entrance a Norman gate can be seen inside them, and in the adjacent wing Gothic rooms. In 1991 there were guides eager to show you as much as you wished to see, amid signs of the use of the bastions for conferences, and many empty rooms awaiting the collections that might make the castle a museum.

Trani

Trani is Puglia at its very best. It is all stone and whitewash, blue sea, blue sky, sultry sun. Its cathedral, isolated on its promontory by modern clearance, stands in pure and tall silhouette unforgettably photogenic, particularly at sunset. Of all churches in Puglia, it best embodies the medieval metaphor of a shining beacon. Beside it the sea beats and the birds wheel against Frederick II's castle. In the wide basin-shaped harbour ropes are coiled on the quay and the wooden boats have cracked paint. Beside the port the old town is run down but not to slum – in the state probably it has always been – except where a few buildings house tourist restaurants. The old town gives way to the newer town with easy transition; the newest town is beside the next bay to the south-east. You might consider staying in Trani rather than BARI, which is easily visited from it. Trani is known further for its *moscato* or medium-weight sweet wine of honeycomb colour, and for its marble, which has been used widely since the Second World War as a cladding.

Though it had no significant Roman history, Trani became a place of some importance under the Lombards, as the presence beneath the cathedral of a dank shrine dedicated to St Leucius is living testament. The relics of this first bishop of Brindisi were brought here in the late 8th century after the more southern city's sack by the Saracens. The walls of the apse are pierced to give access from a pilgrims' ambulatory. However, the shrine seems to have been dug within a much larger basilica dated to the 4th/6th century, of which traces were found in the post-war restorations. It seems to have occupied virtually the same plan as the present church, and probably the twin columns of the upper church arcade are a throwback to it. A sign of the town's prominence from the end of the 10th century is the activity of its bishop, or sometimes archbishop, who from this time entered into diplomatic and diplomatist conflict with the archbishop of Canosa and Bari, and briefly in the early 1060s took over the see of Siponto. After Bari had obtained the bones of St Nicholas from Myra in 1087 – and Trani seems to have played a part in the struggle for their possession once they had arrived – the bishop of Trani more or less manufactured the cult of St Nicholas the Pilgrim, forcing through the canonization of the saint while pope Urban II was in Bari in 1096, and initiating the new cathedral dedicated to him the following year. However, while St Nicholas of Myra was an antique saint worshipped all over the Balkans and eastern Mediterranean, Nicholas the Pilgrim was virtually nobody, a Greek youth who, despite his stammer, had the gift of healing and on his way in pilgrimage to Rome had died in Trani in 1094. Similarly, in the traffic of pilgrims and commerce Trani was second to Bari. By contrast to Bari its policy was often pro-Greek, and it seems to have had close links with Venice. Certain laws of the sea according to Trani are among the earliest surviving maritime codes. There were Norman counts of Trani, descended from Peter I or Pietrone, an energetic builder of fortifications in the 1060s.

The new cathedral was slow in building: not even the crypt seems to have been completed until 1143, the date of the translation of St Nicholas's relics. It is above ground, with windows, airy and light, with a fine forest of slender marble columns and carved capitals. It is entered from an abutting underchurch, this windowless, transformed from the old basilica and retaining the former dedication to the Virgin; it has a couple of 14th-century bishops' tombs and a few frescos. After 1143 building seems to have been much swifter, for the body of the upper church is dated to about the 1160s by the fragments of mosaic surviving in the floor of the choir: they are by the same workshop as those in Otranto cathedral, signed and dated 1162–5 by Pantaleone. Generally, the church is on the pattern of its rival, San Nicola in BARI, but in several aspects deviates and was evidently always to be taller. It has the same open transept and boxed-T plan, but no dome over the crossing (in Bari an afterthought, and here too risky – the building is fairly unstable anyway, and even since the major campaign of restoration of the 1960s has had to be closed again). Like San Nicola it has galleries or *matronea* over the aisles, which are reached by stairs in the tower attached at the west and are true galleries, with a floor, unlike those of many other clones of San Nicola. It has its own double columns, as mentioned, the capitals of which were destroyed in the 19th-century superfetation, now removed. Externally, like San Nicola, it has deep buttressing arches along the nave and matching blind arches round the transepts, but it has no external galleries and no flat east end. It has no flat east end because there were no eastern towers intended; the western belfry must always have been envisaged, or already have existed in some form. Instead of external galleries it has abundant decoration in the form of a cornice running round the top of the transept, as well as round the windows and portals and in outcrops in the blank wall.

By around 1180, work was proceeding on the western end:

Barisanus of Trani, author of the bronze doors in the western portal, signed and dated 1179 another pair at Ravello (he made yet a third pair for Monreale). One might suppose him to have made his first doors in his native city, but the three sets are so similar there is no telling. His signature and self-portrait appear shrunk in humility at the feet of a figure of St Nicholas the Pilgrim, one of the panels at about eye-level. The other panels of the door display single or static figures or affronted beasts or other patterns typical of silks and brocades or, down below where one would have to be a child or stoop to see them, scenes of levity such as two figures fighting. Unlike the earlier doors at TROIA or MONTE·SANT'ANGELO or CANOSA the decoration is in relief, and without silver or niello insertions; and Barisanus's work is conservative and unambitious compared either to those doors or to those of Bonannus of Pisa, who at the same date provided other doors for Monreale and for Pisa cathedral. At Trani, the stonework round the doors is more interesting: the sculptor can be identified without doubt as a Frenchman, specifically from Toulouse. Those Old Testament figures that have not been too badly weathered elegantly perform antics, crossing their legs, their faces beaming, as artificial and unworldly as Pugliese creations but with so much more charm and grace; and they are human, not mythical. The employment of an unnaturalised craftsman in Puglia is an unusual case, which an exodus of western artisans after the fall of Jerusalem in 1187 is generally assumed to explain.

The richly decorated arches that once supported a porch or narthex in front of the portal are not by the same hand or workshop. Similar porches (at BARLETTA or BARI or at Ognissanti here in Trani) belong to the 13th century. These arches harmonise with the rebuilt tower, which is signed 'Nicolaus sacerdos et protomagister', presumably the same Nicholas the priest who in 1229 worked at BITONTO. However, the last of the tower's five further storeys was not completed until past the middle of the 14th century. In the course of the 13th century, decoration continued around the upper parts of the church, which displays, unfortunately at an enormous height, some of the finest examples of Pugliese Romanesque sculpture. The oxen and some other animals that appear begin to approach the stature and naturalism of the oxen lowing from the towers of the French cathedral of Laon, and remarkable among them is a full-size stone copy of the spinario (the nickname of a Hellenistic bronze Boy removing a thorn from his foot that in the Middle Ages stood outside the Lateran palace in Rome). Such work anticipates the achievement of Nicola Pisano; and in Trani there was once an octagonal pulpit, in that way at least a precusor of Nicola's hexagonal and octagonal pulpits of 1260 and 1265 for Pisa and Siena cathedrals. Otherwise the repertoire is the usual Pugliese comic-book of monsters, adorning, however, a cornice recalling Roman imperial buildings (compare those of FOGGIA and TROIA). It is difficult to date such sculpture at all precisely: the prevailing view is that church building and decoration came to a stop during the last two decades of Frederick II's reign, and therefore that the sculpture is Angevin, following the fall of Manfred in 1266, but Frederick's quarrels with the pope need not have materially affected the activity and financing of ecclesiastical workshops. There is a rich, heavy cornice running all round the transept – its architect well judged the size and weight of decoration needed to crown such a tall building. Since the cornice disappears under the gable of the nave roof, the nave must have been heightened subsequently, and a clear break in the masonry can be seen below the western rose window.

There are various other monuments in Trani besides the cathedral. There is a diocesan museum nearby, though I have never gained entrance to it. Most of the several other churches are again not easy to enter. The castle, too, has long been closed, though restoration is proceeding and so one day may be concluded. Built between 1233 and 1249, it is one of Frederick II's most attractive castles, not greatly altered, with one wall still sheer to the sea and the moat in which it washed still deep; the walls studded from top to base with swelling rustication; the towers and keep square and broad, clean and unparapetted. The great open paved space in front of the cathedral and beside the castle is memorable. The few passing cars or visiting Italian tourists do not disturb the solitude and peace in which one may contemplate the view.

Going inland from the castle (via Alvarez), one finds the flank of San Giacomo, adorned by a sculpted window, now blocked; its almost square façade has a portal in style rather like the arches on the cathedral façade, so late 12th-century, and above it a picturesque disarray of protruding animal and human heads. Just by is the via Pagano, which divides the old town by the port from the newer grid streets; further down it Sant'Andrea, a small 11th/12th-century church of Byzantine type, central-domed under a Pugliese pyramid roof, with re-used antique columns and other parts inside; shortly past Sant'Andrea San Francesco. This originally Benedictine church, consecrated in 1184, has a three-domed nave, each dome again under an external pyramid, like San Leonardo di Siponto or other Benedictine foundations such as Valenzano and Conversano (see SOUTH OF BARI). Opposite San Francesco the via Ognissanti, pointing back towards the cathedral, leads to the Ognissanti church, a foundation first mentioned in 1170 and belonging to the Templars. Its large 13th-century portico, two bays deep, would have communicated with the Templars' nearby hospital and probably served as a refuge during the night as well as the day; today one has to make out its grimy sculpture through high railings. The church juts a pretty three-apsed posterior on to the harbour front. Several of the surrounding *palazzi*, some of them isolated by modern clearance, have a history. There is also an 11th-century San Martino.

Across the harbour, occupying the other horn from the cathedral, is what is now the town's *villa comunale*, which is properly for once a small park, formerly a fort. However, the piazza Repubblica, inland along the via Plebiscito/via Cavour, is the focus for the daily *serata*. Downtown Trani happens further along the coast, in the adjoining, much wider bay to the south-east, along the road leading to Santa Maria della Colonna. Here may be found the native restaurants, among which the best food is accompanied unfortunately by white-jacket entertainment, with piano and microphone. The church of Santa Maria della Colonna, another Benedictine monastery passing in early modern times to the Franciscans, includes older, Romanesque parts in its essentially 13th-century structure; should one visit, it has Pugliese quadrant vaults in the aisles, but the rose-window visible from the road is its finest feature. Beyond Santa Maria della Colonna is the town beach. All this stretch is unbelievably busy on a Sunday morning: everyone comes out, in cars or on motorcycles, driving deliberately at idling speed so they may salute their friends, or halting unconcernedly to converse or buy cakes or flowers. Once upon a time no doubt this was part of going to church, but now the crush is so dense it must take an hour to get there: the ritual of promenade seems for most an entirely adequate substitution for religious ceremony.

Bisceglie, Molfetta, Giovinazzo

Eighteenth- and 19th-century travellers between BARLETTA and BARI described the road as enchanting. Johann Hermann von Riedesel found 'every four miles a small village, and the countryside around highly cultivated. Giovinazzo and Molfetta are beautifully situated and charming.' Fruit-trees, cornfields and vineyards were pleasantly set against the deep blue of the Adriatic. Often the travellers had suffered a tedious journey across mountains or the deserted pastures of the Tavoliere, so were the more surprised and delighted. Nowadays it is the opposite. It remains largely true south of Bari, but on the coast to its north the countryside has been eradicated. The road conveys a ceaseless belt of traffic past factories and warehouses, old tyres, garages, lorries, junk-yards and building-sites, which occasionally give way to dry-stone walls, within which the fields are bare and the few trees barren. There are still fields and orchards inland, rendered enormous and monotonous by intensive farming, but along the coast between Trani and Bari only commercial and industrial fall-out.

At Bisceglie perhaps the most interesting monument is the church of Sant'Adoeno, a saint imported by the Normans from Rouen, where he was bishop and is known as St Ouen. In the time of Robert Guiscard Normans seem to have settled in comparatively large numbers in the country of Trani, judging by the number of fortifications count Peter I of Trani erected – Bisceglie was walled in 1060 – and by this church, which tradition reports Norman soldiers to have built themselves. Of the original structure, founded in 1074, not much remains, except the door and the tomb beside it of Bartholomew, the founder; the upper parts, including the rose-window and the statue of St Ouen, were redone in the 14th century, and the interior in the 17th. It is known, however, that the church was built for the use of the inhabitants of the *casali* or hamlets of Cirignano, Pacciano and Zappino; the territory of Bisceglie (and of TERLIZZI to its south) is particularly rich in the towers or fortified refuges such *casali* had. Pacciano has both its tower and its church, of the specially Pugliese 'contracted cross' type, having a single nave with a raised central dome (like San Vito, CORATO, or Torre Santa Croce between Terlizzi and Bitonto). Another such 11th-century *casale* church is the so-called 'temple of Janus'. Also in the countryside round Bisceglie, the dolmen di Chianca is the northernmost of the large group of prehistoric monolithic tombs to be found in the Salento peninsula.

Among other churches in Bisceglie is the cathedral, of the type of Bari San Nicola and Bari cathedral, begun in 1073 but wholly 13th-century in character, first consecrated in 1297. Various pieces of sculpture adorn the exterior; in the 1970s the interior was stripped of its 18th-century superfetation and its galleries or *matronea* were once again brought to light. Santa Margherita is another 'contracted cross' church like that of Pacciano just mentioned, though later: it was owned by the leading family of medieval Bisceglie, the Falconi, whose fortunes seem to have been founded by the eponymous Falco, who had been an official of Henry VI's court, and who in 1197 founded the church, too. It has remained in the family (twice by a married daughter's inheritance), and has three surviving Falconi tombs, one largely ruined of the warrior Basilio or Mauro Falcone; another small one for children of the family dated 1276 and signed by Anseramo da Trani, who was active again at TERLIZZI; and a third of the earlier 13th century by Pietro Facitulo of Bari, to whom is attributed the refortifying of the castle at Bisceglie under Frederick II. Pietro Facitulo's tomb is in an extraordinarily ornate and lacy but idiosyncratic Gothic (now also rather mossy). Many other Falconi were prominent as soldiers, courtiers and bishops, though none of those, as it happens, were buried here.

Molfetta was the birthplace of Corrado Giaquinto (1703–65), an accomplished artist-decorator of the late Baroque Neapolitan/ Roman school. He led the kind of peripatetic career typical of Italian late Baroque painters, for instance Tiepolo, who, like Giaquinto, went to Madrid; Giaquinto also worked at the court of Turin. Like those of Tiepolo, his oil-sketches are often more lovely than the grander canvases for which they were preparatory. Outside southern Italy and Spain, he is not represented in the major galleries so well as he might deserve, though there is a picture of his in the Ashmolean Museum, Oxford; in this part of the world there are several of his pictures in the Pinacoteca in BARI, also in Terlizzi, where they 'shine, solitary gems, in the sea of mediocrity' that is painting in Puglia in the 18th century. In his own town there are two altarpieces by him in the church of San Domenico and a documented *Assumption* of 1754 in the new cathedral.

The old town of Molfetta – not as old as some, since the town was sacked by French troops in 1529 – is divided from the new by the via Dante, on which the 'new' 17th-century cathedral, entirely Baroque, is a landmark. The old cathedral or Duomo Vecchio is by the port on the promontory occupied by the quiet old town; it has a picturesque profile of three pyramidal domes and two east towers, achieved in a unique combination of two local prototypes, the three-dome nave and quadrant-vault aisles church (for example San Leonardo di Siponto or Conversano) and the buttressing arches, flat east end and associated twin towers of San Nicola, Bari, or Bari cathedral. It is predominantly 13th-century, but there are no records by which to date its perhaps spasmodic phases of building. It is very dark inside, presumably because windows were too risky in what is a wide church with no nave arcade, only the walls and four great central supports to carry the broad domes. Over the entrance by the side the sculpture typifies the folk-art crudity of the local Renaissance.

There are fine views across from each horn of Molfetta's very wide harbour basin, from the quay by the Duomo Vecchio to the Madonna dei Martiri or the other way. With the exception of its 14th-century choir, the Madonna dei Martiri is a frigid rebuilding of the second quarter of the 19th century, but recent excavations in the nave attest its Norman and pre-Norman history: the dig has been left exposed now that no-one needs the pews and large white cards with numbers relate to a leaflet with which an unctious friar will gladly issue you. The convent is now a geriatric home, but, with the friar's aid, one can gain access behind the church to a pilgrim's hospital of 1095. Its three long barrel-vaulted corridors have well pointed masonry and well proportioned pilasters. It appears to be all underground, but that is because the windows have been blocked in. The upper floor also survives but has been converted into cells for the present needy.

Mention should be made of the Pulo di Molfetta, to which there are sporadic road-signs. It is a karst swallow-hole 500 by 400 ft across and 100 ft deep, in which traces of neolithic settlement have been found. In 1788 it was investigated and described at length by the natural scientist E.A.W. Zimmermann, by commission of the Bourbon king of Naples, who wished to mine its saltpetre, then at a premium in Europe for the making of gunpowder. It is one among a considerable number of subterranean curiosities in Puglia.

Giovinazzo is a smaller town and has a much smaller, steeply walled harbour. It is much more like a resort than any other port on the coast, and its old town has been restored. So it is a pretty place to walk around in. Off the main piazza of the new town San Domenico holds an altarpiece by Lorenzo Lotto which is both signed and dated 1542 and recorded in the artist's surviving account-book under the same year. It was commissioned by 'Luigi Catalan, merchant of Barletta' on behalf of 'the men of Barletta', whither it was sent by Lotto from Venice. Only the central compartment showing bishop St Felix, crouching stoutly on a throne, survives. Beside the harbour, the cathedral was built on the model of San Nicola and of the cathedral in Bari and consecrated in 1283, but its nave has been considerably altered and its interior remains entirely Baroque. Its east end, with flanking twin towers on the pattern of San Nicola, is decorated with interlacing arches, a 'Greco-Norman' motif more common in Sicily and Calabria. In the old town the late 14th-century church of Spirito Santo has once more the Pugliese type of pyramidal domed nave.

Andria, Ruvo, Terlizzi, Bitonto

Besides the towns along the coast between BARLETTA and BARI, there is a parallel string of towns five to ten miles inland: Andria, Corato, Ruvo di Puglia, Terlizzi, Bitonto, Palo del Colle, Bitetto. All are historic, and have something to show for it; Ruvo (Rubi) in particular was a Greek and Roman town known for its ceramics. It was a stage on Horace's itinerary to Brundisium: he arrived dead tired from Canosa (twenty-five miles), on a road unmade by rain, setting off the next day to Bari (twenty-four miles) on a road still worse, but beneath more clement weather.

Andria, in Roman times no more than a village on the via Trajana, was walled by the Norman count of Trani in 1064. Frederick II gave the town privileges; on the late 16th-century Porta Sant'Andrea his attributed words 'faithful Andria, cleaved in our marrow' are mounted. His son Conrad (IV) was born here in 1228, and he buried two of his wives here, but no tomb survives. The Del Balzo dukes of Andria were the first of the Kingdom to be created, by Joanna I, from outside the royal house – one of her many mistakes weakening royal power. The centre is worth a stroll, passing some *palazzi* and visiting the cathedral (of various dates), San Francesco, San Domenico, Sant'Agostino, which have fine portals. In San Domenico there is an early Renaissance bust (1472) of outstanding quality, of duke Francesco II Del Balzo, attributed by some to Francesco Laurana, but more reliably to his one-time colleague Domenico Gagini. It is a rare example of Aragonese court art reaching the provinces.

Born in Andria in 1705 was the most celebrated of all Italian male sopranos, the castrato Farinelli (baptized Carlo Broschi). After a promising start in Italy, he travelled with rapidly increasing success to Vienna, London and Paris. His effect on audiences was legendary: women fainting from excitement at his performances, and there were stories of such fantastic displays of vocal virtuosity that it was rumoured that he had hidden on his person some mechanical contrivance which accounted for the extraordinary length of his breath. At the age of 32 he accepted an invitation from Philip V of Spain to move to Madrid, where he was paid 50,000 francs a year to sing nightly to the king to soothe his melancholia – some said always the same four songs. He became a valued confidant and adviser of the royal family, with responsibility for many matters other than singing, and remained at the side of Philip's successor Ferdinand VI. After Ferdinand's death he spent the last 20 years of his life in cultured retirement in his villa at Bologna, where he was visited by the great and good from Gluck, Mozart and Casanova to emperor Joseph II.

Corato, the next town south, is smaller, but again with an old town, in which Santa Maria Maggiore is 13th-century. Corato was particularly favoured under the Normans, and Edris, Roger II's Muslim geographer, notes it in his list of Apulian cities as 'a well built, populous and beautiful city with a territory abundant with fruit and produce' – which is almost as much as he has to say of Bari. The 11th-century church of San Vito is now in the new town: in the middle of its single nave ending in an apse rises a dome, flanked by vestigial cross-arms; outside, the dome rises into a four-sided pyramid of the stone tiles called *chiancarelle*, though modern terracotta tiles roof the rest of the nave. Though it has more or less close parallels in Greece and other parts of the eastern Mediterranean, this is a uniquely Pugliese type, generally unacknowledged both in Romanesque and in Byzantine handbooks. It is assumed to have evolved from the Byzantine 'cross-in-square' and is known as the 'contracted cross' plan.

On a much grander scale, Ruvo has a beautiful late Romanesque cathedral and is a particularly pleasant, peaceful backwater, though it is busy enough on market days. The old town is a sunny, whitewashed backdrop for widows, old men, washing-lines and playing children, in which it should not be permitted to park anything more modern than a Fiat 500 'bubble'. Throughout the day the benches of its leafy *villa comunale* are besat by benign old men, emanating tradition, security and contentment. In the middle of their garden is an underground public lavatory of which even an English town council could be proud.

The ancient ceramics industry, which began by imitating Archaic Corinthian and Attic vases, flourished until the 2nd century BC. A panorama of Ruvestine vase production is offered by the Museo

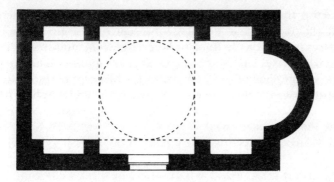

San Vito, Corato

Jatta, which holds more than 2000 local pieces; many are a rich plain black, but there are also shaped vases (*rhyta*) and others with figurative painting. The pride of the collection is a large painted Attic *crater* or wine-mixer of the late 5th century BC.

Because the façade of Ruvo cathedral extends beyond the width of the nave and aisles, the church's similarity to TRANI or other tall thin churches of the same Pugliese type is disguised; inside, where the additions are not apparent, the nave may be seen to be extremely narrow in relation to its height. The entire south side-wall is false, but from the passage between it and the original external wall there is access to the church's newly excavated subterranean history, which extends back to the Roman houses. Over these rest the sleeper walls and pillar bases of a preceding church on the same plan, the whole of which can be explored, picking one's way on catwalks laid between the exposed brickwork and the stanchions by which the upper church is sustained. Or from the upper church one can look down through apertures in the floor. The upper church was begun probably towards the end of the 12th century. Once upon a time the date of 1227 was given for its completion, taken from an inscription on one of the bars of its rose-window that was discovered more recently to read 1597, and to be written on an iron-bar inserted in a restoration. The date of 1227 had been plausible, for the sculpture on the cornices both inside and outside and on the façade – those great griffins of the portal, alas much weathered (one is a poor restoration), the spokes of the rose-window – recalls the similar repertoire and abundance of Trani and Bari cathedrals. Right at the top, the seated figure should be the church's patron saint, but recalls statuary of learned men, for instance Aristotle in one of the Chartres portals or the Romanesque Virgil at Mantua, to which it is especially close. The church's completion should be dated perhaps in the second half of the 13th century. The crypt of the Chiesa del Purgatorio was formerly part of a Roman baths, and the church holds a polyptych of 1537 by the local artist 'Z.T.' (by whom there is more in the Pinacoteca at BARI).

In Terlizzi the 19th-century church of Santissimo Rosario preserves an elaborate late 13th-century portal by Anseramo of Trani, active also at BISCEGLIE and at Bari, where he made a ciborium for the cathedral, now fragmentary; incapable of figures, he was a directionless artist, dissipating the heritage of Frederick II's court in eclectic decoration. Otherwise Terlizzi has a heritage of paintings – a Giaquinto in the Rosario, some 16th-century Venetian pictures in Santa Maria la Nova including a signed *Nativity* by Savoldo and an accredited Pordenone, and a gallery in the *casa natale* of Michele De Napoli (1808–92). Although at the beginning of the 16th century the Venetians had lost the fiefs they had gradually acquired in the area since the later 14th century, the mercantile and other links remained strong, and the rather damaged work by Savoldo for the Scalera family in Santa Maria la Nova is a replica of another he had produced about 1540 for San Giobbe in Venice, which belonged to the same order of Observant Minor friars.

In the territory around Terlizzi there remain several rural or *casale* churches, some of them very old: one, Santa Maria di Cesano, between Terlizzi and Ruvo, is documented to an endowment of 1040 by one Humphrey, one of the numerous Normans who settled early in this region. Cesano had a wooden roof; others, such as Sant'Aneta, Torre Santa Croce, San Basilio and Sant'Eustachio, have or had domical vaults. These four little churches, two of them ruined, lie to the east of Terlizzi; the best preserved is Sant' Eustachio, which, like Santa Maria di Cesano and Torre Santa Croce, is fronted by a defensive tower added at some later date. San Basilio and Torre Santa Croce are of the 'contracted cross' type like San Vito in Corato.

Bitonto's atmosphere is more like BARLETTA's than Ruvo's: its old town is again dirty and risky of *scippo*, and in the surly glances of the men in the *villa comunale* – including unemployed as well as pensioners – the bad old days seem to live on. However, its cathedral is an exceptionally attractive example of Pugliese Romanesque, especially after its cleaning in the late 1980s. It is a reduced copy, like so many cathedrals in the region, of San Nicola in Bari, but has exceptionally rich and fine external sculpture. It was begun perhaps about 1140, and was complete by 1229, the date on the pulpit by the steps up to the choir, signed by Nicholas the priest, presumably the same who signed the tower at TRANI.

From the *villa comunale* and its disquieting stares a fat tower (Angevin, later 14th-century) remaining from the town's vanished walls signals the way to the cathedral. Passing begrimed late medieval and Baroque *palazzi* and a church portal with carved skulls and bones one reaches first the east end of the cathedral, which iron gates prevent one circumambulating. Inside, the chancel is open under a dome: the church has the same 'boxed T' plan of San Nicola in BARI. In the nave it has the same galleries or *matronea* (though the vaulting of the aisles belongs to a much later period), and there is the same kind of crypt, with rich capitals (also a tomb to the soldier Giovanni Francesco Ferrari, whose reclining effigy wears an Elizabethan ruff: he died in 1575). Outside, the cathedral has the same deep buttressing arches and external gallery above, and, round again at the east end, the same enclosed *campanili* and a very fine east window, with heraldic beasts both at the base, on splendid brackets, and at the impost of the jambs, and panes of alabaster instead of glass. The 'crutch' capitals of the external gallery on the south side are particularly rich and varied, deploying all kinds of foliage among which ramp beasts. Below, on one of the doorheads is, of all things, a piece of Anglo-Norman chevron. Above it, a fine stone *transenna* or grille (another on the west front) evokes the contiguous and contemporary Arab world. The central door has a rich hooded arch and what may be a stylized peacock-feather motif, as well as four monsters; the *Harrowing of Hell* in a Byzantine composition is represented in the tympanum. Above, a rose-window hooded by an arch supported by more beasts; still more beasts high up on the transepts.

The cathedral is typical of mature to late Pugliese Romanesque, displaying both an awesome bestiary and more or less anomalous classical quotations, repeating and developing its own vocabulary of motifs in a style almost entirely uninfluenced by Gothic or currents transitional to Gothic; the main external attractions are precious objects and the delights of Oltremar. In this tradition the human figure has no special place; the approach is exclusively decorative and unnaturalistic, lacking any portrait capability – as, inside, the pulpit of Nicholas the priest demonstrates to an extreme degree. The four figures represented on its side, just because they are so very clumsily represented, have given rise to all sorts of interpretations, none of which can be controlled, because there is very little with which to compare them. The favourite theory is that they are the dynasty of Frederick II: Frederick I Barbarossa is seated, then comes Henry VI, next Frederick II (crowned, in the centre of the composition), then his son Conrad IV. Other alternatives include the Adoration of the Magi (but there is no Christ Child) or some reference to the rebellion fomented by the pope during 1229 but rapidly suppressed by Frederick on his return from the Holy Land in June that year; the indiction date on the pulpit is September 1229. Parallels to coins suggest that the seated figure should be a city, perhaps the city of Bitonto, and she seems to be wearing a type of crown that is specific to women; the central, differently crowned figure would still be Frederick, but who the other two might be remains unexplained. The pulpit would be a declaration of loyalty, not rebellion, and would be related to a sermon that exists, preached in Bitonto perhaps from this very pulpit, eulogizing Frederick II and his expedition to Jerusalem. Quite apart from the figures, it is also not easy to decide whether the eagles on the head of which 'Conrad IV' is standing bears significance or is there to fill the space or even to support Conrad, since telamons or propping 'Atlas' figures are abundant in Puglia, and others may be seen by each of the stairs to the crypt (also on one of the brackets of the east window, not upright!). In other ways Nicholas's pulpit is for its time by no means *retardataire*: its foliage and other motifs, such as twisted colonnettes and glass or paste sequins, will remain an integral part of Giovanni Pisano's vocabulary, and on the front of the pulpit the nude male figure supporting the eagle supporting the lectern shows, by contrast to the effigies on the side, precisely the kind of classicism textbooks underscore in the work of Giovanni's father, Nicola. The figure's bent legs derive perhaps from the Lateran *spinario*, a motif noticed in TRANI. The second of the two pulpits is composed of pieces of the former altar and ciborium, signed and dated 1240 by Walter of Foggia. Other churches in old Bitonto include the early Franciscan church – new built within the 13th century – and the small two-domed pyramid-topped aisleless San Valentino of the 11th or 12th century.

Born in Bitonto, five years after the still more celebrated Farinelli in Andria, was the castrato Caffarelli. Caffarelli by contrast was an extremely unattractive character, who was more than once imprisoned for outrageous conduct on the stage and off it, and cordially disliked by his colleagues, whom he treated with arrogance, insult and ridicule. At the age of 14 he was discharged by the celebrated Neapolitan singing teacher Nicola Porpora with the words: 'My son, I have nothing more to teach you. You are the greatest singer in Europe.' Brilliant successes attended him all over Italy, and in Paris, Madrid, Lisbon and London, where his engagement by Handel to create the title role in *Serse* ensured that his was the first voice ever to sing Handel's *Largo* in public. Caffarelli was reputed to have received the highest salaries then ever paid to a singer, and at the end of his life bought himself an estate in Calabria, a palace in Naples and a dukedom.

There is another Romanesque cathedral of the type of San Nicola and the cathedral in nearby BARI at Palo del Colle, set beside the pretty main square, but it has been adulterated. Less adulterated and now restored is Bitetto, a bit smaller than Bitonto; it has a grossly decorated portal to rival that of Terlizzi, donated by one Lillo da Barletta and dated 1335, even though the style is still resoundingly Romanesque. The 11th-century church of San Domenico is another 'contracted cross' one. Nearby Bitetto there are also Bitritto and Binetto. The road between Bitritto and Modugno passes beside one more 'contracted cross' church, San Pietro di Balsignano, a masonry jewel of the late 12th century.

That other uniquely Pugliese variety of church, the basilica with three domes along the nave and quadrant or half-barrel vaults buttressing them in the aisles, needs to be sought out among the olive groves outside Valenzano. To gain entry to the church of Ognissanti is still more difficult: I had to make an appointment with the parish priest (whose residence is the Casa del Clero in Bari), whom I accompanied very early one morning to see the church while he heard confession of a young man he was going soon afterwards to marry. I might have reflected on the continuity of tradition in the countryside despite the proximity of roaring Bari. The church was originally monastic. It belonged to a community of Benedictines founded by Eustace, who later became Elias's successor as bishop of BARI. However, the conventual buildings have altogether vanished. The church had been completed by 1080, and remains very largely unaltered, inside and out. Throughout the stone is beautifully cut and the pointing very even, with very little mortar. Characteristic is the roof-line of three low pyramids built of

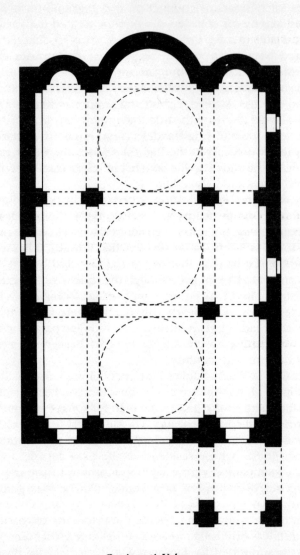

Ognissanti, Valenzano

stone tiles or *chiancarelle* on square bases, corresponding to masonry domes inside. (It can be seen that the roof has been restored, but
there remained sufficient traces to warrant its accuracy.) The east
end terminates in three shallow apses. At the west end the portico
has fallen or was never built beyond the one bay that remains – of an
uncertain date, but certainly an addition. The decoration is sparse
but elegant: beading round the windows, little hoods over them of
inlaid coloured stones (less elaborate than those of the similar
monastic church of San Benedetto at Conversano), and a favourite
motif of the 10th and 11th centuries, a 'saw-tooth' frieze created by
the simple means of setting the stones at 45°. Inside, the church is
unusually well illumined by its little round windows, adapting the
Roman device of piercing the spandrels of arches to relieve the
weight on them; the bare, trim stonework turns the bright white
light of the Pugliese sun warm and mellow. Blind arches and
pilasters with minimal capitals order and articulate the structure,
which is impressively harmonious despite a slight change in the
decoration of the western bay, indicating a slow rate of building. The
domes are neatly set off by a thin lip circling above the four arches
and the pendentives.

Castel del Monte

Around Castel del Monte there is plentiful countryside: the castle
has remained gloriously isolated, still commanding the 360° view it
was built to command, its enemies still without any possible cover.
The approach to it, as the road vaults the switchbacks of the MURGE
plateau and the almost incredible sight of an upright, intact
stone octagon is repeated and confirmed by longer and longer
views, is memorable. These fields bounded by dry-stone walls,
either planted with orchards and groves or open with occasional
stone huts or *trulli* (see MURGIA DEI TRULLI) and gnarled ilexes, were
formerly, one may suppose, forested, as the land is known to have
been in Frederick II's time below Foggia and again around Gioia del
Colle at the southern end of the Murge. There should be little doubt
that it was built as a *domus solationis* or 'hunting-lodge' as the phrase
is rather inadequately translated, and that from it Frederick intended
to enjoy falconing.

Castel del Monte is the only building from this part of the world
Nikolaus Pevsner discussed and illustrated in his *Outline of Euro-*

pean Architecture. He placed it in a context of new ideas in castle
building stimulated by experience on the Crusades, and of an
interest throughout Europe in symmetrical planning, of which he
declared it the most accomplished example. Indeed its geometry is
extremely exciting if geometry can excite: the plan of the building
can support all sorts of compass drawings creating wholly symmetrical and concentric squares, circles, triangles, octagons and stars. It is
not merely an octagon but an octagon with eight satellite octagonal
towers wedded to its eight points and with an internal octagonal
courtyard. One superimposition is a star of eight points coincident
with the centres of the satellite towers: the lines from the centres
forming the star also coincide with the octagonal courtyard. The
drawing can be made not merely on a surveyed plan, which is
usually corrected, but on an aerial photograph. It probably corres-
ponds to the masons' own triangulation. They would have generated
the eight satellite centres from a circle within a square. Circle and
square can be laid out with the same string (the radius of the circle
= half one side of the square); then four satellite centres can be
found at their tangents and the other four at the section of the
circle's circumference and the square's diagonals. That was the
method used for such buildings as the 6th-century San Vitale at
Ravenna, but while the technique had probably remained alive in
the east it had fallen away in the west (the clumsiness of Santa Sofia
in BENEVENTO is a sign of that). Castel del Monte has no close parallel
in Europe, but its triangulation could have become known to
Frederick's court through the contacts he had forged on his 1228
crusade to Jerusalem. Frederick, according to Arab chroniclers, put
mathematical questions to Islamic court philosophers and went to
see sights of Islamic architecture.

One of the innovations of Crusader architecture was the provision of towers protruding at intervals in order to deny the enemy
any blindspots at the base of a plain wall. But the octagonal towers of
Castel del Monte cannot have been for that purpose, since their
windows are not suitably oriented nor adapted for firing – the
embrasures are too deep for anyone on the stairs and not high
enough to stand in – while the windows in the wall between each
tower are too large: they are for viewing and have benches beside
them. That is not to say Castel del Monte had no military purpose at
all: it has enormously thick walls (the external walls are 2.55 m thick
and the inner courtyard walls are 2.4 m) and has a portcullis. The
present stairs to the main portal are not original: there would have

been a wooden one. In the interior, while all the rooms are identical in plan, not all are interconnecting: the fact that the main entrance gives on to a room with only one exit, and that into another exiting only on the courtyard, must reflect precaution. Between the rest of the ground-floor rooms there is free passage. To gain the upper floor, one has to re-enter by another door off the courtyard to reach one of the staircases, which are only in every other tower (the others contain *garderobes*, which are plumbed; there is also a system of conduits conveying water from the roof to the cistern beneath the courtyard). On the upper floor there is again a door through every party wall except one, belonging to the room above the main entrance, from which one raised or lowered the portcullis. The three openings from the rooms on to the courtyard originally gave access to a wooden gallery interconnecting them. The stairs in the towers continued up on to the roof, and again there would have been wooden covers to their exits.

The masonry of Castel del Monte consists of almost seamless blocks of accurately cut ashlar (with no holes or purchase for scaffolding) left entirely plain, except for a string-course between the two storeys. Though the towers might have had covers, there was no parapet or battlement, and the roof is flat. However, the main entrance and each of the eight windows on the upper floor have or had mouldings of marble, and panels of a pink and white marble magnificently, extravagantly, wainscotted the walls of the interior. Though the purpose of Castel del Monte is disputed, these panels (or revetments) mark it as a palace; and LAGOPESOLE, which also had marble veneers, is a documented *domus solationis*. Some of the marble, for instance of the portal or flanking the fireplaces, is so bitty as almost to be like *scagliola*, but that used for the column shafts and the mouldings is of high quality. Sometimes the pink in it looks like a stain resulting from fire, but it is natural. Both marbles are local, some kind of *pietra di Trani*, but I do not know that the quarries have been identified. Although most of the revetment of the walls was stripped by the Bourbons, the edging pieces and membering usually remain, so that one may imagine an intoxicating sequence of chambers of imperial purple, shining and cool against the suffocating heat.

Castel del Monte's masonry of huge, sharp-hewn ashlars is characteristic of Frederick's architecture everywhere. Of his many castles, most were rebuildings and adaptations, but where he was building from new the style of his reign seems always to have involved patently geometric plans, for example the symmetrical and concentric castles of Syracuse, Catania, Augusta or Prato. However, these are all beside towns, are much larger, are square, have functional towers and would have held a garrison. Only the keep at LUCERA seems directly a precursor of Castel del Monte: that was a residence, and though it is square its proportions are much closer, and it is known that at the level of its top storey there were walls across the angles of the square inner courtyard to form a kind of octagon. Most other known residences used or built by Frederick have disappeared; those that do survive, for instance Lagopesole or Gravina, were less ambitious. However, a building such as La Zisa in Palermo, a *domus solationis* of his grandfather Roger II, may be cited as a more remote precursor, symmetrical in plan though simpler, with plain walls, well plumbed, with provision for taking the view, and partly decorated – and perhaps designed overall – by Islamic craftsmen.

The masons who built Castel del Monte were, however, certainly not Islamic. Its structure and detail are as securely western as the philosophy of Thomas Aquinas, for all that he recovered a knowledge of Aristotle ultimately from Arab sources. Is it then a product of Frederick's presiding genius harnessing Pugliese skills? That may be doubted. Castel del Monte outclasses what remains of the work of a native master like Bartolomeo da Foggia. Although Frederick is known to have attracted southwards German metalworkers, it is not easy to find any obvious precedent in Germany, either. It has seemed to many that France is the only possible source. Emile Bertaux, whose historic *L'Art dans l'Italie méridionale* appeared in 1904, interpreted Castel del Monte as an essay on the theme of a French Gothic chevet, sliced from a church and rejoined with its mirror image. Though that is a little contrived it boils down to much the same thing as Pevsner's version. Specifically, Frederick, having returned hurriedly from Jerusalem in 1229 in order to quell both invasion from without and rebellion from within, and realising that such a danger would always be present, would naturally have turned to the precedent of king Philip II Augustus of France (1180–1223). Philip, former crusader in the company of Richard the Lionheart (also a great castle-builder), victor in 1214 against Otto IV of the battle of Bouvines, by which Frederick was enabled to gain Germany, had built a range of castles in order to defend his conquests in France from John of England. An example such as Caen fully anticipates the square plan and interval towers of Frederick's later garrisons, though Islamic sources are often cited and there may also have been surviving Byzantine ones, perhaps still surviving at Miglionico or Santa Severina. Philip had already standardized and centralized military design in order to fortify programmatically and defend strategically from both within and without. Philip's centrepiece was the castle of the Louvre and its round *tour maîtresse*, which, reproduced in other royal strongholds through the country, became an architectural symbol of the newly vigorous monarchy. Frederick's military castles are similarly recognizable and calculatedly magnificent, and Castel del Monte might be a revision of Philip Augustus's *tour maîtresse*, adopting a supplementary, Byzantine and Carolingian association of octagon with empire.

It is reported that in 1220 Frederick obtained papal permission to use Cistercian *conversi* or lay-brothers to help him build. Cistercian influence is clear in Castel del Monte in the capitals of the interior, of a ball-flower type that finds many parallels in Burgundy as well as in Italian Cistercian abbeys such as Fossanova in Lazio. It can be found again even in the fluted pilasters of the main portal, which are derived, it has been suggested, not directly from classical example but from the Romanesque imitations of classical fluting that are common in Burgundian churches (Autun, Paray-le-Monial). However, Cistercian motifs are not ubiquitous and other classicisms (such as the egg-and-dart heads of the first-floor portals on the inner courtyard) derive instead from the Byzantine-staffed, classicizing workshops established in William II's time (1166–89) at Monreale, where work had continued under Frederick's orders, or from the 'school' of the 'master of Elias's chair' at BARI; those courtyard portals present many parallels with the round-arched arches of Nicholas the priest's 1229 portico for TRANI cathedral. The main entrance portal is also close to contemporary church portals, and has more of a Gothic gable than a classical pediment. The only direct borrowing from the expired classical past in the architecture of Castel del Monte is, arguably, the imitation of Roman *opus reticulatum* or 'network' brickwork in the upper parts of some of the interiors.

Most of the figurative carving is, again, either French Gothic, like the 'green man' of more than one boss, or native Pugliese, for instance several 'Atlas figure' brackets; one 'green man' given a classical faun's ears shows a synthesis between them. However, the fragment of an equestrian figure above one of the portals in the courtyard is patently classical, in a toga – an effigy recalling the statue in BARLETTA or the north portal in FOGGIA cathedral. A relief high up on the wall represents a procession or reception, that can only be modelled on such classical examples as the interior of Trajan's arch, if it is not actually a classical spoil, as would better accord with its remote position. (There is a cast in the museum of BARI castle.)

Although Castel del Monte is Frederick II's greatest monument, it is unlikely he ever set foot in it; the only document on the matter is one ordering the materials for the foundations dated 1240, and it can only just have been complete on the emperor's death in 1250. However, since Frederick's personal interest in the progress of his architecture is abundantly documented, he must have visited and chosen the site himself. Its purpose is debated, but it is difficult to evade the conclusion that Castel del Monte was built as it was chiefly in order to look as it does. Some small sign of the impression it made in its own time – or would have done later, had anyone seen it! – is the imitative octagonal tower at MONTE SANT'ANGELO. It was used by the Angevins to imprison Frederick's descendants.

The Murge

Murgia means rock, in particular the eaten white rock that pits and scars the red soil of the unchanging, undulating plateau that lies between the Appennines, the Ofanto, the Adriatic and the Gulf of Taranto, and is known as Le Murge. The cretacious rock swallows all the water and there are no rivers, only ravines (*lame*) or gorges (*gravine*). The Murge have always been sparsely populated, though they are not barren and are irrigated today by water held in man-made lakes in the adjoining Appennines: one passes acres and acres of olive groves or cornfields. However, the beds of the *lame* and *gravine* have long been cultivated, by peasants who often made their homes in the caves usually to be found in the upper reaches of a gorge. MATERA is the capital city of such troglodytism.

Due south of CANOSA, Minervino Murge is situated above the great rift between the Appennines and the plateau or *altopiano* of the Murge known as the Fossa Premurgiana. It is an historic bishopric and has a cathedral and a castle, and spectacular views. The Fossa runs from Minervino to Massafra near TARANTO, but is blocked, just south of Minervino, by the rock on which sits Spinazzola. Again historic and high, but not a bishopric, though it gave birth to pope Innocent XII, Spinazzola is a watershed: above it the rivers flow east to the Adriatic; to its south the Basentello flows south-east towards the Ionian sea. Travelling down the Fossa between Spinazzola and Gravina in Puglia one sees the Murge rise in a cliff, cut by *lame*, above one of which are the ruins of the 13th-century castle of Garagnone. Gravina in Puglia also produced a pope, Benedict XIII Orsini, whose family held several fiefs in this part of the world. Set over its plunging gorge, it was in part a troglodyte city or *città rupestre* like Matera or Laterza (see below).

Frederick II made Gravina the seat of one of four parliaments convened twice annually to utter grievances and to be told what they had to find in taxes – beside Salerno for Campania, Sulmona for the Molise and Cosenza for Calabria. He built the modest castle, usually characterized rather as a 'hunting-lodge', that is set above it, a narrow rectangular building rising two storeys. The town's old centre was around the cave church of San Michele dei Grotti, virtually indeterminate in age: the city had a bishop in the 9th century and before that both a Roman and a pre-Roman past, though that was in the caves on the other side of the gorge in the rock called Botromagno. Through this Roman town of Silvium passed the via Appia Antica, and its course can still be followed south-east of Gravina towards Taranto. The archaeological museum holds artefacts retrieved from the Botromagno, and a reconstructed chamber of a cave church with frescos of the 13th century. Gravina cathedral is a rebuilding following a fire in 1447; though there are Renaissance details, the building is essentially Gothic, incorporating or echoing parts of the original Romanesque building. The Baroque Chiesa del Purgatorio, with skeletons in the portal, has an Orsini tomb of 1660, also one of the few altarpieces in Puglia by a leading artist, the Neapolitan Francesco Solimena (1667), also one of the few autograph works by the local painter Francesco Guarino (1611–54), who was up-to-date with Naples and influential in Puglia. Another grand Orsini tomb, of the early 16th century, is in the little church of Santa Sofia.

Nearby Altamura is a Pugliese equivalent of better known Etruscan cities such as Volterra or Perugia, incorporating remains of megalithic walls built by the indigenous Peucetans in defence against the Greek colonies in the 5th century BC. (Another Peucetan city has been excavated at Monte Sannace near Gioia del Colle – see below.) Altamura was inhabited continuously through the neolithic, Bronze, Iron, Dark, Greek and Roman ages, disappearing in the Middle Ages but re-founded by Frederick II within the recognizable remains of the older town in the 13th century. Frederick also endowed its cathedral, rising high over the houses, and from this time the typically Pugliese lion window survives transferred from the apse; then after an earthquake in the early 14th century the cathedral was rebuilt with a large rose-window, and received its richly sculpted portal. Though it is figurative (the story of Christ), the portal's squat and crude figures are disposed much as if they were decorative ornament, up and down every limb of the architecture. Our Pugliese sculptor, one might expound, shows once more – following on such as Anseramo da Trani – that he has no understanding of form, but only a baroque 'bad taste'; though the portal may be as late as the early 15th century, it has not yet caught up with the Gothic style. However, it is the richest in Puglia, one that in its time and in this place must have been unusually costly and conspicuous, though it lacks any elegance.

Despite his later claim to be a Neapolitan, Altamura was the birthplace of Saverio Mercadante (1795–1870), one of Italy's most important 19th-century composers. His operas are little known nowadays, but Mercadante more than anyone else bridged the gap between Rossini, Donizetti and Bellini on the one hand and Verdi on the other. His influence on Verdi, who as a young man witnessed the success of several of Mercadante's best works in Milan, is beyond question; but his operas have an interest of their own, as occasional performances and recordings are beginning to demonstrate.

Like MOLFETTA, Altamura has a Pulo, a few miles north of the city: this one is circular, 1500 ft across and more than 200 ft deep to a level floor. Towards Cassano delle Murge, there is a modern forest. Acquaviva delle Fonti once had a castle, now encased in its Baroque town hall, and has a cathedral rebuilt in the 16th century but still adhering to the pattern of Bari cathedral and San Nicola. In Santeramo in Colle the Chiesa Madre has fragments by Francesco Laurana or Domenico Gagini or the author of the Del Balzo bust in ANDRIA.

Around Gioia del Colle, the medieval forests have gone, but the castle rebuilt by Frederick II survives unaltered by later modernizations. Particularly fine are the two massive square towers which rise above the ranges surrounding its crooked square courtyard, and the rusticated stonework throughout, and a few windows in the hall reached by the grandiose external staircase in the courtyard. The castle houses an archaeological museum holding finds from Monte Sannace, an archaeological zone to the north-east of Gioia. The name of the site has not been identified but it was native Peucetan rather than Greek and flourished in the central centuries of the 1st millennium BC: the city walls, occasionally reaching a considerable height, and the plan of several streets and houses have been laid bare.

South of Gioia del Colle, Castellaneta claims fame as the birthplace of Ridolfo Valentino: the filmstar's *casa natale* is shown and the main street has a statue of him. It is photogenic in its own right, with squat white houses piled around a cathedral set above one more *gravina*. Nearby Laterza claims fame as the eponym of the Bari publishing house. It, too, occupies a *gravina*, and has a deserted *città rupestre* or rock city that can be visited with a guide from the tourist office or Pro Loco. Above ground, the Assunta is the shell of an early 12th-century church containing a modern interior; it has a Romanesque carved font. The cave church of Sant'Antonio has, unusually, a Greek-cross shape. One more city set on a *gravina* is Ginosa to the south, which has a castle of Renaissance date and more cave churches, including one more, Santa Domenica, of Greek-cross shape.

On the eastern side of Castellaneta, the cities of Mottola and Massafra are the southernmost of the Murge, within reach of Taranto and the Taranto-Bari *autostrada*. Close on the motorway is Palagianello, with a castle above and cave churches within its spectacular *gravina*. Set high on the cliff, Mottola is recorded in Lombard times and as a Byzantine fortress and bishopric in the early 11th century. Its present cathedral is an early 16th-century rebuilding, with a façade of Venetian type. Outside the town to the south-west there are more cave churches, notably San Nicola (with frescos), San Gregorio and Santa Margherita, and the medieval troglodyte village of Petruscio. Massafra, too, has characteristic examples of the cave churches in which the Murge abound: those of Madonna della Scala, San Leonardo, the Candelora and San Marco are the equal of Matera's. The little church of Santa Lucia to the south of the town has a simple two-domed pyramid-roofed nave and apse, documented to 1080.

Bari

The early history of Bari is on display in the museum of Santa Scolastica, situated on the far tip of the promontory of the old town, beyond San Nicola. Santa Scolastica was a convent of nuns first recorded in 1102, when the church and cloister that house the museum were probably already standing. Within their stripped brick shell amid black metal and in glass cases, finds from the prehistoric, pre-Roman, Roman, Lombard, Arab, Byzantine and Norman periods are presented beside maps, photographs and blurbs. Some of the finds came from within the precincts of the convent itself, including an extra Romanesque church (for which there is no name) laid bare beside it. Roman Bari was not an important place, though at Bari the via Appia Trajana and its precursor over which Horace travelled reached the sea; he and others went on to Brundisium to take ship. Horace visited a walled city where the fishing was good – his half line, '*Bari moenia piscosi*', is the fullest description handed down from antiquity. Bari's rise to capital status began with the Arab emirate, 847–71.

The Berber occupants of Bari, subject to Aghlabid Kairouan, where just in these years the Great Mosque was rising, may well have built and shaped virtually a new city. Its inhabitants are reported rich, and to have traded in the east as well as raided in the west. Its walls were adjudged mighty, and thwarted attempts led by the Lombards and the Holy Roman emperor to remove this dangerous base of a hostile power. Louis II took the city in 871 only after a long siege. Five years later, his successor lost it again to the Byzantines in alliance with the Lombards, and under a Byzantine governor it became the capital of the *theme* of Longobardia, the old Roman province of Apulia. Henceforward Puglia was reconquered for Constantinople, though gradually and with setbacks including the brief loss of Bari itself. Not much of this can be evoked in the old town, though it vaguely resembles a kasbah: its streets are narrow and wind a bit and its houses coated in a grimy whitewash are dateless; but there is no smell of spice. In Santa Scolastica a fine disc of Arab metalwork is preserved.

There are signs during the waning of the high Middle Ages of a vigorous culture – a mercantile community like that of Amalfi and Salerno on the opposite coast, or of Venice further up the Adriatic. At Bari they not only sailed but built ships. However, Bari was ethnically more various – Greek, Arab, Lombard and probably Jewish – and never quite shook off subjection to greater powers. Recurrent revolts during the later 10th century failed to dislodge the Byzantine governor, even though his position was often precarious: the Arabs of Sicily might have taken Bari in 1003, had not a Venetian fleet sailed in to the rescue. In the early 11th century Melos, or Ismael, of Bari led two further revolts, in the first of which

(1009–12) he held Bari against the Byzantines for more than two years, in the second of which (1016–18) he for the first time called in Norman soldiers. According to the story he met 40 of them returning from the Holy Land at the shrine of MONTE SANT'ANGELO on the Gargano. He also courted the Holy Roman emperor Henry II, whom he presented with a mantle embroidered in gold that is still in the cathedral treasury at Bamberg. In return Henry created Melos 'duke of Puglia', and Melos obtained the support of the pope, then Benedict VIII, who blessed his Normans as they passed through Rome, but all to no avail: he was defeated in 1018 at CANNAE by the *catepan* or Byzantine governor Boioannes. Boioannes pursued the rebels as far as the river Garigliano above Capua, securing the submission of the Lombards and of the abbot of Montecassino at the same time. Melos fled to Bamberg, where he died in 1020. The Byzantine ascendancy lasted until the 1040s, from which time the Norman presence became increasingly noisome.

The Norman capture of Bari dates from 1071. It was virtually the last city in Puglia to hold out against Robert Guiscard, who had besieged it for more than four years. He was undemanding in victory, probably because he wished for the moment to quieten the region in order to continue his operations in Sicily: and Palermo, a still greater prize, fell to him in 1072. Under early Norman rule Bari's merchants were able to achieve in 1087 the city's greatest ever coup – beating the Venetians to it, as the chroniclers remark – the theft of the body of St Nicholas from his tomb in Myra in southern Turkey. St Nicholas by a different route became 'Santa Claus', but he was most important in the Middle Ages in the Balkans and Italy for his healing powers and interventions in storms for sailors. Of the band of 70 who stole the relics from Myra, a certain Matthew it was who shattered the tomb, releasing an odour of sanctity such as to bring on ecstasy, while 'the venerable remains glowed like coals of fire'. On arrival in Bari the relics created a riot, when bishop Urso, returning from TRANI, attempted to seize them from Elias, the abbot of San Benedetto at Bari, who had been the first to welcome the sailors. The bishop was defeated, and the relics were lodged not in the cathedral but in a private church in the precinct of the '*praetorium*', the governor's palace. The Norman ruler, Robert Guiscard's son Roger Borsa, then ceded to Elias the castle and its court as the site for a new church, which was made 'palatine', removing it from the bishop's jurisdiction. It is difficult now to chart the politics behind the chroniclers' simple-minded narration of the

squabble, but one suggestion is that Urso may have been intriguing
with citizens of Trani, who were also on the expedition to Myra but
were excluded from its spoils, and Urso seems also to have been the
ally of Bohemund, Roger Borsa's rival. At any rate the hereditary
'company of St Nicholas' of which Elias was president became the
city's oligarchy and aristocracy, enjoying virtual autonomy beneath
Norman rulers either weak or crusading – and in any event having
no castle in which to lodge a garrison.

During the lifetimes of Elias (died 1105) and his successor
Eustace (died 1123) the great church of San Nicola rose rapidly,
although only the crypt was ready for use at the Council of Bari in
Bari in 1098. Convened in order to heal the schism of the Eastern
and Western Churches, the Council coincided with the first success
of the first Crusade, the taking of Antioch just south of Myra by Bari's
Norman overlord Bohemund. One who attended was St Anselm,
archbishop of Canterbury, who might have found St Nicholas's crypt
still more splendid than his own fine church. Judged by their
capitals, the taste of the two crypts is remarkably similar. The rest of
Canterbury was transformed by rebuilding in the late 12th century
for the cult of St Thomas à Becket, whose tomb was destroyed in the
Reformation; at Bari, though the metalwork has gone, St Nicholas's
relics are still beneath the altar and even the chest in which St
Nicholas's bones were carted through the city is preserved. In 1111
the rival sons of Robert Guiscard, Bohemund and Roger Borsa, both
died and higher rule was not effectively imposed until in 1132 the
city was forced to recognize Roger II. Shortly afterwards an enamel
representing his crowning by St Nicholas (a design similar to the
famous mosaic in the Martorana in Palermo, representing his crowning by Christ) was placed in the centre of the new ciborium over the
high altar, which is intact, though the enamel has been detached.
Roger promised not to build a new castle, but then began the
present one importing Saracen labourers; he suppressed the revolts
that followed with less kindly terms. After Roger's death, Bari rose in
1154 with most of Puglia and with papal and Byzantine support in a
concerted attempt to shake off rule from Sicily, but was punished in
exemplary fashion by William I 'the Bad' in 1156: 'Thus the ruling
city of Apulia, illustrious in fame, rich in wealth, proud in most noble
citizens, wonderful in the fitment of its buildings, now lies reduced
to heaps of rubble.' William forbade the inhabitants to return to their
city for the space of 20 years. Only St Nicholas's church was spared;
and although the cathedral and town were rebuilt before the end of

the century, Bari under the Hohenstaufen and the Angevins never recovered.

At the end of the Angevin period Bari was a minor port no longer trading but only shipping out local produce through the offices of foreign merchants. By Alfonso the Magnanimous it was bartered for support from the Milanese Sforza, whose possession it remained even after the French had taken Milan, until the death of Bona Sforza in 1557. After plague in 1657 the population of the city fell to a mere 3000. Its history begins again in the Napoleonic period, when in 1813 the French viceroy Joachim Murat laid out the corso Vittorio Emanuele II alongside the old city and projected the new town. It was soon the administrative capital of the province and of the region of Puglia in the republic of Italy, but remained politically dyspeptic until the end of the century. It has now fully ingested northern capitalism, following rapid economic growth and industrialization under Mussolini and after the Second World War. Architecturally it is now a very modern city, since it was bombed, and the buildings of 'Murat's quarter' between the Corso and the station are for the most part concrete and glass, loud and brash with shops, bars and restaurants in every street. Things are a little quieter and the grid-plan looser in the adjoining Madonnella district eastwards along the coast, where most of the building dates from between the World Wars; the same is true of a small area to the west, adjoining the old town and on the same side of the Corso, called Marisabella. But there is much more of Bari than this, built since the Second World War as the town expanded phenomenally, rising from tens of thousands to nearly 400,000; its rapid expansion has recently come to an end, but the commerce and industry continue for some miles along the coast and on the western side of the city.

The old town, as usual, is run down, and the restaurants, shops and hotels are in Murat's new town; a few hotels are further flung, or along the coast. All are business hotels. The central shopping street is the partly pedestrianized via Sparano, which runs through the centre of Murat's town from the Corso to the station. Most shops belong to national chains; an exception is the bookshop of the Laterza publishing house which has occupied the corner of via Sparano and via Dante since the beginning of the century. It stocks not only Laterza textbooks and editions of Italian literature, but also has several shelves of publications about Puglia. Restaurants are plentiful but mostly mediocre or fusty; their trade is chiefly the very large groups in which people in this part of the world like to dine. An

exception is the newer Ai Due Ghiottoni, via Putignani 11: this is to
date Bari's best restaurant. There are several that specialize in fish,
but none are outstanding. Bari, though smart, is not fashionable; it
has plenty of life, but little character; it is a businesslike, business-
man's city.

On the broad boulevard of the Corso, there are bars and cafés and
institutional buildings including the Teatro Piccinni, as well as a
statue of Piccinni. Niccolò Piccinni of Bari (1728–1800) was a
central figure in the history of Italian and French opera in the later
18th century. He was immensely prolific (more than 120 operas
altogether), but his greatest triumph came early with *La Buona
Figliola*, also known as *La Cecchina* (The Little Magpie), one of the
most successful comic operas of the entire century: taverns were
named after it, and for many years its tunes were sung and whistled
all over Europe. By the middle 1770s his popularity had begun to
wane and he accepted an invitation to Paris, where he immediately
found himself enmeshed in the quarrel between the supporters of
'French' and 'Italian' opera – a war of words that had as much to do
with court rivalries and chauvinism as with music. He was set up as
champion of the 'Italian' faction in opposition to Gluck, and inevitably came off worse when the two men were persuaded to com-
pose rival versions of *Iphigénie en Tauride*. His best French opera,
Didon, appeared after Gluck had left Paris. With the Revolution
Piccinni returned to Naples, but ran into political trouble and
eventually went back to Paris where he died in poverty.

Down past his statue is the castle, and from the castle the
cathedral is visible. From the round Trulla on the north flank of the
cathedral it is straight to San Nicola, and past San Nicola is Santa
Scolastica. The medieval port was beside the castle, where the
industrial port is now. A wide road, built in the 1930s, makes it
possible to walk or drive round outside the 16th-century walls of the
old town. The road continues round the wide bay to the west to the
Fiera del Levante, the complex housing the trade-fair by which the
city is convulsed during September.

Another way to enter the old town is to walk round from the south-
east end of the Corso through the open market along the sea-front to
the east end of San Nicola. The east end is a good place to begin study
of the most famous church in the region. It is unusual, being flat.
Inside, there are three apses, a larger central one and two lateral
ones, but they are boxed in by a separate external flat wall, inside
which one may walk round them. The arrangement seems original

to abbot Elias's church, though it is imitated in several other churches of the region, including the cathedral in Bari when it was rebuilt after the razing of 1156. It has been supposed either that the wall was added after the apses had been built or that the apses were added inside the wall, which would have belonged to the governor's palace on the site. However, the remains of a band of coloured stones round the lowest windows giving on the crypt resemble the windowheads of the church at Valenzano not far inland, founded about 1080. In fact apses and walls are contemporary: the point was to build bell-towers over the side apses, and to incorporate them into the building harmoniously. Bell-towers once rose in the gap on the corners left by the gables of the transept, which stop short; they were removed when they became unsafe. Their equivalents were eventually built at the new cathedral, at BITONTO, at MOLFETTA; conversely, churches otherwise similar to Bari but without a flat east end, such as TRANI or RUVO, have detached *campanili*.

The monsters adorning the main window of the east end directly recall those of Romuald's throne in CANOSA for bishop Urso (died 1089): two elephants with the same ribbed trunks and *houri* eyes support columns on which rest griffins with the same feathers as Romuald's eagles, and beneath the window sill there are two sphinxes affronting a potted plant, as in a side panel of Romuald's throne. However, there also appear intertwining tendrils bitten by beasts, a northern motif, although among them one finds traditional Byzantine peacocks, and at their base the tendrils grow out of a vase, a classicism found earlier at Salerno cathedral, the major precedent for abbot Elias's church. On the Porta dei Leoni on the north flank the jambs, lintel and inner arch are of the same period; on the inner arch there appear warriors mounted fighting others on foot, defending a shrine at the top – Crusaders versus Moslems? More likely Latins pillaging Greeks! The outer lions bearing columns, capitals figuring a reaper and a vintner and top arch of open flat leaves were added probably shortly after the church's completion, before the interruption of 1156.

Inside the church, the transept is open, without partition between crossing and wings, forming a T with the stem of the nave. It belongs to the type sometimes called 'Gregorian', because it was adopted in churches built by associates of pope Gregory VII, such as Montecassino consecrated in 1071 or Salerno cathedral begun in 1081, in imitation of Constantinian 'great churches' such as Old St Peter's. However, San Nicola follows local tradition, for example

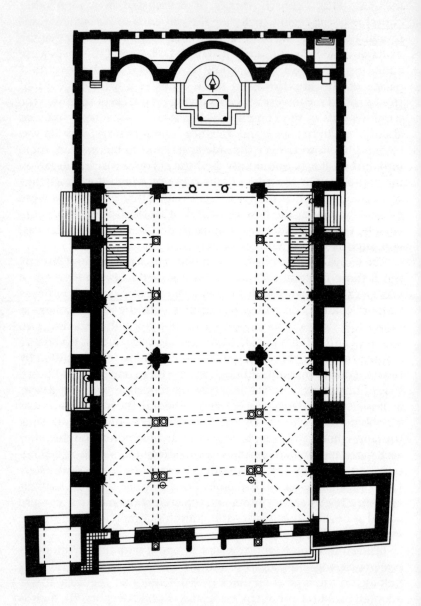

San Nicola, Bari

CANOSA or GERACE or again Salerno, in protruding the span of the transepts a little beyond the width of the aisles; St Peter's and Montecassino were unvaried oblongs. Or more exactly San Nicola reconciles the two usages, for it is filled out into a pure oblong by a series of shallow arches buttressing the outer nave. Surely the same aesthetic induced Elias both to 'box' the bell-towers at the east end and to iron out the bump of the protruding transept by these arches along the nave, continuing the pattern of the blind arches lining the transept (see plan). The use of blind arches belongs to Apulia's Byzantine or even earlier heritage; the deeper arches are sometimes supposed to have belonged originally to the governor's palace, and above the middle arch of the southern side slits meant to be firing slits are pointed out, but more of them would have been needed and these are merely a couple of windows lighting the internal corridor. Though there may well be something older invisible inside or underneath, it is likely that the Byzantine buildings were demolished (excavations have revealed much re-used material) and San Nicola built from new, with the sole exception of the north-western tower (see below). However, a second purpose of the unprecedented, though soon widely imitated, external arches must have been to buttress the first three-storey nave to appear in Puglia. A third purpose may have been to provide space for tombs, reviving an Early Christian practice – in this case tombs for the members of the 'society of St Nicholas', who had the precious entitlement of burial near him.

There was perhaps some brief pause between the completion of the crypt and the continuation of the nave, since the impost moulding changes between transept and nave arches. There is a more definite break on the south side in the stonework to the gallery above the nave arches, which was a second thought of the advanced 12th century, added as an adornment – and stabilization – of the completed church and not in communication with the inside galleries. The last arch to the west on the northern side is squeezed in beside a protruding tower, which must already have been there in some form, and was kept in order to provide access to the internal galleries or *matronea*; it is not a bell-tower. The tower does not align with the west façade either, unlike its southern companion which was built afterwards. On the western façade, the inner parts of the central portal correspond in style and date to the east window and the inner parts of the Porta dei Leoni; once again the outer parts were added in the course of the 12th century. The angels in the spandrels recall Byzantine ivories and their imitations, but the source of the two telamons or 'Atlas figures' who strain to support the jambs at their base is not so familiar; they seem to be the first of their kind in South Italian art, though in Puglia the idea is widely repeated, not least on Elias's throne inside the church. So, too, the later gable crowning the arch over the central portal is probably the first in Puglia; together with the oxen supporting the columns on which it rests and the sphinx at the peak of the gable, it may be dated to the later 12th century, after the razing of 1156. The façade has no rose-window, for they do not appear in Puglia before the 13th century. Both the numerous protruding bosses of the portal and the oxen surely derive from metalwork, the main source of Pugliese sculptors' motifs – the oxen are not so far from the bronze oxen of Reiner de Huy's extraordinary font for St Barthélèmy, Liège. There are signs of an intended portico, never built; the attached columns incongruously underpinning two buttressing strips are a first groping attempt at the greatest problem facing Renaissance architects, how to make a church look like a classical temple.

Inside, the church is dark, though lofty. The openings of the gallery or *matroneum*, of blind arches hooding three smaller arches on columns, repeat in microcosm the larger rhythm of the nave arcade, divided into two lots of three arches on columns between heavy piers. In San Nicola this more old-fashioned system (used earlier for instance at BOVINO) did not yield to the northern Norman system of alternating or uniform piers, because there was evidently no idea of vaulting the nave: if things had gone according to plan the strong piers would have carried stone diaphragm arches at roof level, but all between would have been of wood. Plans were changed: it was decided to heighten the nave and to place a dome over the crossing (though that was never built, either). Unforeseen stresses resulted, and in the 15th century arches were inserted across the nave at a lower point, permanently disfiguring its space. The gilt wooden ceiling, dating from the 1660s, is the sole vestige of a more extensive Baroque refitting; its invisible paintings by Carlo Rosa, a mediocre Neapolitan painter widely employed in Puglia between 1650 and his death about 1678, tell of the miracles of St Nicholas.

At the east end of the nave a 'screen' of three arches decorates the entrance to the transept (and again consolidates the structure); it features beautiful capitals one of which can be attributed to the master who carved Elias's chair, installed behind the ciborium in the middle of a mosaic dais. Elias's chair is justly the most famous work of South Italian Romanesque sculpture. Until recently it was dated to the time of the Council of 1098 on two compelling grounds, first its inscription, 'In this seat sits our illustrious and good lord Elias, bishop of Bari and Canosa', and secondly a chronicler's notice that at the Council pope Urban II gave a magnificent chair to Elias. Now it is argued that the passage in the chronicle was an interpolation, and the throne's stylistic affinity to works datable to the later 12th century is stressed. It was made not for Elias but to commemorate Elias (the words around it seem partially to echo the epitaph on his nearby tomb); but also, installed in San Nicola, this bishop's throne-like throne must have asserted a claim usurping the bishop's and the cathedral's jurisdiction. There is an extraordinary history of antagonistic rivalry between San Nicola and the cathedral, continuing to early in this century; in the context of the sack of Bari that had just taken place, the chair would have been a potent symbol of order and continuity under palatine power, while the cathedral lay in ruins and the bishop and the townsfolk wandered in exile.

The unnamed artist of the throne, while undoubtedly versed in the local repertoire, was up to date with classicizing trends in William II's court to such a degree that he directly anticipates the accurate resort to classical models under Frederick II. Examples are two heads attributable to him on the southern external gallery of the church (unfortunately hardly visible except in photographs), which copy Roman busts of an identifiable period. At the same time the forcefulness of the figures on the throne suggests that he knew the immediate antecedents of Benedetto Antelami in Emilia, while a detail such as the outstretched tongue of the screaming man gnawed by a lion at the back of the throne even recalls the yelling devils of Vézelay in Burgundy. But whatever his training and journeymanship, he enriched it by igniting, with greater flair than any successor in Puglia, the vital spark of sculpture – the appearance of strain, or some kind of movement through the figure. The two nudes and one mailed soldier who strive to support the vacant seat are its outstanding feature. The throne is all one piece of marble: it therefore has as well an appealingly crooked and expressively individual quality.

It is not known where exactly Elias's chair was originally placed. The porphyry disc on which it rests at present is modern. The mosaic around it antedates it, having been laid by Eustace, who commemorated himself in the inscription on the riser of the last step: 'By these steps ascent on high is denied to the proud: by these steps it is given to the meek to seek higher things. Therefore you should not fear, who seek to climb up: be humble, suppliant and guileless, and you will rise, as did father Elias who earlier conducted this church, which father Eustace now rules and decorates.' Round the extreme edge the name of Allah is written in Kufic script. The ciborium is inscribed 'This citadel is the equal of heaven: enter good and faithful servant: pray devoutly to God for your own sake and for the people'; between 'this citadel' and 'equal to heaven' St Nicholas originally crowned Roger II. It is not of great quality, but it is the 12th-century original, unlike so many imitations in churches up and down Puglia. Behind, the Michelangelesque tomb is of Bona Sforza (died 1557), daughter of Isabella the daughter of Alfonso II of Naples and the widow of Giangaleazzo Sforza son of Francesco Sforza duke of Milan; Bona herself was married to Sigismund I of Poland, on whose death she returned to Bari. It was completed by the Neapolitan team of Sarti, Bernucci and Zagarelli in 1593.

On the way down to the crypt on the right-hand or south side is Elias's tomb, marked by a long inscription and four fine figures of philosophers from the front of a Roman sarcophagus of the 4th century. His epitaph reveals an exceptionally distinguished man: 'A great ornament to the world lies here buried in peace; kings have lost a father and the laws have lost a judge. Fallen, o Bari, is the crown of your estate; know that you flourished only while bishop Elias flourished. An illustrious father is enclosed in this beautiful tomb who ruled you well, and carried you up to heaven. To one and all he was a good master, lowly and prominent, local and foreign. The equal of Solomon both in good sense and in building, in his pious life he was the equal of Elijah; he constructed this temple, which shone out even like a golden lamp. Here he fell asleep while his spirit sought the stars.' It is significant that the high quality of the sarcophagus is mentioned, and that he is remembered for building the church: 'the equal of Solomon both in good sense and in building' implies that his was the inspiration of its design. The metaphor 'shining out even like a golden lamp (or beacon)' also occurs on an inscription surviving from a perished church built by a Byzantine governor at the beginning of the century.

Today in the crypt there is likely enough to be a mass in progress, attended by tiny black-clad widows. Pilgrims are no longer so frequent; MONTE SANT'ANGELO has many more. The twenty-eight serried coloured-marble shafts were 'spoils' from Roman or Byzantine buildings, but all have capitals newly carved to a high finish after models of varying dates and kinds – some after Byzantine capitals, others incorporating animal motifs from a wider range of sources – some of which re-appear on the jambs and lintels of the church doors. The porphyry column now kept aside is said to have followed St Nicholas of its own volition from Myra, and was already fettered in its cage in the 15th century: the legend would have arisen because porphyry was of enormous value and rarity in the Middle Ages. Behind the modern altar is an icon of St Nicholas, given in 1319 by tsar Urosius of Serbia, who with his tsaress prays beside his patron. In 1087 the pious Matthew was dissuaded from taking the icon of St Nicholas they had in the church at Myra, but it undoubtedly looked like this: the iconography is standard in countless copies. The earlier, fantastically rich fittings of the tomb were stripped by later impecunious rulers, but according to reports the pilgrim looked down on the saint floating in his oily 'manna', which was sold in bottles, while above everything was of silver, the altar, the walls, the vault.

A few frescos are visible in the apses of the upper church. There is also in the north apse a more important panel altarpiece signed and dated 1476 by Bartolomeo Vivarini: there are several mediocre workshop Vivarini altarpieces to be seen in Puglia, but the canon who commissioned this work, the Venetian Alvise Cancho, was able to ensure that Bartolomeo himself painted it. Saints John the Baptist, Francis, Nicholas and Benedict are represented beside the Madonna in rather forced attitudes of liveliness, painted in bright, clear colours but drawn in a style of wiry line then at its zenith in northern Italy (and Bartolomeo was influenced by such Ferrarese painters as Cosimo Tura). There are other pictures, and in the Museo Nicolaino in the galleries numerous other bits and pieces, including stone sculpture retrieved or ormolu removed in the restorations, and items from the depleted treasury – of some interest, were the museum to be open.

Outside the church, the so called Portico of the Pilgrims is largely a work of restoration. There was once hereabouts a hostel for pilgrims, built by Elias, which had an inscription insisting that lodging and board were free, but that the pilgrim should not expect comfort. All the conventual buildings, having fallen into decay, were drastically restored at the end of the last century. Further restorations to the church followed in the 1920s and 1950s, which were by today's standards perhaps insensitive, too keen to sweep away the debris of later generations in order to re-create a kind of neo-Cistercian purity. So again the little church of San Gregorio, by the

14th-century arch from the town into the precinct, is all neat and trim. Though recorded in the early 11th century as the property of a local magnate, the church looks to have been rebuilt after 1156 presumably on the same plan. It has the same three-arch between two-pier system as San Nicola; the sacristan there has the keys. The church shop retains a strong flavour of genuine pilgrimage devotion, in all its glassy gaudiness, though it does sell postcards of the *exultet* rolls in the cathedral.

From beneath the relief *St Nicholas* on the entrance arch to the precinct the via delle Crociate leads to the cathedral, passing by the church of San Marco, a 12th-century building with a later portal and rose-window. The cathedral's history goes back ultimately to Early Christian times, since the first bishop of Bari, St Mauro, was supposedly a disciple of St Peter, and it becomes recoverable from the 5th or 6th century, the probable date of a mosaic found beneath its west end. The present church has not only a crypt but an underbody running the length of the nave, roughly corresponding to a basilica of about the same width but considerably shorter, which bishop Bisanzio is known to have 'broken down' in 1034, in order to initiate a new cathedral. The nondescript round building protruding anomalously from the north flank was then already in existence, since it must be the baptistry mentioned 'next to the church' in 1032; now adjoining, it is used as a sacristry and is known as the Trulla (a feminine form of the *trulli* of the MURGIA DEI TRULLI). Bisanzio's church was destroyed in 1156. In 1171 archbishop Rainaldo began rebuilding, on the same foundations, although in 1178 he bought out some houses behind the church in order to extend the east end with two towers and a wall between them on the model of San Nicola. Again in order to make the older structure conform with the new ideal, buttressing arches were added outside down the nave (but they are not flush with the transept, which is a betrayal of their *raison d'être*), and inside galleries were inserted (but they never had a floor).

In 1267 there was an earthquake – at any rate, one of the towers fell down, and during the restorations, which continued into the early years of the 14th century, archbishops Romuald and Landulf rebuilt the upper parts of the church and inserted its rose-windows. The window in the south transept had to be redone in 1613 when the other tower fell down – though its replacement looks convincingly Romanesque – and the rose in the west façade was abolished in the mid 18th century when the entire front was updated. In fact the whole present appearance of the church is a reconstruction,

since under the same archbishop Muzio Gaeta in the mid 18th
century its eternal aspect was transformed by stucco and paint of the
species that still englobes the crypt and the inside of the Trulla.
Considerable damage was wrought to the carving in which the
church is so rich. Restoration began in the early 20th century and
continued into the 1930s. It is most apparent in the unhappily plain
and discordant new rose-window of the west façade (the line of the
late medieval heightening is still visible towards its upper half),
although the 14th-century crouching monsters, influenced by
northern Gothic gargoyles, have survived on the eaves of the aisles.
The columns and pediment of the portals remain Baroque, but they
surround jambs and lintels of the 11th century, retained in the new
church from the old. Their simple foliage or pattern relief has
parallel in the work of Acceptus at CANOSA, active in this same second
quarter of the 11th century. On the south flank not only the lintels
and jambs but also the columns standing in front of the westernmost
portal belonged to Bisanzio's church, though they now support a
13th-century porch. The south flank has been extricated from the
seminary dormitory into which the external gallery had been absorbed, and there is once again a clear view of the sculpture on the
upper windows of the south transept, from the early 13th century.
Four different magnificently fierce creatures crouch at one signal to
devour their victims. The east end window has more tranquil pairs
of elephants (repeating those of the same window in San Nicola) and
sphinxes (recalling the pinnacle of San Nicola's main portal) lording
before a dense bramble of carved foliage.

Inside the cathedral is lighter, thanks to its rose-windows, but
otherwise deliberately similar to San Nicola; however the dome
projected in the 12th century at San Nicola was here realized. In the
1950s the considerable fragments of the original screen, pulpit and
ciborium, torn out in the early 17th century, were reassembled,
which is perhaps better than nothing, but inevitably is a disappointment after San Nicola. The pulpit on the way up the right-hand aisle
incorporates fragments both 11th-century and 12th-century. Two
lions who presumably once bore the columns of an outside porch
flank the steps up to the transept. Surrounding the crossing is a screen
reconstituted with fragments of the 13th-century original by one
Peregrino da Salerno, with marble slabs or *plutei* of venerable
tradition, ornamented in low relief with motifs deriving from Byzantine silks. The reconstituted ciborium is just like that in San Nicola,
but so, it seems, was the 1233 original by Alfano di Termoli, from

which three of the capitals survive. Fragments of frescos of the same date are visible on the wall of the apse, also amphitheatrical choir-stalls after the high medieval pattern, and a reconstituted bishop's chair. More frescos have been retrieved in the north apse, where the sarcophagus of archbishop Romuald (died 1309) occupies proud place. In the south transept the large detached fragment of mosaic is not from the earlier church or churches, but 17th- or 18th-century.

The crypt was rebuilt and amplified in 1156, a few months before the destruction of the city, in imitation of San Nicola's. It is now all pink and creamy stucco, except in the north apse where some 13th-century frescos have been scraped clean. This crypt houses St Sabinus, once bishop of CANOSA, whose bones the saintly Elias found while rummaging in the church's underbody, which had since served as a necropolis. That was in 1091, immediately after he had become bishop. His piety was political, for the translation of its local saint was another twist of the screw in the once greater town of Canosa's subjection to Bari. The icon behind the main altar may be extremely old (supposedly it was smuggled out of Constantinople in 733, escaping imperial Iconoclasm) but it is transfigured by repainting.

The cathedral archive conserves several precious ancient manuscripts. They include a *morgincap*, or Lombard marriage settlement, of 1028 and three *exultet* rolls, the best of these the one known as Bari Exultet I, dating from 1055–6. The *morgincap* displays in its midst an image of Mele, son of Natale, and Alferada, daughter of Bisanzio (not the bishop; it was a very common name), each holding on to the snake-like scroll by which he promises her a fourth part of his wordly goods, according to Lombard custom. The liturgical Bari Exultet I, which is nearly 20ft long, was unrolled from the lectern of the pulpit to hang down to the floor of the nave: accordingly it was painted with illustrations the wrong way up to the script and the reading deacon, but the right way to the congregation. Altogether 32 of these rolls survive from the late 10th to early 12th century in southern Italy, the vast majority *exultets*, so called because they begin with the prayer, 'Let the angelic host now exult'. They constitute an early stage in the evolution of the great Last Judgements by which the west walls of Latin churches came to be engulfed in the 12th, 13th and 14th centuries, for their central episode is the Harrowing of Hell, which in Byzantine iconography proved eventual resurrection. They were read and displayed on Easter Saturday while the Easter candlestick and the holy water were blessed, or miraculously activated with Christ's redemptive power. Bari Exultet I even contains an image of the deacon reading from a pulpit, with the priest behind him under a ciborium (simpler in kind than the San Nicola construction), holding the Easter candlestick; behind him another deacon censes and a bishop presides on a chair somewhere up there – the illustrator was incapable of conveying the spatial disposition more accurately. Another image shows the earth before the descent of the tetramorph of the Apocalypse – not naturalistically, but as a matronly figure looking balefully mystic thanks to the black eyeshadow used in Romanesque illumination, in a floral robe, in a bouquet hat, holding on to two lily-like trees on a hill with quadrupeds around her feet. It is an image with its origin in Ashtaroth or Ninkhursag or the thousand designations of the Near-Eastern mother-goddess, a fossil preserved by the Roman convention of allegorical representation. Like abbot Desiderius at Montecassino or, later, king William II at Monreale, the patrons of these Bari manuscripts wanted the forcibly superior language of the latest Constantinopolitan art, in preference either to the inherited Greek forms of their own province or any Latin, that is to say evolving Romanesque, idiom.

There remain to be seen in the old town several churches of ancient foundation but more modern appearance, besides Santa Scolastica. Several early Romanesque reliefs are immured in the façade of Santa Pelagia. San Michele has a much older crypt and adjacent to it a small stretch of the cloister of San Benedetto, where Elias had been abbot. The castle, founded by Roger II, was rebuilt by Frederick II in 1233, and again after storm damage in 1240. Originally its north wall gave directly on to the sea. The ground floor of the north wing belongs to Frederick's time; the external staircase and courtyard are typical of his castles, for instance Gioia del Colle. The rest of the main block is Angevin; the castle was refurbished in the 16th century, and its bastions were added then. In the room beneath the staircase there is a gallery of casts, in which it is possible to have a closer encounter with creatures otherwise remote on the skyline of cathedrals.

Facing on to the *villa comunale* in piazza Umberto I on the way up the via Sparano is the university. In it is the archaeological museum, housing glass cases mostly of vases, but also of bronze armour from Bari itself, Ceglie, Ruvo, Canneto and Canosa. The Pinacoteca or picture gallery is on the seafront (lungomare N. Sauro) in the Madonnella district in the new town. In its current disposition, the first two rooms are given over to medieval sculpture of good quality and to paintings up to and including Antonio and Bartolomeo Vivarini, though there is nothing of the quality of Bartolomeo's San Nicola altarpiece. In a room almost to itself the life-size standing image of St Peter Martyr is by Giovanni Bellini, but the simple effigy gave him little scope. In the next two rooms local artists reflect trends either from Venice or from Naples: when from the latter, the influence is rather from the Netherlands, Naples in the 15th century falling, like Provence, Spain and Sicily, within the ambit of Eyckian art. The prolific local master known by his unresolved initials ZT, active 1500–39, is represented by a polyptych based closely on Memling. Room 6 contains 16th-century Venetian works, by Veronese (a ruin), Tintoretto and Paris Bordone (commissioned by the local Tanzi family about 1538, and the best of them). Interesting is a Caravaggist work – perhaps by the Fleming Matthias Stomer, who worked in Sicily – on an easel in room 9. Room 13 holds works by Luca Giordano, including a *Deposition* of about 1660 showing off his Venetian colours. Room 14 has work of some note by the 18th-century peripatetic Corrado Giaquinto, native of MOLFETTA.

There is also the football stadium, built 1987–90 for the World Cup in Italy, by Renzo Piano, otherwise known for the Pompidou Center in Paris. It is a suspended saucer of an amphitheatre (the architect compared it to a space-ship), surrounded by pine-woods designed to mitigate the environmental disadvantages of its asphalted car-parks.

The coast south of Bari

South of Bari, there are no populous, thriving coastal towns like those to its north, until you come to Brindisi: it is still much more as the northern coast once was a century ago. For stretches the sealine is very monotonous, but every so often it relents, and there are several pleasant and picturesque small towns either on the coast or immediately inland from it, of which the best known is Ostuni. There are beaches, but the adjacent towns have not been cari-catured into resorts: the less brash pace of the intensive agriculture – orchards, olives, vineyards – predominates.

The coast road leaves Bari quite swiftly, and then reaches Mola di Bari, a fishing port on a promontory in the usual pattern, only on a smaller scale; it, too, was once a pilgrim and crusade port, and has an Angevin castle and a Renaissance cathedral. On the way to Polignano sul Mare there is the isolated monastic church of San Vito, with three domes over the nave in the usual way. Polignano has a beach and nearby some blue grottos (in one of which is the novel dining room of a hotel, the Grotta Palazzese), with a pretty old town on a cliff and Renaissance pictures, local and Venetian, in its churches.

The next town, Monopoli, is rather larger, in the usual pattern, and once a Holy Land port as a pilgrim attested as early as 1002: 'Some go by Bari, others Barletta, others also Siponto or Trani, others Otranto the last port in Apulia; but we went on board at Monopoli, not far from Bari . . .'. Here, too, an Amalfitan colony was numerous enough to have its own church, the surviving Santa Maria Amalfitana, nave-and-aisled and apsed, wooden-roofed, 12th-century. The cathedral houses, in a land of many miraculous icons, one of the most famous, the 13th-century Madonna della Madia. It was rebuilt in the mid 18th century in a florid Baroque and decorated at the same time with paintings by such as Pietro Bardellino, a follower of Giaquinto, Francesco De Mura of Naples and Carlo Rosa. There are some Venetian paintings of the later 16th century and three works by Antonio Verrio the elder in the church and in the sacristy, which holds a veritable picture collection.

A little inland, historic hamlets near Bari such as Triggiano and Capurso have escaped engulfment but inevitably have become somewhat dormitory. Rutigliano is more properly a town, set on a hill, with an odd single tower in the main square and a church, Santa Maria di Colonna, consecrated in 1108. Its portal bears on the lintel contemporary, rough figures of Christ with the apostles and the Annuniciation; the outer parts are later. Inside there are remains of frescos, a 13th-century icon of the Madonna, and an early 15th-century Venetian picture (Antonio Vivarini?).

Conversano is still more of a town and still older: it was a Peucetan settlement, as its megalithic walls attest, and was known in Roman times as Norba. As Cupersanum, it appears in Lombard chronicles from the 7th century and by the mid 10th century was the property of an important Benedictine monastery. The monastery church survives in the present San Benedetto, which has a three-domed nave and quadrant-vaulted aisles of the late 11th century and closely resembles the contemporary Benedictine church of Valenzano, but was greatly altered in the 17th century. Its interior is entirely Baroque, the choir and the central dome have been rebuilt, and the floor of the nave was lowered in order to improve the view to the altar for the nuns in the gallery over the west door – the monastery became a convent of nuns in 1266. However, the exterior remains 11th-century, and is interesting for its contemporary inlaid decoration, some of it figurative and richer than the comparable examples on the exterior of the crypt of San Nicola or again Valenzano or at the Patirion near ROSSANO. The present cloister is later, but from it there is access to the crypt, which undoubtedly antedates the present church. The crypt's equal width suggests that its Lombard predecessor was already large, and perhaps already had the same vaulting system, known now from at least one example (Seppannibale, see below) to go back to the 8th century. Indeed traditions linger in Puglia: on the flank, lions still support the portal columns in Romanesque fashion though it is 17th-century.

In effect the convent of San Benedetto ruled the town until the Napoleonic period, although it has a castle that was once Norman, transformed and aggrandized several times before the 18th century. It has, too, a cathedral dating from the 12th century, though rebuilt in the later 14th century, as its frilly eaves confirm; inside it has galleries imitating San Nicola of Bari and a 14th-century crucifix. The entirely 17th-century church of San Cosma is wholly decorated, in a co-ordinated scheme of furniture, stucco and painting.

On the last leg of his journey from Bari to Brindisi Horace mentions only Gnathia (Greek) or Egnatia (Latin) or Egnazia (Italian), of which the site, south of Monopoli, has been excavated. His sophisticated company was greatly amused by the kind of miracle to which the credulous resorted before Christianity was available, namely an altar where incense burnt without being set alight. Horace preferred the orthodox belief that the gods stay in their heaven, and says he leaves it to the Jews to suppose they operate on earth – presumably Jews were relatively numerous here, at the ports through which they immigrated. Quite when Egnazia disappeared is not known, but the city of the archaeological zone is mostly Early Christian. The forum is identifiable, and at one end of it runs the very road along which Horace drove. Everything is built of tufa blocks. Besides the base walls of houses, there are several traces of the city wall, and the plans of two basilicas, the larger Early Christian, the other (by the forum) earlier and pagan. The inscription on a little monument erected by bygone antiquaries reading '*iratis nymphis exstructa*' (built by angry nymphs) is taken from Horace: he meant to say that Egnazia had poor water, and there are frequent cisterns among the ruins.

Not far from Egnazia towards the main road is the isolated church of Seppannibale (a modern name, derived from the former owner of the nearby farm), which has now been dated to the late 8th or 9th century and is therefore significant, despite its small size, for its use so early of the characteristically Pugliese formula of domes over the nave and quadrant or half-barrel vaults buttressing them from the aisles. The domes and vaults depend on arches and pilasters sparely ornamented but clearly articulated; there are remains of contemporary, Lombard frescos in one of the cupolas. Its small windows in the domes and niches in the angles, otherwise uncommon in Puglia, remain more usual in Sicily, where the design is therefore directly or indirectly Lombard and not derived from an Arab source. Outside, the domes again look Sicilian but their peculiar base is plausibly a stage towards the later typical Pugliese pyramid of stone tiles or *chiancarelle*.

Inland, the town of Fasano forms part of a tourist constellation orbiting the Castellana caves and Alberobello (see below). The coast now offers no towns, only marinas, for instance Villanova, with a castle to recall its foundation by Charles I. From Villanova the town of Ostuni is visible – a delicious confection of whitewashed houses ringed by Angevin walls and topped by a late Gothic cathedral. Round its curved upper façade of Venetian form the cathedral has a dense frieze of eave arches, and beneath it three fringed rose-windows and three moulded portals, in stone that has ripened to a honeyed texture. Its Baroque interior, however, is cheap nougat. Other churches, though of no great note, blend prettily with the urban fabric: one has a coloured majolica dome. St Orontius, bishop of Lecce, stands high on an 18th-century pedestal. Round the city there are ribbons and quilts of green cultivation, and on a brilliant day (frequent enough in Puglia) Ostuni may enrapture. Other such white towns are Locorotondo and Martina Franca (see below).

South of Ostuni the coast grows dreary in preparation for Brindisi. Inland, Carovigno has a tract of megalithic wall, built against the Greeks not by the more northern Peucetans but by the Messapians indigenous to the Salento peninsula (more such Messapian walls are further inland at Ceglie Messapico and, most extensively, at Manduria; also in the remote countryside south-east of San Vito dei Normanni). San Vito dei Normanni is so named to disguise its history: in the last century it was known as San Vito degli Schiavoni

(Slavs). Nonetheless it has a castle that once was Norman. Respectively north and south off the road between San Vito and Brindisi there are two more cave churches with a number of frescos, San Biagio and San Giovanni.

The Murgia dei Trulli

Disgust and shock were the reaction of one Pugliese whom I told I had no desire to see the Grotte di Castellana or Castellana caves, which he regarded as the most impressive sight the territory has. Its next most attractive feature would undoubtedly, had we pursued the conversation, have been the stone huts called *trulli* abundant in the same district (see below).

If the region around Alberobello is the most highly developed touristically in Puglia, that is not without reason. 'The Murgia dei Trulli' is neither deserted like the rest of the Murge and the Tavoliere, nor brutalised by large conurbations, but has a pleasant rhythm of small towns punctuating its hills and vales. Most houses and *trulli* are whitewashed, the land is variously cultivated with orchards, groves and vineyards within dry-stone walls: it all looks fresh and peaceful under the gorgeous sun. Of course there is modern development, but the towns, however grimy their outskirts, are still unspoilt once you have reached the top of their hills. Putignano, Noci, Locorotondo, Martina Franca, Ostuni, with their white stone houses in crooked cobbled streets – pretty names as well – have a kind of Mediterranean seaside charm that tourism elsewhere has ruined.

Off the road (SS 100) south from Bari towards the Murgia dei Trulli, Adelfia contains the old Norman settlement of Canneto, and has a square Norman tower; Casamassima has a little 13th-century church, Il Soccorso; Sammichele di Bari has a modernized castle and a museum of peasanthood. Turi has a little Romanesque church, San Rocco, with two domes over an aisleless nave; of course, outside, the domes have the shape of *trulli*. To the south and the west of Turi lie the deep MURGE and their empty acreage of vast estates; to the east the Murgia dei Trulli.

Until the opening of its nearby caves in 1938 Castellana was an old, but out-of-the-way town, passing most of its history as a fief of the Benedictine monastery of Conversano: constitutions to which his tenants were to be bound were issued by abbot Eustace in 1162

. Trajan's Arch, Benevento.

2. Troia cathedral.

3. Bishop's throne in Canosa cathedral.

4. Bohemund's tomb, Canosa cathedral.

5. Trani cathedral.

6. Detail of Trani cathedral portal.

7. Bust of Frederick II in Museo De Nittis,
Barletta.

8. Old cathedral, Molfetta.

9. Ruvo cathedral.

10. External gallery of Bitonto cathedral.

11. Pilgrims' hospital at Madonna dei Martiri, Molfetta.

12. Aerial view of Castel del Monte with superimposed, geometrical eight-pointed star.

13. Castel del Monte with *trulli* in the foreground.

14. Façade of San Nicola, Bari, taken during the Festival of St Nicholas.

15. The translation of St Nicholas's relics on a cart into Bari, re-enacted every May.

16. Elias's chair, San Nicola, Bari.

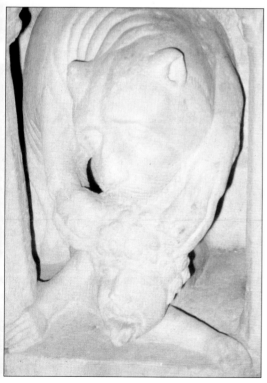

17. Detail of Elias's chair, San Nicola, Bari.

18. Courtyard of seminary on the cathedral square, Lecce.

19. Prefettura and Santa Croce, Lecce.

20. Cathedral crypt, Otranto.

21. Capital in cathedral crypt, Otranto.

22. Detail of the façade of Santa Croce, Lecce.

23. Amphitheatre, Grumentum.

24. Craco.

25. San Marco, Rossano.

26. Detail of mosaic, the Patirion, Rossano.

27. Holy Saturday procession with flagellants, Nocera.

28. The Riace bronzes, National Museum, Reggio.

29. Ruined fortifications at Locri.

30. The Cattolica at Stilo.

31. Interior of Gerace cathedral.

and survive (they are much like those of Torremaggiore, see NORTH OF FOGGIA). Its centre still has several decent *palazzi*. Not far from the town, an enormous car-park marks the entrance to the caves. The Grotte di Castellana are a long series of karst caves, which are remarkable not simply for their size and extent but for their rock flora (so to speak) – the variety and especially the colours of the alabastrine cave walls and of the stalagmites and stalactites. Visits are guided, departing regularly during the season. At Putignano there is only one cave and it is smaller, but has its own special range of coloured alabasters. At Fasano there is an extensive safari-park zoo; the Selva di Fasano is a suburb of holiday villas.

Alberobello is capital of the *trulli*. It is the only real tourist trap in Puglia. Although *trulli* evidently have a special appeal for some – though not the author – culturally they may be ranked beside cave houses, to which indeed they are a kind of successor: they can be traced back to about the 13th or 14th century. The name is derived from the late Latin for a footless wine-cup or round measuring ladle, and is traditionally applied as well to round ancient tombs in the Roman Campagna; also the former baptistery of the cathedral in Bari is called the Trulla. *Trulli*, then, are round buildings resembling the archetypal grass hut, but of stone: the conical roof, often crowned by a needle pinnacle, is built of stone tiles or *chiancarelle*. *Trulli* are found throughout the Terra di Bari and the Terra d'Otranto, where the rocky terrain and the small size of the trees encourage their construction, but nowhere else in such extraordinary numbers as in the town of Alberobello, in the long shallow valleys north to Putignano and south to Locorotondo, and again in the Valle d'Itria between Locorotondo and Martina Franca and on the road towards Ostuni. In this region *trulli* abound almost incredibly: Alberobello is built entirely of them, and in the countryside they are in places the only form of house visible. Limited by the nature of their rubble-and-cement dome to a standard size, *trulli* are very commonly grouped in little bundles, and have been adapted with great success to modern convenience, making garages and living rooms and family houses beside a drive and a lawn.

Alberobello's masterpiece is its *trulli* cathedral, a garden orna-ment elevated to life size. In its kempt *trulli* streets where *trulli* potpourri and *trulli* honey are sold, *trulli* restaurants offer delicately delicious local pasta specialities with agonizingly slow service, during which I have speculated on the possible derivation of *orecchiette* (local 'little ear' cup-shaped pasta) from the old-time peasant's winter-night contemplation of the dome of his *trullo*. The connection to the domes of Pugliese Romanesque and pre-Romanesque churches is perhaps better grounded. Living proof of it is the little church of San Rocco at Turi mentioned above, where *trulli* tops cap the domes.

Locorotondo is true to its name, a 'round place' on a round pimple of a hill, very pretty, and it makes a wine that has made its way to the avantgarde Italian restaurants in London. There are signs in Puglia of the advent of modern vinification and DOC, but much of its grape-juice is sold anonymously – in particular as the base for aperitifs such as Martini and Dubonnet. I have been told in Puglia that others, in particular the French, need southern Italian wine to bolster their own production: for Pugliesi, their soil and its fecundity are *'forti'* – the peasant may expressively brace his shoulders when telling you this, as a resentful pride rooted in centuries of unthanked labour becomes vivid in his nut-brown wrinkles.

Martina Franca has a labyrinthine old town enlivened by Rococo balconies and portals, and also a worthwhile music festival in late July to early August. Visiting the old town, it is advisable to obtain a map from the tourist office just inside the gate from the *villa comunale*, though the labyrinth is not very large – the area only of the old city wall, which had 24 towers. Both wall and former castle were subsumed into the city's fabric in the 17th and 18th centuries, masked and disguised by curvacious window hoods and scalloped balcony railings. The streets, mostly impassable to transport except Vespa vans and the donkeys for which Martina Franca is also known, are clean, and fat cats – no starving strays – sit at the top of the steps to the front doors. The inhabitants, in the day mostly little old women in black who flit like shadows among the universally white sunbeaten walls, will smile and say good day. In the churches, one has an inkling of LECCE *barocchetto* – the Salento peninsula is not far away – though the stone here is poorer.

3

The Salento peninsula

Taranto

Disappointment awaits seekers after Greek Taras, Roman Tarentum, city of fabulous riches and notorious softness. However, modern Taranto (pronounced Táranto) would be a tolerably pleasant town if you were ignorant it had a history: probably you would not go near its old town where there is nothing Greek to see except two repaired but very bust columns re-erected on a derelict site; you would not contemplate what its harbour would once have been and so fall to melancholy; you would not scavenge among the exhibits of its archaeological museum for any titbit worthy of its fame. You would be caught up instead in the extremely busy and clogged streets of Taranto new town, a town entirely transformed both from its ancient and from its later past, even from its pre-1945 state, by the creation of the enormous steelworks of Italsider on the opposite promontory. Its population is now close to a quarter of a million; the single-span dual carriageway Punta Penna bridge flies you over the famous land-locked harbour known as the Mare Piccolo; express-ways convey you into the heart of the thriving city, its affluence indicated in 1990 by advertisements for Sony camcorders on the sides of its buses. American influence, or more exactly Italo-American influence, is strong, shaping sharp suits, cocktails, a taste for pool-side decor. The ideal of life seems to be a country club provided with every possible '*relax*', in Italian a noun and a range of facilities. Their manner is hospitable and broad, with a strong hint that they are very busy and are making time for you.

The modern city has turned its back on its historic site and its famous harbour: it faces the Mare Grande, as the open sea is known by contrast to the Mare Piccolo, along the shore of a wide bay. The better hotels are along this sea-front – none of them beach hotels, but for the businessmen with their portfolios relating to metalwork-ing, oil refinery and naval dockyard business – and the better shops are nearby, many blocks away from the grand square and *villa comunale* built adjacent to the old town in the last years of the 19th century. There instead the portals of the National Archaeological Museum and the Law Courts and a school and a second-class hotel look on the palm-trees beneath which life is more tranquil, its peace disrupted only by the flux of schoolchildren. It is the typical main square of a provincial small town, such as Taranto once was. It is still quieter in the extensive gardens by the Mare Piccolo known as the villa Peripato.

The archaeological museum houses comparatively little from Taranto; much of its stock is regional. On the upper floor rooms I and II (overlooking the piazza) are given over to Greek marble sculpture of quality and to mosaic fragments: finest are some female heads and one svelte male torso. The Roman material and architectural and tomb sculpture that follow are of no more than browsing interest. Then begins a long series of rooms devoted to Greek vases, many of them with figures of great beauty or else with unusual subjects. Corinthian and Attic vases of the highest quality are represented; it is one of the most important collections of Greek vases in the world. But room XI, the last of the sequence, is probably the most interesting, not so much for its small, intact Archaic-period Greek male bronze, with very muscular, stubby thighs, as for the elaborate and ingenious jewellery in the central cases. Here at last there is something more truly reflective of the Tarantine reputation for luxury; although the finds are from tombs all over southern Puglia, it is claimed that Tarantine workshops made them. The ground and upper floors hold study collections, of prehistoric material and of secondary classical material arranged by area of finding.

Taras was a colony from Sparta, consisting, according to legend, of a generation that had been fathered on their wives by the lower orders while the fighting men were away at an interminable war. At any rate the Tarantines were universally regarded in antiquity as effeminate, for which one reason was their wealth, rivalling Sybaris (see THE COAST OF THE GULF OF TARANTO); another was their preference for hiring mercenaries rather than fighting themselves as a citizen army against the Peucetans and Messapians of the interior and against Rome, with which Taras clashed in 281 BC. Pyrrhus, king of Epirus, entered the war on the side of Taras, earning his proverbial victories at an expense the Tarantines themselves by their effeminacy avoided, until he betrayed the city in 272 and it was brutally sacked. However, it is evident from the pages of Livy that it was still the leading city in the south in the time of Hannibal, and that its retaking by Fabius Maximus in 209 BC was the beginning of the end of the Carthaginian occupation. Thereafter it lost both its riches and its regional hegemony, though the large number of prosecutions in Tarentum in the 2nd century BC for indulgence in outlawed Bacchic rites suggests that it kept its morals. Taras was the main destination of the via Appia Antica, though it was a couple of easy further stages across to Brundisium. But as Brundisium became the greater port, the favoured road from Naples became the via Appia Trajana, descending instead down the Adriatic coast.

Somewhat oddly, Taranto's antique reputation for luxury and decadence was still alive in the 18th century. Lampriere's classical dictionary (1788) adds gratuitously that the city's modern inhabitants 'still maintain the character of their forefathers in idleness and effeminacy'. In 1767 Riedesel found the only occupation among the Tarantines to be fishing, and most of them not to have one; every business or labour, especially cultivation, was done by immigrant Calabrians or by Neapolitans. He wondered whether their idleness was atavistic or environmental, due to the sweetness of the air and balmy climate. Now, in the presence of the naval dockyard and the steelworks, these notions are hardly suitable for airing even in the bar or the train-carriage.

Riedesel also, like many other travellers to the region, took steps to witness and dutifully reported the phenomenon of tarantism, the insane desire felt by peasant women around Taranto to dance the tarantella after being bitten by a tarantula. The southern Italian spider is, however, not nearly so vicious as the South American varieties that later took its name, and it was doubted from early on that the spider's bite was really the cause of the hysterical dancing. It began to be noted that the same women fell victim more or less regularly; they were almost invariably unmarried; despite their belief of having been bitten and their neighbours' willingness to accept it, outsiders thought some psychological motivation more likely. All accounts seems to agree that the experience was a melancholy one: the dancing was solitary and compulsive and monotonous rather than hysterically wild, performed by the victim joylessly and gloomily and sluggishly and endlessly, 18 hours or longer once it had started; it was even commented that hiring the musicians required to accompany the dancing was an annoying expense. In his book of 1969 H. V. Morton reports witnessing a tarantism, and then reports, in his usual way, other people's reports; I confess I did not seek one out.

The ancient city was founded on an ingrowing peninsula, enclosing except for a narrow channel to the sea a great basin (the Mare
Piccolo) fed by freshwater streams, one of them the river Galese
(Galesus) which Virgil called 'black', much to the confusion of
Neoclassic travellers, who sought some mineral reason. Then only a
century after Virgil Martial called the same river 'white'. Virgil's
epithet is now taken to mean densely shaded by trees; Martial was
referring to the whiteness of the wool that was washed in it. In
classical times the Mare Piccolo was evidently an area of great
beauty, which has now been more or less buried. During the later
4th century BC Taranto was, too, virtually a philosopher's city like
that of which Plato dreamed, under the benign rule of his friend and
fellow philosopher the Pythagorean Archytas, also an engineer who
was meant to have made a model pigeon that flew. Its riches derived
from the fish and especially molluscs, a valuable source of dye in
antiquity, which the mixture of fresh and salt water in the Mare
Piccolo encouraged – and still encourages in their extensive cultivated modern beds; and from the wool of its sheep, incomparably
white thanks to the detergent action of the river Galese. In Riedesel's
time it had only goats, but was known for its curious *lana penna* or
'feather wool' gloves and stockings, made from a 'silk' extracted
laboriously from a local clam: the stuff was both very warm and
exceedingly soft. Currently a local speciality worthy of export are
taralli, small hard bread rings which may have various flavours, even
sweet, but are best when piquant or flavoured with olives.

In 1481 the peninsula on which the Greek town was built and the
medieval town remained was severed by the channel that still
divides old town from new, and is crossed by a raisable bridge. Old
town and port are unaffected by the modern harbour, which is out in
the Mare Grande alongside the steelworks, and is served by a
motorway that reaches it directly from the north. Nonetheless both
are in a sad state; there are signs of refurbishment in the old town but
so there have been for some time and nothing refurbished has
emerged. The inhabitants seem to be those precisely who have not
benefitted from the new port and steelworks, despite the continuing
presence of the navy in the castle beside the new channel. There are
still fish restaurants along the Mare Piccolo sea-front but they are
spiritless: it is not the fashion in the new town to come here at all, let
alone to eat. The old, natural channel on the north side of the old
town is now the smaller; on the north side is also the station, the
terminus of a branch-line from Bari not frequently served, one more

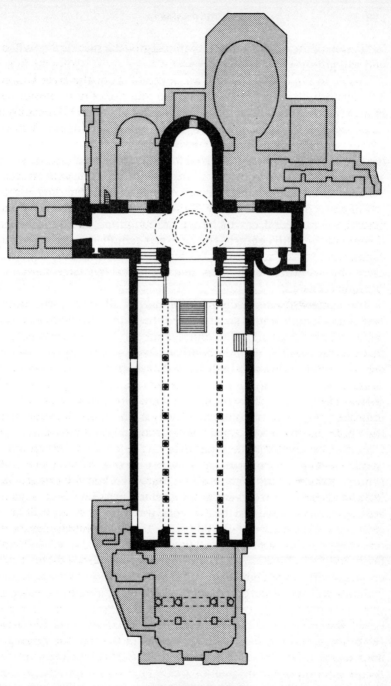

Cathedral, Taranto

indication of the city's former provincialism – the main line was laid
and still goes via Brindisi to Lecce.

To see in the old town there are several Baroque palaces which
have the potential to take on the charm of those of nearby Martina
Franca but are dirty and run down when not under scaffolding. The
castle, rebuilt when the channel was dug – both were undertaken in
a fever of fortification after the Turkish capture of OTRANTO in 1480 –
has round bastions, newly evolved for and against cannon but very
soon to be superseded by arrow-shaped ones; it cannot be visited
because of the navy. San Domenico, a 14th-century building at the
top of a steep stair, is the only church of interest in the old town
besides the cathedral, of which parts are Byzantine, datable towards
the end of the 10th century. The nave was rebuilt after the Norman
capture of 1063 by archbishop Drogo, and the harmonious façade is
early 18th-century, with lines like those of the later Baroque
churches of LECCE.

The narrow Byzantine choir and transepts, all three of the same
height and length, with a small dome at the point where they meet,
most probably had originally some symmetrical western extension;
that was replaced by the new Norman nave, presumably because it
was too small. The nave built by archbishop Drogo, who would
attend the consecration of Montecassino in 1071, was of a 'Gregorian reform' Early Christian-revival kind, with aisles created by an
unbroken sequence of columns. However, the nave had to match
the choir, and therefore is narrow by comparison, for instance, to
Otranto's, though it is the same height. The columns are antique
'spoils', several of them made up of more than one Roman piece; the
capitals are also many of them spoils, but reworked – for example,
little heads have been carved among Corinthian foliage; others again
are copies or variations. In the choir and transepts, the original blind
arches have been revealed inside since the Baroque redecoration
was stripped; the crypt is also original, though floor and vaults have
been redone. Outside, the blind 'hanging' arches and the half-
columns with simple but fleshy capitals are Byzantine, although the
cylindrical shape of the dome and the carvings of its cornice suggest
the late 12th or 13th century. The Norman blind arches running
down the nave have been rendered irregular in parts by later
reworkings, and there are only fragments in the nave of a mosaic
floor dated 1160 (much like that of OTRANTO). The bell-tower is a
reconstruction of the original of about 1133. Off the transept, the
chapel of San Cataldo (St Cathal) is an extremely lavish piece of

Baroque decoration, gradually compiled from the second half of the 17th century until the beginning of the 19th. The relics of St Cathal, an 7th-century Irish saint who stopped over in the region on his way back from a pilgrimage, and died here, were 'rediscovered' by archbishop Drogo. As the many dedications to him reveal, he enjoyed a considerable cult in the Salento.

The prince of Taranto was a title first created for the king's second male heir, the first son becoming duke of Puglia under the later Normans, duke of Calabria under the Angevins. The first prince of Taranto was Tancred, early deceased second son of Roger II (Bohemund had the power, but never the title). From Charles II's fourth son Philip the principate passed instead to his sons Robert and Philip II (all three were also dead-letter Latin emperors of Constantinople), and then the male line died out; the title was picked up by the formidable Raimondello Del Balzo Orsini, a second son and adventurer who became the foremost baron of the Kingdom in the last years of the reign of Joanna I. His tomb is in Galatina (see SOUTH OF LECCE). Until the Napoleonic period the princes of Taranto figured among its very largest landowners, owning not only enormous estates functioning virtually like the slave *latifundia* of ancient Rome but numbers of towns, so atavistically feudal were they.

Messapian cities and the Tavoliere di Lecce

Between TARANTO, BRINDISI and LECCE the roads are straight and monotonous and the territory unchanging and flat, populated in small towns where the shops are hidden away and there is little coming and going even in the central bars. This is the Tavoliere di Lecce, so called by analogy with the northern TAVOLIERE, though the soil is much rockier, like the MURGE. Olive trees predominate. Both the Adriatic and Ionian coastlines are sparsely populated and developed, as if miles from anywhere. Nevertheless several historic towns offer points of interest, some set on pimply hilltops as enchanting as those further north – particularly those that were once centres of the indigenous Messapians.

Off the main road between Taranto and Brindisi, Grottaglie is by long tradition a pottery town and has a colourful pottery quarter. Its Chiesa Matrice is a pretty church, its façade datable to 1379 incorporating an older portal, and with works of art inside, too. The castle was built for the bishops of Taranto, of the 14th century going on

17th. The town's name is justified by caves in the nearby *gravina*, a couple of which had been put to religious use. There are more such caves throughout the region, and notably near Francavilla Fontana, which sprang into being in the early 14th century round an icon of the Madonna said to have been discovered in 1310 by prince Philip of Taranto himself. Its Baroque palaces and grand cathedral outdo those for which Martina Franca is better known: among them the palazzo Imperiali takes pride of place, a massive moated grange of 15th-century foundation but 18th-century completion. Genoese in origin, the Imperiali had acquired both palace and town from the Milanese Borromeo in the 16th century: the vendor was St Charles Borromeo, who gave all the money to charity and plague relief.

Ceglie Messapico north of Francavilla and south of it Oria and Manduria were important centres of the indigenous Messapians, who successfully resisted the ancient Greek colonists politically, though inevitably they Hellenized culturally and later Romanized. Ceglie's old quarter occupies the former acropolis of Caelia, and small tracts of the Messapian walls (4th/3rd century BC) accompany the modern *circonvallazione* or ring-road; it also has a fine late medieval and Renaissance castle which preserves a Norman tower. In the countryside the towers called *specchie* or look-outs are also Messapian; the most conspicuous is the Specchia di Miano halfway between Ceglie and Francavilla.

Oria (Uria), another whitewashed hill-top town, is on a pattern like Ceglie's, though it has no surviving walls except the so called Torre Palumba. A Hohenstaufen and Angevin castle occupies the former acropolis. In the high Middle Ages and Byzantine times it was a regional centre, to which even Brindisi was subordinate; of those days there remains within the castle bailey the now sunken 9th/10th-century church of Santi Crisante and Daria, in a Greek cross-in-square plan (one of the five domes has been lost). The 18th-century cathedral replaces a Norman one of which some stonework is preserved in the nearby bishop's palace courtyard. Dominating the town, the castle retains almost intact its curtain walls, its square keep built by Frederick II from 1227 and three round towers of the 14th century, also a fine external staircase. It houses a museum of Messapian remains, and one can climb to a terrace to admire the panoramic view.

Manduria has lost its ancient and medieval heart, but the tawny blocks of its three miles of Messapian walls, still reaching 20ft in places, are some of the finest examples of ancient fortification to be found anywhere. They were built primarily in defence against Greek Taras, and successfully: beneath them died in 338 BC the Spartan king Archidamos fighting for the Tarantines. There are three distinct walls, the inner the oldest, of the 5th century BC, the middle of Archidamos's time, the outer and not so well made of the 3rd century BC and the time of Hannibal. Numerous tombs are to be seen at the apex of the curve made by the circumventing modern road, some of them upset by the more recent wall. Leaving the road, and following the walls to the south and east, one finds two surviving gates which have further tombs round them. At various points there are original passages under the walls, and there is also within the walls a subterranean grotto that has revealed signs of ancient use and is known as the Fonte Pliniano because it may be one that Pliny records. The modern town of Manduria has several Baroque palaces and a Renaissance cathedral, still conforming, despite changes in ornament, to the Venetian or northern Adriatic late-Gothic pattern; the interior, too, has been restored to its 16th-century appearance.

On the road again between Taranto and Brindisi, Latiano has a museum of Pugliese folklore, and in the countryside to the south-east another Messapian site; there is another again (Baletium or Valesium) in the same direction at San Pietro Vernotico. Mesagne, the next town, was also Messapian (Messania), and is of interest now for the animated decoration of its church façades, the Chiesa Madre, Sant'Anna and Santa Maria in Betlemme, of the 17th and 18th centuries. There is also a castle built by Manfred from 1256 but rebuilt by others, and a small museum of things Messapian. From the town the road follows the original course of the extension of the via Appia Antica to Brundisium. On the outskirts of Latiano, the approximately 7th-century church of San Lorenzo has a domed choir triconch (three-lobed) in plan, giving on to a barrel-vaulted nave: it resembles the still earlier church of Casaranello (see SOUTH OF LECCE) or rather perhaps Cassiodorus's church of Vivarium near SQUILLACE. Off the road south to south-west from Mesagne to Torre Santa Susanna, the le Torri farm has the half-ruined Lombard church of Santa Maria di Crepacore, with two domes over the nave – like those of Seppannibale (see COAST SOUTH OF BARI) or Sant'Ilario a port'Aurea at BENEVENTO, but with barrel-vaulted aisles. Halfway between Oria and Latiano, the Madonna di Gallana, with three domes over the nave, is a third little church hardly much later in date.

Down the coast from Taranto, the scenery is so unspoilt as to be deserted: there are nevertheless several small resorts or *stazioni balneari,* mostly along the strip near Taranto, between the points of Capo San Vito and Torre dell'Ovo, fewer after Torre dell'Ovo and Porto Cesareo. The coastline may have been more densely inhabited in ancient times than it is now; the via Salentina, which divided from the via Appia somewhere near Grottaglie, passing through Manduria and brushing the coast near Porto Cesareo, led somewhere, but there is no modern equivalent of the road. At Torre Saturo near Leporano the remains of a Roman villa; at Torre Castelluccia near Lido Silvana traces of an ancient walled settlement. More than two centuries of unchecked Saracen raids depopulated the coast during the high Middle Ages, and then during the later Angevin, Aragonese and early Spanish rule the incursions of Barbary corsairs. Much of the land was brought back to cultivation only in this century. Against the corsairs various towers were erected along the coast; there are castles further inland, surviving generally in an altered state (Pulsano, Avetrana). The Knights of Jerusalem had the fief of Maruggio and built the Palazzo dei Commendatori and the Chiesa Matrice. The nature of the coast is rocky and broken, with few beaches; the sea is blue, the land bare.

At Roccaforzata between Taranto and Manduria was born Giovanni Paisiello (1740–1816), one of the most successful and influential composers of the 18th century. After a promising start in Naples he accepted a lucrative invitation to St Petersburg, where he produced eight operas, the last of which, *Il Barbiere di Siviglia,* achieved such popularity in Italy that it proved a serious stumbling-block to Rossini when he brought out his own version 34 years later. Returning home via Vienna, he excited the admiration of Mozart (who undoubtedly felt his influence in the operatic field) and then re-established his reputation in Naples with some of his finest works, among them *Nina* or *La Pazza d'Amore* (Mad for Love), the best sentimental comedy of the period. A rather naive involvement in politics in 1799 put him in difficulties, resolved by leaving for Paris in 1802 where he enjoyed a brief spell of glory as Napoleon's favourite composer. But his only opera there was a failure and Napoleon reluctantly allowed him to return to Naples. His last years were embittered by further changes of political fortune and by the dazzling success of the young Rossini.

In the northern vicinity of LECCE, among the occasional towns punctuating the flat but peaceful countryside, Squinzano makes a good white wine. To its north, off the road to Cellino San Marco, the church of Santa Maria dell'Alto stands whole in a ruined village of the

7th/9th century; the church is of the same date but has had various medieval improvements. To its north-east, on the road to the coast, the abbey of Santa Maria delle Cerrate is supposed to have been founded by Tancred count of LECCE·(died 1194) after a vision of the Madonna between the horns of a stag he was hunting at the spot. However, leaving aside the point that the story has been borrowed from St Eustace (or St Hubert), the abbey is already documented in the early 12th century. Its portal is in some respects like that of Santi Nicolò e Cataldo in LECCE which Tancred did found, but the type is diffused (for instance, at MATERA) and this example must date well on into the 13th century, judging by the bulky figures representing the life of Christ round the entrance portal. The loggia on one side of the church, with figurated capitals, is presumably of the same date. Numerous frescos adorn the walls of the restored church, and it has a surviving ciborium. There is a rustic quality throughout, and the adjacent building houses a museum of peasanthood in which some further detached frescos are displayed.

Brindisi

Still greater disappointment than at TARANTO awaits the seeker after Roman Brundisium, where Caesar's armies took ship, and so did Walter de Brienne's, where many thousands of sandalled feet trod down to the harbour in pursuit of empire, riches, learning or relics, and no doubt stood and waited, and where Virgil died. 'Mantua bore me, the Calabrians took me, Naples has me now' (*Mantua me genuit, Calabri rapuere, tenet nunc Parthenope*) – indeed Brindisi (pronounced Bríndisi) would have been no suitable last resting-place for the greatest of poets (the Salento peninsula was known as Calabria in antiquity). There is no more a stirring past left in Brindisi than there is philosophy in Athens. By Tancred's fountain one can sit down and weep 'the dew of a pious tear', but it is likely to be for more pressing problems than Virgil's loss. Ships still sail from Brindisi to the Piraeus and other ports of Greece but today Brindisi's links across the water are limited rather to Albania: Mussolini built it up as naval port when he invaded, an invasion reversed by refugees from the Communist regime and its aftermath at the end of the 1980s and early 1990s.

Old and modern Brindisi are squeezed in uncomfortable proximity on the arrowhead of a peninsula jutting into a split inlet of sea.

At the point of the arrow, two columns (one a stump) at the top of steps above the waterfront supposedly mark the end of the via Appia Trajana, but all that seems genuine about them is an inscription on the base of the one that stands, which commemorates the rebuilding of the city in the 10th century by the Byzantine *dux* Lupus Proto-spata. Brundisium had been so reduced by Saracen raids, uncurbed for the two preceding centuries, that it had to be refounded. It is difficult to believe that the surviving capital, with its four angle deities identified as Jupiter, Neptune, Minerva and Mars, is Roman; if it is, it inspired those carved in Santa Croce in LECCE by Gabriele Riccardi – or perhaps it was carved when in the 17th century the second of the two columns was removed to serve as a pedestal for Lecce's bronze statue of St Orontius. Past the columns a narrow street leads back towards the cathedral, the 'Portico of the Templars', and the heart of the old town.

From beneath the columns one looks out to the narrow passage between the projecting headlands to the open sea. This is the passage that Julius Casear in 49 BC, during the opening stages of the Civil War, barred to prevent Pompey, who held the town, from escaping to Greece; by abandoning the town Pompey gained the sea but on the other shore, at Pharsalus, he met final defeat. The severe problems of dredging the passage were sometimes blamed in mod-ern times on Caesar's siege operations, although the true cause was a deliberate blocking of the passage once again in the middle of the 15th century in order to prevent sea-borne raids on the town. For Brindisi has a second good harbour the other side of the headlands, where the inlet widens only gradually to meet the open sea. Besides the castle built by Frederick from 1227 on the western waterfront in the inner harbour a second fortress was built by Alfonso of Aragon on the outer, western side of the passage from 1445; both are preserved (Frederick's having been extended in the later 15th century and given bastions under Charles V) but neither is visitable because the armed forces still use them. The passage remained effectively blocked until the initiative was taken to canalise it in the late 18th century; by which time the whole town reportedly stank and its inhabitants were grey with disease because the inner harbour was virtually stagnant. If now once again both inner port (used for ferries and small-scale cargo) and outer (industrial) are flourishing, that is due mostly to Brindisi's naval base, and since the Second World War to the construction of an oil refinery and plastics factory behind the eastern headland on the Capo Bianco. From the 16th to the 18th century Brindisi had once again almost ceased to be a port or a town.

However, during the Middle Ages the passage (now named after the 18th-century engineer Pigatoni) was open and Brindisi became a leading Crusader port – though no longer the predominant Adriatic port it had been in Roman times. The destruction of Bari in 1156 helped, and it was favoured particularly by Frederick II, who in its cathedral in 1225 married his second wife Iolanda de Brienne. He thereby acquired the crown of Jerusalem, or a claim to it at least, and in 1227 set forth to the Holy Land – only to turn back in illness. He set out again in 1228, now excommunicated by the hostile new pope, Gregory IX, and already once again a widower but also once again a father, of Conrad, later Conrad IV king of the Romans (died 1254). He returned from the east to Brindisi in 1230, having regained Jerusalem (or more exactly having obtained the consent of the Muslim powers that Christians should occupy it), if not the communion of the Church.

Of the cathedral in which Frederick married, only the foundations, lower walls and plan remain, in consequence of the earthquake of 1743. Just a small section of mosaic floor in the choir survives, with grossly drawn, entirely unmodelled beasts just like those in Pantaleone's mosaics in the cathedrals of OTRANTO or TRANI, and dating from 1178. The road, bridged by a pointed arch, passes under the *campanile*, as it once did at TRANI and BARLETTA. On the other side from the church are the remains of a hospital run by the Knights of Jerusalem, a 14th-century loggia known incorrectly as the Portico of the Templars. It constitutes the entrance to the archaeological museum, and contains several enormous 12th-century capitals more interesting than anything farther inside. The capitals come from the monastery of Sant'Andrea dell'Isola, founded in 1059 on the extreme edge of the outer headland and demolished in 1481 when the fortress begun by Alfonso of Aragon was extended – OTRANTO had just been sacked by the Turks. Their size indicates an ambitious building, had it survived, and assuming it was completed.

Further into the old town, there are two churches of interest, San Giovanni al Sepolcro and San Benedetto. San Giovanni is a round one, built by the Canons Regular of the Holy Sepulchre not later than 1128. Its plan reflects the Holy Sepulchre more closely in not being completely round, but cut across by a straight wall originally providing three apses at its eastern end. A central ring of columns sustains the roof, which was perhaps always wooden, as now.

Various levels of frescos survive on the walls. Outside, the late 12th-century main portal has been newly cleaned, and is interesting for its gabled frame of a type that would become ubiquitous in the 13th century, for its capitals which echo the dancing men capital of Sant'Andrea dell'Isola, and for the populated foliage of its jambs, stemming from a pot at the base in classical fashion, and incorporating some clear classical reminiscences such as a descendant of Hercules throttling a lion with his knees and with his hands forcing open its jaws. San Benedetto also has a 12th-century portal, a little earlier, with men hunting beasts from an enchanted forest along the lintel and bands of strapwork around the arch and down the jambs: though individual motifs may be oriental, the inspiration for almost all the decoration is western, or even northern, rather than eastern. Inside, one of the capitals repeats the four-animal capital from Sant'Andrea dell'Isola; as for the architecture, this is a fully Romanesque church of French type anticipating or perhaps contemporary with Santi Nicolò e Cataldo in LECCE, with rib vaults in the nave and only the quadrant vaults in the aisles to prove it is in Puglia. The ribs are broad and solid and would indicate an 11th-century date in Normandy, but here they belong to the second half of the 12th century. The church is certainly later than the cloister, which plausibly might have been begun immediately after the monastery was founded, in 1080; so much is argued by the form of the capitals (of the kind known as 'crutch' capitals – *a stampella* – from their shape) and the groups of little colonnades running between piers and hooded by blind arches unevenly, and by the rather mole-faced little oxen on a capital that have close kin on capitals in the crypt at OTRANTO. The cloister is pretty, and worth seeking out with the aid of one of the church's indefatigable cleaners.

Heading into the modern town centre, past the 17th-century church of Santa Maria degli Angeli, richly decorated inside and out, and across the piazza Popolo where the three main thoroughfares meet, one may visit Santa Lucia, a gloomy church now Gothic but incorporating parts of a Romanesque and of considerably older building: the crypt is high medieval. There are 13th- and 14th-century frescos in the crypt and in the nave and some Renaissance works of art as well. There is also the Chiesa del Cristo of the 13th century, as the rose-window and cornice decoration demonstrate (it was founded by one friar Nicola Paglia in 1232); and it contains inside two 13th-century wooden sculptures.

The so called Fountain of Tancred is well outside the centre of town on the road to the north-west towards San Vito dei Normanni; it is a not particularly curious fountain dating from the 16th century, though associated by tradition with Tancred and perhaps intentionally antiquarian, like the one at Gallipoli (see SOUTH OF LECCE). This same road will lead to the large church of Santa Maria del Casale, founded by Philip I prince of Taranto, fourth of the numerous and pious sons of Charles II of Anjou, at the end of the 13th century. The façade is colourful, in a manner resembling Tuscan churches such as Siena cathedral, or the decorated brickwork of Greco-Norman monastic churches in Calabria; and, like La Roccelletta near SQUILLACE, it is a great barn of a building, a huge broad nave without aisles. On its tall walls there are considerable remains of early 14th-century frescos – the most significant of their time in Puglia. However, it is difficult to catch even a faint scent of the new art of Giotto in the air breathed by Rinaldo da Taranto, author of the *Last Judgement* on the west wall. The frescos of the east end are of the same date but apparently by another hand.

Lecce

Lecce is a town of surprises, gentle ones perhaps, but genuinely unexpected. Here at last one begins to feel remote: it is well down into the Salento peninsula and although communications remain open the rest of the world is all in one direction, the one you came. And Lecce looks different, not just in its churches – in an individual Baroque or *barocchetto* of which the greatest master was Giuseppe Zimbalo known as lo Zingarello – but also in the idiosyncratic Art Nouveau villas that line a stretch of its *circonvallazione* or ring-road; or in its sporadic palm-trees and orange trees and the vaguely North African reminiscence of its sometimes labyrinthine backstreets, set with houses all of two storeys, all whitewashed; or in its De Chirichesque emptiness during the longer noon break, for the latitude has palpably changed and the churches do not open till five in the afternoon – though there is less to see inside them, and the outside is all their reputation.

There was a Roman Lecce (Lupiae, becoming Litium during the Middle Ages), but virtually nobody knew of it until a 2nd-century amphitheatre was discovered beneath the town's central square in 1905 and partially excavated in 1938. About one quarter of the ellipsoid has been exposed, and a few pieces of sculpture are now preserved in the Museo Provinciale. Lecce became the capital of the Salento under the Normans, partly because they had occupied it for some years before managing to take Otranto, the Byzantine capital of the region. It was a Norman county, and the county in particular of Tancred of Lecce, who remains commemorated on the portals of his foundation of Santi Nicolò e Cataldo, outside the town in what is now the cemetery. It is not clear why Tancred is known as Tancred of Lecce and not as king Tancred (ruled 1190–4), or why it is usually implied that he was defeated by emperor Henry VI, as if Henry, the husband of Roger II's daughter Constance, had successfully upheld his claim to the Norman throne after the death of William II without issue. In fact on William's death Tancred brought most of the kingdom under his allegiance and twice defeated generals sent against him by Henry, in 1190 and 1193. Son of Roger, Roger II's early deceased first-born, Tancred had been William's heir designate before the change of policy by which Constance was married to Henry, and as such had led his army on William's ineffectual expedition to the east; he was a grizzled commander and politician enough to have his succession recognised by the pope and to arrange the marriage of his son Roger with the daughter of the Byzantine emperor. But first Roger and then his father died in the early months of 1194, and after that Henry was able brutally to enforce his less accepted claim.

Tancred's foundation at Lecce dates from 1180, while he was still a courtier. Although the façade was redecorated by Giuseppe Cino from 1716, the Romanesque church is visibly intact beneath and through the Baroque screen. The west portal is matched by one only slightly less elaborate to the south, the monks' door leading into the cloister, but that door is now blocked and the cloister was entirely transformed and enlarged with a second court in the 16th century. The western inscription has this to say: 'Since the life that inhabits this flesh is vain and fleeting, take care, Dives, that for the sake of the flesh it does not fall asleep. For himself Count Tancred establishes an eternal pledge of life in these buildings, endowing these shrines with villains'. The jambs and head are carved with fine precision in the receptive Lecce stone in four bands with motifs ranging from classical acanthus to Islamic hexagons; the lintel has a row of heads amid more acanthus, broken. The inscription of the south door provides chiefly the date, 1180.

Inside, the church is vaulted throughout and fully Romanesque in the sense that it forms a logical and organic whole generated from

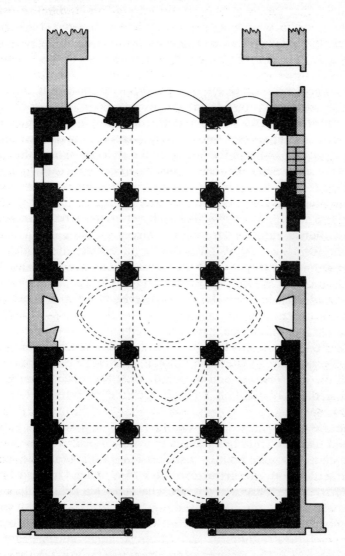

Santi Nicolò e Cataldo, Lecce

the unit of the bay. Its gently pointed arches and rather slender proportions recall certain Burgundian churches, and it might be assumed that Tancred obtained the aid of a French abbey, possibly Cluniac, for his new Benedictine foundation. However, the church has an unusual plan of a kind that could, perhaps, only have arisen in Puglia by the fusion of Greek and Latin tradition. For this longitudinal aisled three-apse church (Latin style) contains a central transept and domed crossing (Greek style): it properly contains it, since the transept does not protrude and the lower supports of the dome are not different from the others, and the transept is formed only by the interruption of the dome into the long barrel vault of the nave and of the transverse vaults of the arms into the succession of groin vaults over the aisles. Since the screen must have been west of the transept, and the monks' door is in the second bay from the west, the monks' choir would have formed a kind of cross-in-square extended to the east. It is difficult to imagine that such a church was built for French choir monks, rather than for local Greek-speaking clergy; and a hybrid form such as this gives the lie once again to the idea of a programmatic extirpation of the Greek rite by the Normans. Tancred's forebear Bohemund, whose land this had been, is known to have endowed not only Latin monasteries but also a Greek one. Behind the east end, through doors cut in the side apses, are later extensions to the church that are now redundant; the church itself is little used and can only be entered with the keys of the grumpy and elusive sacristan. Its later decoration in *grottesche* is contemporary with the new cloister, and the statue of St Nicholas of Bari is also 16th-century, by Gabriele Riccardi, architect of Santa Croce in the town.

In the town, Santa Croce was the first to be founded of Lecce's famed Baroque churches and is a convenient place to start a tour. The churches were built by a succession mostly of ascetic orders who settled convents in the town after 1539, when Charles V began its fortress and transformed it into a barracks and military depot for the war against the Turks. Gabriele Riccardi had already been employed to build the chapel of San Marco in the main square beside the amphitheatre, next to an odd ogival loggia and beneath the column topped by a statue of St Orontius (Oronzo), bishop and patron saint of the town. (The bronze-clad wooden bishop is of 1739 and the lower part of the column was brought from Brindisi in 1666 to commemorate the end of a plague.) San Marco served the town's Venetian merchants and has a 15th-century Venetian style of doorway, though it dates from 1543; at Santa Croce, for the strict Celestine Benedictines, Riccardi seems to have been given a freer hand. The church has been called Brunelleschian but really its nave colonnades are a throwback to Romanesque, not the early Renaissance: Riccardi's model might as well have been the town's 12th-century cathedral (rebuilt later by lo Zingarello). Lecce's churches in general are architecturally unsophisticated, and all their effect proceeds from their abundant and exuberant decoration. Santa Croce is decorated not only outside, by three different workshops working over the period of a century, but inside, where its plain box hall is transformed by the bright white figuration of the capitals of the arcades. These are by Gabriele Riccardi himself or his school, and so is the equivalent, first story of the external façade; then Francesco Antonio Zimbalo added in the three portals in the first decade of the 17th century, and finally his son Giuseppe lo Zingarello ('the little gypsy') in the 1640s supervised the upper parts, that is, the balustrade with its bestiary brackets and busy putti (all in a kind of fairground style recalling English bargeboard carving), the rose window (inscribed 1646), and the eave statues fluttering against the skyline. Among the supporter beasts are one or two that appear to have been modelled directly on Pugliese Romanesque examples: down here there was effectively no Renaissance, but the late Middle Ages persisted into Baroque – a Baroque that is a long way, too, from Bernini or Borromini, or even from that of a centre such as Naples, whence Zingarello's patron bishop Pappacoda might have sought artists, but preferred his own local man. There is a parallel perhaps to 18th-century South German or Austrian Baroque, an ecclesiastical style practised by virtual illiterates animated by nothing more edifying than the glory of God.

Beside Santa Croce the Celestines built living quarters grand enough to have become now the 'Government Palace' – a long austere building made less austere by its decorated windows, the work of lo Zingarello succeeded by Giuseppe Cino during the second half of the 17th century. After Santa Croce, the next new church was the nearby Gesù of the Jesuits, 1574–9, which is sparsely decorated on the façade but inside has altar upon altar with flanking spiral columns in Lecce stone – an extremely soft calcareous ('calcarenite group') stone which can be sawn and turned on a lathe and with which effects more normal to stucco can be achieved. These many altars inside the churches attest the devotional piety of the town's capitalist farmers, who had invited most of the various orders to found their convents in Lecce. In the left transept the *Joseph in Egypt* is an early work (about 1660) by the Lecce painter Antonio Verrio the elder, and the *St Agatha* on the ceiling may be by his brother or cousin Antonio the younger, a preliminary to his later work (usually derided) as court painter to Charles II in England between 1672 and 1707. Close by the Gesù is Sant'Irene, for the Counter-Reformation Theatines, who dedicated their church to a patron saint from the town's Byzantine history, St Irene of Thessalonica; the suckling wolf on the façade is also an emblem of the town, punning on its Latin name. Begun after 1586, this church was dedicated in 1602 and finished in 1639; like the Gesù, it was designed by a member of the order, not a professional architect. It contains a *St Stephen* by Antonio Verrio the elder and a large canvas of the *Ark of the Convenant* by a local painter of the next century, Oronzo Tiso (died 1800). Also not far from the central square is Santa Chiara for the nuns of St Clare, which Giuseppe Cino, lo Zingarello's more restrained follower, designed in 1687. Behind the church, in the grounds of the former convent, the auditorium of the town's ancient Roman theatre has been excavated intact.

The cathedral is hidden away, and the square on which its main entrance faces is a cul-de-sac with a narrow, concealed entrance off corso Vittorio Emanuele. As one enters, the view opens out quite dramatically, but the effect is more the product of chance than design – however delightful, it was not planned by a scenographer like the Baroque vistas of Rome or Paris. But in Rome or Paris one does not find a *campanile* such as lo Zingarello's, built 1662–82 – it might seem to belong better in New Delhi. It is a minaret rising in four retreating stages marked by lo Zingarello's personal repertoire of balustrades, pyramids and cornucopiac vases, which sometimes achieve a fecundity resembling Hindu art – superficially. 'The little gypsy' also rebuilt the cathedral from 1659 on the pattern of Sant'Irene: it has a richly decorated northern portal (and another with unusually competent figuration on the opposite, southern flank, giving entrance from outside the enclosed square). Inside, it is dark, decorated with the usual Lecce stone spiral-column altars and Neapolitan-style coloured marble. The choir-wall pictures are by Oronzo Tiso; in the right transept, the *St Orontius* is signed and dated 1656 by Giovanni Andrea Coppola, but he seems to have been assisted by Antonio Verrio the elder (see above), who thereafter established himself in Lecce. Other buildings in the square are the bishop's palace, an older building face-lifted in the 18th century, and the seminary, built 1694–1709 by Guiseppe Cino. The seminary, in which priests are still trained, has a charming courtyard with orange trees around and in the centre a richly carved well-head. This is perhaps not the right context to repeat the vile calumny that long after their creation had been banned, Lecce kept the Vatican choir supplied with castrato singers.

Exiting the cathedral square, the corso Vittorio Emanuele leads to the left to a succession of three Baroque churches, Santa Teresa, Sant'Anna and Santa Maria del Rosario. Of Santa Teresa, for the Descalc Carmelites, another poor, reformist, 'spiritual' order, the unfinished façade is attributed to Zingarello: it has motifs seen again on the cathedral *campanile* and at the Rosario. Sant'Anna is just a chapel; the Rosario is probably Zingarello's finest work, designed in 1691 and finished 18 years after his death, in 1728. The vases are still more superabundant, the friezes overflow their entablature, the columns are encircled with ballet-dancers' tutus. In the same quarter of the city is the church of the Carmine in piazza Tancredi, 1711–17 by Giuseppe Cino. The more central San Matteo was built by Achille Carducci from 1667 to 1700 to a design imitating, in its convex façade, the Roman works of Borromini; but inside the unfortunate Carducci was able to create neither Borromini's geometrical discipline nor his pulsing spatial shapes: it resembles a theatre waiting for a set. That is not to exhaust the number of Lecce's Baroque churches, nor hardly to have mentioned its palaces and a hundred lively windowheads or portals. Then again the same *barocchetto* style can be found in numerous churches and palaces (mostly religious institutions) virtually throughout the Terra d'Otranto. However, the best within Lecce can be seen within the day.

Outside the 16th-century town gates, the modern town extends beyond the *circonvallazione* on three sides and beyond the Castello on the fourth. At one corner of the line of the old walls the Museo Provinciale may be mentioned, for its archaeological holdings arranged didactically (by far the majority of its visitors are schoolchildren) and for its pictures, which include some known names but not any important nor autograph works by them. One of the best pieces is perhaps the bust of *David* by Gabriele Riccardi; the altarpieces once imported from Venice are of low quality; the numerous paintings by local artists or even a Luca Giordano with the familiar visionary subjects painted in the usual visionary style are not likely to warm a cold gaze. There are further pictures by the Lecce-born

Oronzo Tiso and by the Gallipoli-born Giovanni Andrea Coppola, leaders of the local ecclesiastical decoration industry.

South of Lecce

At Lecce the state railway ends, but a network of local railways takes over. The main road ends, having no further capital to reach, but the traffic is still busy, in fact down towards the point of Santa Maria di Leuca it is very congested. There is no industry, but the agriculture is intensive and the numerous market towns – Copertino, Nardò, Galatina, Galatone, Soleto, Martano, Vernole, Maglie and others, not counting the coastal centres of Gallipoli and OTRANTO – scurry with life. Most offer something at least to see: they will have a *barocchetto* parish church and probably also a decorated palace, and notably there are several fresco cycles preserved from the high to the late Middle Ages.

The region immediately to the south of Lecce has been as Greek as any in the toe, and seemingly from ancient times. Greek colonies in the interior may have remained Greek under Roman rule and into Eastern Roman or Byzantine rule, and then certainly after the Norman conquest continued Greek: Greek religious rites were not suppressed in villages such as Calimera, Sternatia or Corigliano until the later years of the 17th century, and the local dialects are reported Greek rather than Italian. At Carpignano the frescos of the cave church of the Madonna delle Grazie include two dated by inscriptions to 959 and 1020; the first declares 'Be mindful, Lord, of your servant the priest Leon and his consort Chrysolea, and all his house. Amen. Painted by the hand of the painter Theophylact in the month of May indiction [tax-month] 2 of the year 6467 [from the creation of the world]'. In style it is a provincial version of the 'Middle Byzantine' style evolved after the interlude of Iconoclasm, that is to say about 100 years earlier; but it is wholly and truly both Greek and indigenous – unlike the Byzantine art in Italy of the following two centuries, which was imported from Constantinople or, if made locally, imitated Constantinople. The fresco represents Christ enthroned between angels robustly painted in an energetic and richly decorated manner, but still innocent of the deliberately flat and heavy patterning of Romanesque – though something more like that characterizes the second fresco, by Eustathios, of 1020, because it is essentially a copy of the Christ of the earlier one.

In the other direction, to the west, frescos of later date and greater extent are to be seen in the churches of Santo Stefano in Soleto and Santa Caterina in Galatina. In Soleto, the Guglia di Raimondello is conspicuous – a church tower of five storeys endowed by the prince of Taranto Raimondello Del Balzo Orsini in 1397 and highly decorated in an overloaded taste to which, arguably, Zingarello's Baroque work at LECCE still conformed – there is another church by Zingarello at nearby Melpignano. In Soleto, behind the 18th-century church which Raimondello's tower accompanies, Santo Stefano is a pretty, patently 14th-century church, entirely covered inside by closely contemporary frescos – those in the apse a little earlier, those in the nave belonging to the 15th century. However, the programme of decoration is still largely Byzantine: on the west wall, the *Last Judgement* includes the Byzantine Etoimasia or preparation of God's throne; in the body of the church, heavenly visions such as the Trinity or the Celestial host occupy the upper regions while saints and Doctors of the Church are placed below, in a reflection of Greek mosaic schemes.

The portal of the larger church of Santa Caterina in Galatina recalls that of Santi Nicolò e Cataldo in LECCE even though it is more than 200 years later: it was founded by Raimondello in 1391 according to an inscription on the south door. Its structure, too, is not so far from Santi Nicolò e Cataldo, though it is higher and longer and has more shafts to the piers since it has refined Gothic vaults, and has double aisles. Covering the whole nave and populous in the aisles as well, the 15th-century frescos are here decidedly Latin, by Neapolitan or Tuscan artists: in the first bay, crude representations of the Apocalypse; in the second and third, more accomplished scenes from Genesis; Sacraments; angelic choirs and the Life of Christ. In the third bay, it is a study in metaphysics to see angels in Roman legionaries' uniform in the vault while the soldiers who harry Christ on the walls are in contemporary armour. In the choir, the painted tomb of the prince of Taranto, the founder, on the left is rivalled by that of his son Giovanni Antonio further inside, in an extension to his father's choir: these monuments of the local lord are among the finest in southern Italy outside Naples, though the tomb of Filippo Sangineto at Altomonte near CASTROVILLARI is comparable. Raimondello is shown dead in Franciscan habit, as he would have been buried according to a common practice, but kneeling in eternal life in armour. Around father and son, further frescos narrate the vicissitudes of the church's dedicatee, St Catherine of Alexandria; in the inner right-hand aisle of the fresco of Raimondello kneeling before Sts Jerome and Anthony Abbot is signed and dated 1435 by Francesco d'Arezzo, who may also have been the author of the choir frescos. The choice of the two saints, known for their solitary flagellant desert meditation, shows a fashionable Renaissance piety.

On the western side of Galatina, the towns of Galatone (pronounced Galátone), Nardò and, further again to the north, Copertino and Lequile, are interesting more for their Baroque churches – particularly Nardò and Galatone. In Copertino the castle is to be seen – 16th-century bastions working out from a quadrilateral courtyard enclosing an Angevin keep, with an intact Gothic chapel with 16th-century tombs. In Galatone the church of the Crocefisso del Pietà is highly decorated both inside and out, from the last decade of the 17th and first decade of the 18th century. In Nardò the major Baroque façade is that of San Domenico, a rebuilding following the earthquake of 1743; the 18th-century façade of the cathedral conceals a medieval church behind, retrieved at the end of the 19th century, with remains of medieval frescos (of various dates) and later altarpieces. An octagonal pulpit-like building, called the Osanna and dating to 1603, is the latest example of a series of odd or unclassifiable constructions in this part of the world: these number, besides numerous prehistoric menhirs, the so called Centoporte of Giurdignano near Otranto, the Cisternale of Vitigliano between Poggiardo and the coast, and the Centopietre by the 11th-century church of San Giovanni at Patù in the extreme southern tip – all three nowadays thought to be medieval in date, however recidivist their art. In the flat, treeless landscape divided by dry stone walls lurk many troglodyte churches and monastic ruins. On the Ionic coast to the north of Gallipoli, around Santa Maria del Bagno, there are passable beaches.

Maglie, halfway from Lecce to Santa Maria di Leuca, is also on the road between Gallipoli to the west and OTRANTO to the east. It has a prehistorical museum. South of it travel is slow, along narrow roads or infrequent one-track railways. The country continues monotonously rocky and flat, though it takes on more character along the eastern coast and at the extreme southern tip of the heel: just south of the Capo d'Otranto (the extreme eastern point of Italy) there is a pretty area around the hillock-top resort town of Castro. Castro has a castle and a modified but still partly 12th-century former cathedral, in which there is visibly incorporated a still earlier Greek-cross church. In the rocks of its coastline are some spectacular caves, including the Grotta Zinzulusa. Other nearby caves have proved to contain prehistoric material, including wall-paintings (the Grotta dei Cervi), and inland near Minervino di Lecce (actually much closer to Otranto) the Dolmen di Scusi is the largest prehistoric tomb in the peninsula. In Minervino itself the church is by Gabriele Riccardi, mason of Santa Croce in LECCE. At Muro Leccese nearer Maglie megalithic walls attest a Messapian city, and among its churches the Annunziata is well provided with altarpieces. Poggiardo has a small museum housing later medieval frescos taken from a nearby cave church, Santa Maria, and there is another such cave church with frescos in the countryside near Vaste.

Though tourists are generally rare, the southernmost point of the heel at Santa Maria di Leuca (three syllables) attracts crowds in the summer season, for no reason except that it is a land's end. However, there are again caves which may be visited by boat. There is report of a Greek temple set on the promontory, where there is now a church, but its dull, plain, chilly 1920s façade dampens any romantic notions the report may arouse. Like the coast south of Taranto, the area was well populated in antiquity, but Barbary raids over a millennium extirpated the centres of population. Ausentum, for example, on the coast south of Gallipoli, was a more important town than Ugento is today: its megalithic walls, of which there are fragmentary remains, had a perimeter of about five miles.

On the eastern, Ionic coast, Alezio, immediately inland from Gallipoli, was the birthplace of Giovanni Andrea Coppola (see below) and has his *casa natale*. Its name is an artificial revival derived from the old Roman town of Aletium, which had been whittled down to the mere church of Santa Maria della Lizza, the authentic survival of the name. As it stands the church is 13th-century, with a 15th-century entrance and frescos and paintings inside ranging up to the 17th century. Again, near Casareno, the so called church of Casaranello lost its parish in the 15th century, even though it dates back at least to the 5th century – the date of the mosaics in the chancel – and it was the birthplace of pope Boniface IX (1389–1404). Despite their antiquity and good quality, the mosaics are non-figurative and therefore have limited interest, but the paintings in the nave have more – the saints on the lower walls, the scenes from the Passion above them and the Lives of Saints on the vault, all early medieval, but of different dates. At least one of the standing saints, inscribed Barbara (newly emerged from a recent restoration), appears to be of the same style as the Carpignano frescos (see above), that is to say 10th-century: her face has a sculptural forceful-ness like that of the Carpignano angel and her cloak many of the same patterns as the Christ. She wears fine, very heavy gold earrings. The fragmentary cycle of the Life of Christ above the arches, including the Kiss of Judas and a round-table Last Supper, is by contrast Latin and of the 11th or 12th century, while the very primitive *Lives* of martyrs in the vault, which have evidently been copied from a manuscript, will be later again, though quite when is difficult to say. The nave was formerly believed to have been a later addition to an Early Christian church in the shape of a cross, or rather a substituion for one arm of the cross; but it has emerged that nave, aisles and choir are of one bond. So the nave church with an eastern dome is primeval in South Italy; and one might compare the plan of the 6th-century church of Cassiodorus's Vivarium excavated near SQUILLACE. At Casaranello the only later modifications have been the substitution of the present barrel vault for an original wooden roof over the nave and the insertion of a small round window in the west end. There is no justification for the assumption that pope Boniface IX was responsible: he would probably have used a Gothic vault and would certainly, in the late 14th century, have introduced a larger rose-window.

Gallipoli, from the Greek *kali polis*, beautiful city, has in its time rivalled Taranto, which broadly speaking it resembles. It has no *mare piccolo*, but is situated on a narrow promontory between two wide and amenable bays, a promontory so narrow at its root that it was cut through at the beginning of the 16th century, rendering the old town an island. The bridge between old town and new is marked by a skyscraper hideous, shoddy and utterly gratuitous, since it has remained untenanted since it was built. The fairly large old town, with sea ramparts a mile in perimeter, is cleaner than most, and is distinctive for its several churches with modern mosaic fronts and its occasional outside stone staircases between the first and second floors.

Eighteenth-century travellers were refreshed to find an active port, one of the most active in a region then generally depressed. It still serves today as an outlet for the region's agricultural exports, notably of wine to France (where it is melded anonymously) and as a fishing port. A few fish restaurants are situated by the bridge to the old town, where there is also a fountain of 1560 incorporating three Hellenistic reliefs of nymphs arbitrarily named Dirce, Salmacis and

Byblis. On the other side of the channel, the 16th-century castle (englobing earlier parts) occupies a position analogous to the castle's in TARANTO. More or less in the centre of the old town is the cathedral, built during the course of the 17th century, with a lively decorated façade and, inside, the finest pictures held by any church in the heel or toe. The main artists are Nicolò Malinconico of Naples (1673–1721) and his son and assistant Carlo and Giovanni Andrea Coppola (1597–1659) who was born in Alezio just outside the town (see above); their quality had already been recognized by Winckelmann's friend Riedesel, who wrote of Coppola: 'The painter knew how to vary his style in every picture: the one representing the *Miracle of St Francis of Assisi* is in the severe and noble style of Guercino, whereas in the *Martyrdom of St Agatha* there is fire in the composition, and all the enthusiasm of Tintoretto. In the *Assumption of the Virgin* he has successfully imitated the grace and delicacy of Albani.' In fact Coppola had visited Tuscany, leaving a signed work in Lucca, and made surviving copies after the Carracci, Guido Reni and Albani. In such works as his *Miracle of St Francis*, in fact St Francis of Paola, there is a pleasant taste almost of Van Dyck; at any rate the paint is fatty and creamy and it is for once a pleasure to study the altarpieces occupying every bay of the aisles, six of them by Coppola. The Malinconico were responsible in the 18th century for the painting on the upper walls and ceiling. Gallipoli has otherwise only its small archaeological museum and the Chiesa della Purità, highly decorated on the inside with both paintings and stucco; there are occasional works by Coppola in this and other churches as well.

Otranto

Horace Walpole had never visited Otranto; its castle is not Gothic; the place is remote but not sinister, in fact it is charming. It is not Gothic but Byzantine: in the darkest centuries of Byzantine rule in Italy it was the seat, or toehold, of government, being lost only once, briefly, to the Lombards in 757–8. It was, too, one of the very last cities to fall to the Normans, about 1070. Otranto (the accent is on the first syllable) is still a metropolitan see, as it became under Byzantine rule, and it still has the cathedral that the new, Norman bishop William rebuilt with emphatic grandeur soon after the Guiscard's son Bohemund had taken the city. It has also in San Pietro an intact relic of the preceding Byzantine era, an entirely Greek cross-in-square church dating to the 9th or 10th century.

In 1480 Otranto suffered a terrible incursion by the Turks that not only scarred the city but traumatized all Italy: the threat of the Turks, who had engulfed Constantinople in 1453 and whose tide had not yet reached a visible neap, materialized with horrid force, washing the town with blood: the bishop was massacred in his cathedral, and 800 Hydruntine 'martyrs' were put to death on 14 August, two days after the city's capture. It was a very Christian victory when Alfonso II retook the city in September of the following year, on a second attempt. The cathedral conserves the martyrs' bones in a special chapel in shelves of boxes rather like those of a pharmacy, and has a commemorative portal in the south wall; and the town has a beautifully kept *enceinte* of Early Renaissance walls, curved and thickened against cannon but predating the age of bastions, which were added only to the castle. So this peaceful, whitewashed city, which still has a medieval size, has twice floated loose between the seismic plates of history – at the furthermost lip of the lava-trail of western barbarism in the 8th century, at the furthermost of eastern barbarism in the 15th. Today to have reached Otranto is to have reached, perhaps, the furthest outpost of triumphant Europeanism; across the strait the mountains of Albania are visible, and Otranto has a touch of the empty patience of changeless poverty *insh'Allah*, except for the geraniums in the window-boxes.

From the small harbour ferries ply occasionally to Greece, and perhaps there will one day be commerce with Albania, so long closed by Communism. From the 18th century Riedesel relates that Albanians during the summer months would bring for barter to the Otranto beaches ice from the mountains visible across the water. From the waterfront through a gate one makes one's way up the central via Alfonso d'Aragona, turning up to the right to find the entrance to the cathedral. Its façade is 17th-century, but incorporates a rose-window dating from immediately after the sack of 1480. Step over the sill of the main door, and you tread on the Latin signature at the bottom of a 12th-century mosaic covering the entire nave and choir and aisles, up between and around a fine arcade with rich capitals, under a late 17th-century decorated and compartmented ceiling. The transept has suffered some alterations, but the splendid crypt, entered by two deep staircases in the aisles, has not, and is not outdone by that of San Nicola at Bari.

A restoration of the mosaic floor, still going on in 1990, has already somewhat altered the accepted history of the cathedral, for it has revealed beneath the 12th-century mosaic traces of another, datable, so an excavator told me, to the 4th/6th century. It is unlikely therefore that the Byzantine cathedral was at San Pietro, as has been supposed: it must have been here, in a building that had survived as hardily, if perhaps also as shakily as eastern Roman rule. And that would better fit the document of the present cathedral's consecration in 1088, in which the remark that the church 'had never been consecrated' would have been redundant if the church had been new. What surely was meant was that it had had no Latin consecration. The exact extent of the cathedral's predecessor will perhaps be revealed by the excavations, but it has been observed already that in the peculiar spurs that jut forward from the west wall at the beginning of the nave there are two buried pilasters and capitals: these presumably belonged to the Byzantine cathedral, and were at first taken over into the new Norman one, until displaced by the present nave arcade with capitals which can be dated to the middle or later 12th century. The original Byzantine church was perhaps nearly square, occupying the present nave; to which the Normans between 1070 and 1088 added the crypt and above the crypt the transept that rests on it, then in a second, 12th-century campaign rebuilt the nave.

The consecration in 1088 was performed by the papal legate and archbishop of Benevento, with the assistance of the archbishops of Bari, Taranto and Brindisi as well of William, the bishop of Otranto, with such a name obviously a Norman. That is an important group of personages, and Otranto is remarkable among Pugliese churches in directly reflecting the cathedral of Salerno, which was, if not technically the metropolitan, then certainly the capital see of Robert Guiscard's Norman kingdom. In its original Norman form Otranto probably had an open transept like Salerno or, later, San Nicola at Bari – the two low arches now dividing the central choir from its aisles being inserted probably for structural reasons at the time when the nave was rebuilt. (Both arches and new colonnade were in place before 1162–5, the date of the mosaic that was set around them.) Perhaps Otranto's crypt also reflected Salerno's (drastically rebuilt since); at any rate, it is one of the most ornate and the earliest of Puglia's fine crypts, which those of San Nicola, Bari, or Trani afterwards rivalled but hardly outdid.

In the crypt, one is immediately surrounded by a forest of elegantly slender columns, in a penumbra glimmering delicately with pale marble. Many of the capitals are re-used, both antique and Byzantine, some left, some partly reworked; others are 11th-century imitations of these and other antique and Byzantine examples; others are standard 11th-century; others again are ostentatiously figurative. The style is still pleasingly close to Acceptus (see CANOSA), not so much in motif (though eagles like his pulpit eagle are here) as in its spareness and economy; nevertheless the more florid taste that created Romuald's contemporary throne at Canosa is also germinating, for instance in the charming affronted lions on two capitals (one by a master, near the central altar; the other in imitation and a little rougher, in not so prominent a position).

By the time the new nave was built and the new mosaic floor laid, the Norman kingdom was secure and ruled from Sicily, and the see of Otranto had declined in importance. Its splendid floor was not so remarkable, since fragments prove similar floors to have been laid at Taranto, Brindisi and Trani (in the latter two cases apparently by the same team). What is remarkable is its largely complete survival. Apparently it took at least three years to lay out, since it is dated 1162 in the middle and 1165 at the west end: the five inscriptions repeat or add that the artist was Pantaleone and the commissioning bishop Jonathan, while William I was king. One of them achieves clumsy leonine verse: '*hoc opus insigne est superans impendia digne* – this is a great work, and fittingly it is worth more than the expense of its materials'.

Most of the mosaic's many figures are disposed rather giddily without hint or sign of containing ground or space, but a great tree provides a central armature, and several are enclosed in roundels. Also iconographically the figures are a jumble – Alexander, Solomon, Arthur, Adam and Eve are all here, according to inscriptions. (Alexander is shown riding his chariot up to heaven, by the device of offering kebabs just above their heads to two griffins – the same image happens to survive at Trani). On the other hand the figures are not purely 'luxurious' in the sense of St Bernard's diatribe against purposeless chimerical decoration: the stories of Jonah and of Samson and the lion, either side of the altar, symbolize respectively the Resurrection (Jonah in the whale was an antetype of Christ spending three days in hell) and the devil's overcoming. Elsewhere as much meaning may or might be drawn from it as the spectator can or could imagine – though the imagery includes the Labours of the Months, widely used out of context as infills and too hackneyed to carry any obstruse message. It seems certain that the various juxtaposed significances and potential symbols did not and will not add up to a coherent message – nevertheless certain themes recur (for instance more than one story, including Alexander's, can be moralized as a lesson of pride) and the imagery in certain signpost positions (above all round the altar) gels into something more definite.

The figures of the mosaic are drawn with blithe unawareness of any third dimension, lacking mass and occupying no space. Not only is there no modelling except a few inapplicable dots and streaks, but a dotted black contour around them all negates any effect of figure against ground. All derive from other art – from the repertoire of contemporary sculpture (the elephants, for instance, at the base of the tree closely resemble those standing beneath the growth of foliage on the jambs of the central portal of San Nicola in Bari), from manuscripts, from classical mosaics (the cupid-fishers around Jonah betray the derivation of both form and iconography from Early Christian church floors), and so on. So much is equally characteristic of Pugliese medieval sculpture, but nowhere else is the tendency so extreme and the awareness of an original existing model so faint.

Descending again to via Alfonso d'Aragona and continuing up it, you will find on the left a sign to San Pietro, and a moment's hovering presence should be enough to produce the custodian, from nowhere but not for nothing. It is a completely Greek church, a Greek cross of barrel-vaulted arms under a single dome. The iconostasis has gone, but numerous traces of frescos remain, and one under the arch to the left of the altar, representing Christ washing the apostles' feet, has been dated to the 9th or early 10th century, by analogy with the signed and dated frescos at Carpignano. The *Washing of the Feet* is told with a Byzantine variation (which occurs also among the mosaics in St Mark's in Venice), showing Peter perplexed: he at first refused to have his feet washed, but then, miffed not to be the first, pleaded for it. The remaining frescos are of a later stratum and date, into the period of Norman rule. One exits from the town at the Aragonese castle, marked as such over the gateway by a finely carved coat of arms.

ITINERARY TWO

THE TOE

On the via Popilia (Eboli)

If 'Christ stopped at Eboli' he cannot have done so for long: Christ turned back at Eboli would be a more accurate translation of the title of Carlo Levi's book. Eboli is not on the border with Basilicata but is the last outpost of the virtual conurbation surrounding Mt Vesuvius, and has still a kind of Neapolitan raciness and perfervid zoom. I arrived there on a May evening and, having found the only business-man's hotel and a room in it without difficulty, walked out into a full *serata*, of the kind that utterly swamp the towns of the South as the participants drive in, park and talk and walk in the main square more densely than feeding pigeons. To eat, it seemed to be either pizza or some other fast food (at 'Cook and Pizza Tony', for instance), consumed by quantities of young Ebolitans on the street, or else the hotel restaurant: restaurants are few and far in the South between the capital cities.

A sortie up into the old town was unsatisfactory and inconclusive. There were the remains of the castle, greatly transformed through the ages, of this church and that, empty spaces and a slight view; as darkness descended lovers flitted and delayed – no other move-ment. It was the usual story of Italian historic city desertion: everybody prefers to live in the valley where the houses are new and the commuting convenient. In the South the dereliction is com-pounded by destructive earthquakes, which are left to the author-ities to repair. Too often there is already nothing left of outstanding interest anyway; Eboli is no exception, despite its past reaching into Roman times (Eburum) and its two small tracts of megalithic acropolitan walls. There is little historical curiosity among the local inhabitants, as the lack of bookshops illustrates: usually books from here southwards are stocked by stationers, and the few bookshops proper carry a jejune stock.

In any case there is no point in trying to treat Basilicata and Calabria fairly, as if they were the equal of the rest of Italy. What is to be seen has to be seen against a blank and inhuman past, against which the people become a caricatured folklore, or a toneless background, against which the monument takes on a conspicuous

colour. Places to go and monuments and events to see are rare but
once found are unfamiliar and exciting. And to drive from one to
another in this part of the world is tremendous fun, since there is
endless scenery and the roads are now often superb in relation to
the volume of traffic they carry. This situation is very new. The
Autostrada del Sole, from Naples to Reggio Calabria, begun in 1962
and completed in 1974, was only a first phase; it has been followed
by numerous secondary motorways or *superstrade* linking leading
towns (*capoluoghi*) in an ever tighter network. Swift viaducts and
tunnels, many just now appearing along more secondary routes, are
dramatically cutting times of journeys down and up again across
valleys from forty minutes to three. The new *superstrade* also offer
wonderful views, even memorable ones, though viewed at motorway speed they are not usually so; of course the old roads remain, so
that one can step off the new ones to seek out and explore at a more
leisurely pace as well.

   Nonetheless, just as there are still seasons despite central heating,
so geography determines the routes to take despite bulldozers,
explosives and concrete stilts. The routes are those of the rivers and
valleys, as one may track them between the tortuous mountain
chains and watersheds that divide Tyrrhenian, Ionian and Adriatic
Italy. The earlier, larger part of this book has covered Adriatic Italy
and a bit of Ionian, that is to say Puglia and the further edges of
Basilicata where the rivers run east rather than south, and the part of
Puglia, south of Taranto in the ball of the heel, that borders the
Ionian sea. This part of the book covers Tyrrhenian Italy and the rest
of Ionian, that is to say both sides of Calabria and most of
Basilicata, in which the rivers flow south. In this part of the book I
have been more selective. I do not believe that random explora-
tions, for the sake of the scenery or the sensation, need a guide;
instead I have included only places about which it is frustrating not
to have information, ordering them according to the abiding geography of the watercourses.

   From Eboli the Autostrada del Sole runs southwards along the
floor of the valley of the northward-bound river Tanagro. The hills to
the east constitute the border with modern Basilicata (the Monti
della Maddalena); the hills to the west initiate the rocky Cilento
region of southern Campania, across which lie eventually Paestum
and Palinuro. At the top of the Val di Diano, near the town of
Lagonegro, Mt Sirino forms a watershed, and from its eastern side
the river Sinni descends to the Ionian.

In Roman times the via Popilia on its way to Reggio came down the same valley, but divided a single province, Lucania, comprising both the Cilento and modern Basilicata. Roman and Byzantine Lucania bordered Samnium around Beneventum to the north and Bruttium, present peninsular Calabria, to the south. Then the name Calabria belonged rather to the tip of the heel than the toe, to the present Salento peninsula in Puglia (and also to some of the instep, present south-eastern Basilicata); but from the time of the Lombard invasions, seemingly by an error of the Byzantines themselves, it came to be applied to the province ruled from Reggio (Rhegion). Basilicata is a name datable to the 10th century, referring to those parts of the old Roman province of Lucania that the Byzantines continued to hold or retook after the Lombard invasion; *basilius*, from the Greek title for the Roman emperor, was widely used meaning effectually 'Byzantine'. Similarly in the 11th century when the catepan Boioannes had reconquered Daunia or northern Puglia that region became known as Capitanata, corrupted from Cate-panata.

In medieval times regions were ruled from strongpoints, in which South Italy is extremely rich; only seldom, during the reign of such exceptionally strong rulers as Roger II or Frederick II, did central power effectively overarch and interfere. A pattern of vicious tax-farming set in with the Angevins – so harsh in Sicily that it occasioned outright revolt in the 'Vespers' of 1282, an absolute novelty for the time; it was no easier in Basilicata, which had also to pay for supporting both Manfred and Conradin against Charles I. Political and natural reasons were plentiful for a fall in population to hardly a quarter of a million overall in the 18th century. Revolts broke out against the Spanish viceroys from the middle of the 17th century and continued, as conditions failed to improve, until Unification; conditions still did not improve, but the door to emigration to America was opened, nearly halving the population in the half century before the First World War. Fascism repressed or sponsored repression, with bloody consequences when reprisals were taken by the peasants after the Allied invasions of 1943. More enlightened government has had still to contend with a collective mentality comparable to that of an underprivileged recidivist delinquent.

4

Basilicata

Latinianum or central Basilicata

The bleak and bitter heart of Basilicata is the former Roman and Byzantine district of Latinianum, through which run the two rivers Agri and Sinni; the more classical name was revived for a time in the 19th century. This land has generally been barren and poor, even for pasturage, because the mountain soil rapidly erodes (the original forests of oaks, chestnuts and beeches finally disappeared in the 19th century, but deforestation began in antiquity), and the valley floors, though watered all year round, are either marshy or gravelly, the rivers running an inconstant course from season to season. In their still pools the anopheles mosquito widely flourished, so that malaria became endemic in early modern times; how far it affected the ancient and medieval world is uncertain. Vines, orchard trees and the lowlier cereals were the only crops of an undernourished, febrile people. Only bandits and hermits have flourished in this colourless country where settlements founded have time and again died out. Although there is fresh green in the upper valley of the Agri around the man-made lake of Pietra di Pertusillo, especially near the Roman site of Grumentum which in antiquity was known for good wine, elsewhere today the quarries and the gravel farms are more dominant. Mostly the hill slopes, ravaged by constant landslip, are a featureless cement grey, hardly relieved by the sparse vegetation.

In the heart of this heartland is Aliano, the village to which Carlo Levi was exiled and about which he wrote *Christ stopped at Eboli*, though he called the place Gagliano in what was often a poetic recollection. Socialist and doctor as he was, he came to love the backward, unregenerate, superstitious people and wished to be buried among them. His house is now a museum, containing memorabilia, agricultural implements of bygone days, and his paintings. It has particularly soulless views over the raw erosions (*calanchi*) and ravines which render parts of Basilicata properly a desert, and is surrounded still on its windy outcrop by unsanitary, tumbledown slums set amongst steep winding alleys.

However, at the other end of the village the 1960s mayory, a curved, grey, concrete building in conspicuous contrast to the whitewashed stone of old Aliano, bustles with didacticism, project-planning and social awareness. The passing of the bad old times is proclaimed if by nothing else then by the numerous signs to the town's attractions – this way to the *calanchi*, this way to the 'historic centre', this way to Carlo Levi's house. There are now in Aliano several shops, more than one bar, a garage, and even a *pizzeria* where I ate an indifferent meal in which the cheese was Kraft. Everyone confirmed to me that 'everything is changed' – except that it was a *dénouement* of Carlo Levi's book that many of the village's primitive inhabitants had actually been to America and returned. In fact not everything has changed. In the 'historic centre', the old houses are still inhabited, not entirely by the elderly; a man led out a donkey as I watched; there was a smell not only of excrement – obviously no lavatories – but also of animals and dank straw, as if men and beasts still shared their habitation. However, the tiny woman all in black who called out in rough dialect was using a supermarket detergent.

I felt a bit silly asking people questions about now and then. Two youths on a scooter took an interest in me and wanted their photograph taken, which was some sign of backwardness, I thought. One had finished school but had not much idea of what he would do; the other had a job 'on the land'. They wanted to earn money to eat, as they put it; neither had a notion of career or of any other life elsewhere, of travel, fast cars or glamorous women, or even of vandalism or politicized discontent. I thought it remarkable that they were not attracted by the lights and evils of the city, that they were apparently so untouched by its lure; but I recalled, too, that the barman in the *pizzeria* had turned to pay attention to the blaring television only when a discussion of a new airport for Potenza had come up. Probably everybody here had been born in the village. So perhaps still in Aliano the world is only Aliano, as it was in Carlo Levi's book.

Roads into Latinianum follow the valleys of the Agri from its rising at Marsico below BRIENZA (SS 276/598) and of the Sinni from below Lagonegro towards Latronico (SS 104). The former was the route of a Roman road linking the via Popilia (to Reggio) with the via Appia Antica (to Taranto), and on it lay ancient Grumentum, today an archaeological site signposted off the SS 103 beneath modern hilltop

Nova Grumento, by the reservoir of Pietra di Pertusillo. Here in 207 BC, after he had failed to capitalize on his victory at CANNAE and the Italian campaign had turned to the advantage of the Romans, Hannibal suffered a defeat at the hands of Claudius Nero, losing four elephants, according to Livy; however, he managed to retreat his army into camp and left a few days later in the middle of the night, successfully deceiving the Romans by leaving tents up and camp-fires burning. But Grumentum as it remains to be seen today is of the early imperial period; a surviving inscription records a stoa or portico which the architect Titus Vettius built in 43 BC, but which is lost. Nevertheless the whole outline or plan of the city is intact, and the course of the city walls is still traceable round its perimeter, though they have not been excavated from the line of trees that cover them. At the south end of the site a large modern museum has been built but is not open (this kind of local government inconsis-tency, ultimately financial, is all too typical of Basilicata and Cal-abria). Entrance is beside the fairly substantial remains of the town's theatre, beside which there is a large patrician house. Following the former main road from end to end of the town, one gains the forum, with adjacent buildings; then further down past cultivated fields is the amphitheatre, preserved at one point to the second storey. The most remarkable aspect of the remains is their robust *opus re-ticulatum* or square bricks laid at 45° in 'network' bond. Later Grumentum declined and was sacked; the Byzantine and Norman town for the valley was Viggiano.

Off the road southwards to San Chirico Raparo, but not sign-posted, the abbey of Sant'Angelo was founded in the 10th century. The 11th- or 12th-century church has a standard high medieval type of nave terminating in a high, small cupola before an apse; modestly decorated on the outside with blind arches, it may be grouped with other larger, more richly decorated monastic churches of brick in Calabria (for example San Giovanni Vecchio at STILO). Its cupola is an unusual, rather clumsy construction rising on the outside through several tiny stages. The monastery may be assumed to have been Greek, but the architecture is not properly Byzantine; at the very least its circumstances were conditioned by the Norman conquest and it seems appropriate to call it Greco-Norman. A ruin of much more recent kind is at Craco, reached from a northward turning just beneath the confluence of the Sauro with the Agri: a landslip of the kind so common in the region rendered the town unsafe on its rock-edge in 1978.

On the southern side of the Agri, Tursi (Toursikon) was the capital of Byzantine Lucania; it preserves a structure of Byzantine period in the crypt of the Chiesa della Rabatana, so called after the name of the Arab quarter it once had. The region was once forested, and further towards the coast, fertile, as both the cultivations and the excavations around the now isolated church of Santa Maria d'Anglona attest. The excavations have dug out chiefly a necropolis with tombs of both the Greek and Roman period; but also beside the present church begun in the late 12th or early 13th century the outline has been laid bare of a smaller predecessor dating to the 10th or 11th. A late 13th- or early 14th-century portico precedes a portal like that of MATERA cathedral and others in the MURGE of Puglia; on the other hand the east end has a rich decoration of coloured-brick blind arches recalling Calabrian Greco-Norman. The nave has a full complement of frescos, both of individual saints on the piers and in the spandrels of the arcade, and of *Lives* of saints under and between the windows above them, all in a loose and careless 15th-century Gothic style. At the end of the nave and aisles one steps over or through the remains of a central and two flanking apses into the later choir: was there originally a dome between the dwarf transepts and before the extended chancel?

The valley of the Sinni features once again a series of hill-top or rock-edge hamlets, several recorded since Byzantine and Norman times; some, such as Colobraro, a corruption of Kyr Onouphrios or St Onophrius, derive from monastic settlements. Greek cenobites settled, cleared, farmed and built in these wild regions from the beginning of the 10th century, much in the same way as would Cistercians in Burgundy, Yorkshire and elsewhere from the early 12th. If seldom there is much to show for it, that reflects partly the ascetic instincts of the hermits or monks, and partly, until after the Norman conquest, the continuing peril of rapine: so much is revealed in a conversation from the second half of the 10th century recorded in the *Life* of St Nilus between the saint and the Byzantine military governor. 'Let me clothe your chapel with precious wall-hangings,' asked the governor. 'I would prefer,' replied Nilus, 'that you should go to the Katholikon of the Kastron (the cathedral of the garrison) where they guard them so they may not be stolen.' 'I cannot bear to see your chapel of clay,' pleaded the governor. 'Then you cannot bear seeing me, since I am of clay. Do not bother about my chapel at all, since the impious Saracens will destroy it anyway.'

A not dissimilar fatalism struck Carlo Levi a millennium later. It seems almost inevitable in the bare landscape of the region, a peculiarly inhuman desert lacking even any Berber red or Tuareg blue. It is difficult to describe one's sensation driving through it. The strong, colourless light floods the mind: its unfolding unchanging-ness, its undulating endlessness, strips away ideas and personality. One feels like a worm on asphalt.

Brienza, Potenza, Acerenza

Brienza is a dream of a fairyland castle rendered to shattered ruin by earthquakes in 1851 and 1980: today scaffolding still alternates with the jagged canines of its broken walls. It is such a pity, for Brienza is an ideal site in this countryside made for castles; its conical hill, terraced and turretted by the clinging houses of the encircling town, rises from the floor of the intersection of three valleys, two made by the northward-bound Pergola and the third by a smaller torrent descending from the pass into Campania at Atena Lucana. Many of the houses, too, still have scaffolding; that should eventually go and then the shoulders of the hill may still rise clear of the concrete mayhem ungreening its outskirts.

The castle is Norman, apparently no older, but founded as a strongpoint in the mid 11th century when the Norman bands began their first inroads into Byzantine Lucania. It was converted into a residence in 1571. On its north side there are substantial remains of outworks extending down the valley; this is perhaps its most picturesque aspect. In this direction, too, there are spectacular views from the high pass and watershed near the Torre di Satriano, unique vestige of a town destroyed by Joanna II the Mad in 1420 and never rebuilt, though modern Satriano di Lucania has appropriated the name. The valley of the Pergola, merging into the Melandro, veers to the east eventually to join the Tanagro; but Potenza to the north-west is at the head of the valley of the Ionian river Basento.

Potenza is a colossal sprawl, a churning heap of environmental violence like an anthill on a lawn. There is, furthermore, nothing there: earthquakes have shaken down its churches and monuments to the mere walls, all baldly and antiseptically mortared and pointed. (Here the ravages of the 1980 earthquake have been repaired.) As the capital of Basilicata it has government offices, a university, an art school, and so on, but it is still culturally poverty-stricken. There are far too many 'men of respect', by which I mean the 'respect'

characteristic of the kind of society that created the old-time Mafia –
not a justified respect but a subservience unable to question the way
things are or are done, trussed by the fear of revenge or ostracism. It
can be seen in the way these men get out of their cars, or talk, or are
greeted – the shiny patina of power, with a reek offensive to Attic
nostrils. It seemed much worse here than in Catanzaro or Cosenza.

Potenza might have been rather like Perugia, since it is similarly
perched on a table-top hill of acropolis shape, and is a wearisome
drive to reach. Using one approach one passes massive brickwork
underpropping also reminiscent of one end of Perugia, and similarly
there is a main square with *cafés de luxe*, then shopping streets,
some pedestrianized. Both traffic and parking are close to crisis in
Potenza, especially during the *serata*. There is much less of interest
to see: San Francesco survives mostly intact from the 13th century
(inside, a 16th-century tomb), and the smaller, bare San Michele is
just about Romanesque. There is an archaeological and other museum: Potenza (Potentia) was already a leading city of the region in
Roman times.

Acerenza, once a city of equal or more importance, the seat of a
metropolitan bishop since Byzantine rule, is still a sizeable town but
now extraordinarily isolated. No main road leads to it: one is lost in a
country of scrubby hills and valleys until eventually its daunting
acropolis appears, approached by a steep, straight ramp. Up on top,
there is little life, but habitation continues at least. You should find a
bar open; I had a decent cup of coffee even though the people were
pinched and grim and there was little on the shelves except bubble-
gum. From the apse of the cathedral there are superb views over a
lofty drop. The cathedral was rebuilt in the last quarter of the 13th
century, on a plan precisely like that of the unfinished abbey of
VENOSA, not many miles (as the crow flies) to the north; however,
unlike Venosa, it has a crypt, refurbished in the mid 16th century.
The use of Venosa's French plan, some 200 years out of date by the
late 13th century, illustrates the new isolation of what were becoming Naples's provinces, an isolation that here has not yet been
broken. A few works of art create an itinerary round the cathedral's
vast, empty, stripped interior; the dome was arbitrarily rebuilt and
the Baroque stucco removed after the earthquake of 1930. There is
some 13th-century bestiary sculpture on the altered west façade.

Acerenza is situated on the further side of the Bradano, the most
northerly of the five main Ionian rivers of Basilicata, rising to the
west of Acerenza in the vicinity of LAGOPESOLE. To the east, as the

Appennines break up, lie MATERA and the Puglian MURGE; further down
the Bradano are comparable acropolis towns, Irsina, Miglionico and
Montescaglioso, which also overlook the VALLEY OF THE BASENTO. Irsina
was known until this century as Montepeloso; from its more illustrious past it preserves its castle, 14th-century frescos in the crypt of
San Francesco, and the contents of the Museo Ianora.

The valley of the Basento

The highest inhabited settlement in Basilicata is Pietrapertosa, soon
seen on the right as one travels the motorway down the Basento
valley from Potenza. Its name ('pierced rock') recalls the even more
remote, isolated and aerial castle of Peyreperteuse in the French
foothills of the Pyrenees. An appropriate inhabitant in the late 10th
century was 'Luke the *kafir* and apostate', that is to say a man at the
same time an infidel for the Arabs and an unbeliever for the
Christians. Such was his nature and that of his band of so called
Saracens (but one may doubt that they were all from overseas) that
the inhabitants of Tricarico on the other side of the river had been
for years afraid to set foot outside their walls – so much emerges
from a document of 1001, in which the Byzantine governor arbi-
trated the boundary between the territory of Tricarico and that of
Acerenza, by then lost to memory, so long had the ravages of the
bloodthirsty Luke continued. The document and its date nicely
illustrate the Byzantine 'reconquest', hardly secured before undone
by the Normans, who took Tricarico in 1048. Predecessors such as
Luke reveal how much more than a bandit was Robert Guiscard.
   As the valley begins to widen on its way to the sea, Ferrandina on
the right is one of the more prosperous small towns of Basilicata; it is
less grim than many, perhaps because the large nunnery of Santa
Chiara above the main square has had serene influence. In the square
the ample late-Gothic Chiesa Madre holds inside its western wall
wooden statues of queen Isabella and king Federico, the unpopular
Ferrante's second son, restored after the French invasions, who
founded and gave his father's name to the town in the last years of
the 15th century. So much an inscription on the town hall nearby
will also tell you. Off the road to Salandra a track leads up to the
ruined castle of Uggiano, the town's precursor.
   The road from the floor of the valley to the left, the SS 7 for MATERA,
first passes, after rising but before descending to cross the Bradano,

the exceptionally pretty castle and pleasant town of Miglionico. On a circular site, linked to the town only by a narrow saddle, Miglionico is gloriously four-square, swelling at the corners into round towers; it also has a couple of square towers between, one restored insensitively. Coming round and up to the entrance one finds its heart has gone, though the remaining covered parts are inhabited, except for an overgrown internal arcade which is crumbling. The castle seems to have no accepted date: its geometric plan suggests the castles of Frederick II, but fortification in this place is certainly older, and the fundamental design is possibly Byzantine, apparently resembling most closely the Arab models that have several times been cited as Frederick's precedents. One might compare Santa Severina in the MARCHESATO. Or does it date from after Frederick II, to the 14th or 15th century (like the decayed arcade), and to the time of the barons who here hatched, in 1481, one of their several attempts against the hated and equally unforgiving Ferrante (Ferdinand I) of Aragon? The Chiesa Madre in the town is a charming mixture of the ages wrapped up together in a bundle difficult to penetrate, and San Francesco has, almost like a bolt from heaven, a polyptych by Cima da Conegliano, dated 1499. It is said to have been brought by a local priest from a church near Bergamo at the end of the 16th century – when one can believe that changing fashions there had brought its value low, but would not have affected its appreciation here. It is an open, clear, classic Cima, with a perfect waxen Madonna on a marble throne against a blue sky.

On the other side of the Bradano from Miglionico, Montescaglioso is not immensely high but seems it, if one looks out from around the venerable abbey of Sant'Angelo at the furthest peak of the town; the drop is almost as sheer as at Erice in Sicily. Unfortunately the abbey church and double cloisters are rather disappointing work belonging surely to the late 16th or 17th century; though the abbey was founded before 1079, there are no more than traces of older building, for instance in the portico or narthex before the spoilt church. Before that there had once been a temple: a *telamon* or male caryatid was found that is now in the REGGIO museum. The town, one long straight street leading up to the abbey, is tedious, belying its long history. The yellow notices on its buildings date them all too early. To the east lie MATERA and the MURGE. Past Pisticci, that, too, an historic centre, and past Bernalda, and one has arrived at the coast.

Matera

Matera is the most outlandish and extensive of the cave cities of the MURGE of Puglia, though its *gravina* runs out into the Bradano and it has been part of Basilicata, rather than Puglia, since 1663. The gorge it colonizes is especially spectacular, and its large *città rupestre* (rock city) was densely inhabited into this century, when most similar cities in Puglia had been long deserted. It was only after the Second World War that the population of the Sassi, as the troglodyte district is called, was systematically rehoused, and now that the Sassi have been rendered sanitary some people are even living there again. It is anyway sometimes hard in Matera to distinguish between purely troglodyte caves, half troglodyte houses and houses wholly above ground. The town is amphibious, with a cathedral of the 13th century upstanding amongst its cave churches, and Baroque *palazzi* and churches adjoining the Sassi on the brink of the gorge.

Cave-dwelling is not civilized – if proof were needed, it is an archeological fact that before the arrival of the Greeks and Romans Bronze-Age troglodytism was widespread in Puglia, during the Roman Empire it was much rarer, and after the Empire's destruction it once again became widespread. In anarchic conditions of Lombard, Saracen and Norman rapine the peasants moved out of sight, away from the roads, away even from the hill-tops, in order to lead a furtive existence; in the same Dark Age the Venetians' ancestors occupied their equally unapproachable lagoon. In the lagoon, however, the tide flushed away the refuse twice daily, while the stink of centuries of human dirt compounds the perennial airlessness of the caves. Even uninhabited and bare cave houses and churches hardly encourage a prolonged visit, though they do not have the still worse, fetid chill of catacombs. Perhaps they might be of greater interest if they were to provide insight into the immediate precursors of Puglia's Romanesque architecture, but the churches seem to reflect, more or less distortedly, only two standard types, the oblong nave-and-apse and the Greek cross-in-square church. The frescos with which they are adorned are of poor quality, repetitive and comparatively late in date – few, for all that they appear Byzantine, are earlier than the 12th or 13th century. To follow the ignorant, poor, timid and superstitious down these holes is unique and a curiosity, to be sure, but can be a pleasure only for archaeologists inured to skeletons and latrines.

One can rapidly descend to the Sassi from any point on the via

Lucana, the ring-road lining the old town and giving little hint of the different world beside it. It is easy enough to pick up the '*strada panoramica dei Sassi*' or as it were the main artery that winds through the endless capillaries of the two main ventricles of the Sassi, the Sasso Caveoso and the Sasso Barisano. The course of this main way through the labyrinth is guided by the prominent Baroque church of San Pietro Caveoso. Frequently there are vertiginous views over the *gravina* and over tracts of the human warren. One can spend a long time there. If that is not enough, there are apparently more than 120 rock churches in the national 'park' round Matera. There is further information about them in the tourist office by piazza Vittorio Veneto, which will also provide a guide to the Sassi. The town no longer has to hide the Oxfam conditions that Carlo Levi described from hardly more than fifty years ago – swollen-bellied, red-eyed, malarial, skeletal children too weak even to brush away flies.

Above the Sassi, the via XX Settembre and its continuation the via Ridola give access to the other sights of Matera – the Museo Ridola for neolithic things or rather bits of things; a 15th-century castle (the other side of the via Lucana); several Baroque churches; two other churches, San Domenico and San Giovanni Battista that are predominantly Baroque but have Romanesque parts; and the cathedral. The cathedral was completed in 1270 but had been under construction for perhaps 50 years, since its main side portal is close to that of San Giovanni Battista just mentioned, which was being built in 1233; and both portals directly recall the portal of Santi Nicolò e Cataldo in LECCE, dated 1180 – in the serried spread leaves of the archivolt and the row of heads along the lintel. It is a type quite widely diffused in the region. One can discern in the other sculpture, of the capitals and of the façade – notably the four utterly ungymnastic figures that support the rose-window – 13th-century (and older) models, but the reflection is dim. Inside, there is little light with which to view the dusty, gloomy furniture of the nave and choir.

The coast of the Gulf of Taranto

Between the mouths of the Bradano and the Basento, just by the modern border between Puglia and Basilicata, the ruins of Greek Metapontion are some of the best kept and most rewarding of Italy's boot, though not spectacular compared with those of Campania. The main archaeological site, just seaward of the junction of the SS 175 descending from Matera with the SS 106 from Taranto, features chiefly a theatre and four Greek temples, of which the best preserved, temples A and B, have no more than their foundations (stylobates) intact. They belong to the early and mid 6th century BC, while the more vestigial temples C and D flanking them are of the 5th century BC, except that D encased an older structure. One vector of the theatre has been restored upstanding, from which there is an excellent view of the site and, beside the viewpoint, an explanatory map. It is easy to envisage the city. As the map indicates, the *agora* or main square lay to the west, and there is another temple, the so called Tavole Palatine, to be seen on a separate site to the north, just off the road to Taranto by the Bradano: this, dating from the end of the 6th century BC and with votive offerings to Hera, has five and ten columns re-erected, of a peristyle originally 6×12, in a splendid archaic Doric like Paestum's. The Antiquarium by it has aerial photographs and maps as well as cases containing finds – the best of which are in Reggio.

Metapontion (Roman Metapontum) seems to have been founded in the early 8th century BC by the Achaeans of Croton (modern CROTONE) and Sybaris (see below) as a bulwark against Spartan Taras (TARANTO). It became wealthy from a rich hinterland – its coins show an ear of corn – though it never quite rivalled Sybaris or Taras. When Pythagoras found it advisable to move from Croton, he settled in Metapontion, and Cicero was shown his house. As an Achaean city Metapontion sided with Athens against Taras and Syracuse in the Peloponnesian War, but after the foundation by Taras of Heraclea on the nearby coast in 433 BC (see below) its independence was compromised. Later it supported Hannibal, who in 207 BC, after his defeat at Grumentum in LATINIANUM, had made his way to Metapontum; subsequently, after the defeat of his brother Hasdrubal and his second army in the north, he retreated still further into Bruttium (Calabria), taking with him the Metapontines and all those remaining loyal to him in Lucania, largely for their own protection against the ensuing Roman inquisition. Little is heard of Metapontum thereafter.

The ruins of Heraclea, not far to the south between the mouths of the Agri and the Sinni, are less interesting, though there is again an antiquarium (Museo Nazionale della Siritide), with maps, diagrams and aerial photographs as well as exhibits. Previous to Heraclea there had been nearby a city founded by Ionian Greek refugees from the Lydian conquest of Asia Minor called Siris (also the ancient name of the river Sinni), which was destroyed about 530 by the Achaean cities of Metapontion, Sybaris and Croton in concert; then in 433 Taras and Thurii (the latter a successor to Sybaris destroyed in the interim by Croton) founded Heraclea, at least partly in order to contain Metapontion.

Occasional *lidos* (di Metaponto, di Scanzani, di Policoro) punctuate the coast: there are sands and swimming. All are served by the SS 106, running from Taranto to Reggio, which is one of those purgatorial Italian two-lane main roads that become the main street of each successive settlement and carry an endless stream of lorries — though some road improvement is being undertaken at various places. There is no alternative to it until the plain of Sibari, whence there is a connection up to Castrovillari and the Autostrada del Sole. Between the Sinni and the Sibari plain the mountains descend directly to the sea, and only single torrents stream shortly between them. These are the mountains of the Mercurio, the highest of the south, reaching 5000 ft, and pretty inhospitable; it was famous hermit country under later Byzantine rule. Their watershed is the border between Basilicata and Calabria, and here, too, the peninsular toe leaves the mainland instep.

Off the SS 106, a few roads lead up the valleys to small settlements: one of these is Rocca Imperiale, a photographically sharp castle above a sketched, blurred pattern of roofs. First built by Frederick II and rebuilt in the 15th century and perhaps again later, the castle is large with substantial parts remaining, though currently deserted and overgrown. The town beneath is built in its lower fortifications. I came, I wandered about, I saw virtually nobody, I left. Further south, dramatically set immediately beside the road, the sea-castle of Roseto is more of a machicolated residence than a castle, but much grander than a corsair tower, though corroded and at present being restored. The small town of Roseto shortly up the mountain retains its medieval walls. Just round the headland, Capo Spulico, another road inland leads to Amendolara, the birthplace of Pomponio Leto, a prominent humanist of the early Renaissance in Rome, so keen an antiquarian that he could be accused and imprisoned by pope Paul II for reviving pagan worship.

After Trebisacce the hills begin to recede and the wide plain of Sibari (Sybaris) opens, irrigated by two main rivers, the Crati and the Coscile, between which lay ancient Sybaris. In 510 BC that city came to a violent end after attacking but being defeated by its neighbour Croton (modern CROTONE), as Herodotus relates, but a second city, Thurii, was founded not long afterwards, on the initiative of Pericles of Athens; that in turn evolved eventually into a Roman *municipium* known as Copia Thurii. Most by far of the remains that have been unearthed belong to this last and least romantic city (the results of a series of excavations can be seen in a couple of archaeological offices or museums in modern Sibari and near the site beside the modern bridge over the Crati). There is, then, little to show for Greek 'Sybarite' Sybaris's alleged six miles of walls, 100,000 inhabitants, and proverbial 'luxury', exemplified by laws against noise nuisance, the use of chamberpots, trees planted to shade roads, and games with better prizes than the Olympics. Its chief memorial is the *staters* it coined from silver mined at San Marco Argentano. In perspective, the proverbial wealth of the Greek cities of the Gulf of Taranto should be seen in relation to the poverty of their origins: to land-hungry emigrants Magna Grecia was an America. For all its sybarism, Sybaris's destruction was no direct consequence of its wealth and ways: it arose rather out of a personal and factional quarrel, and the city was laid waste by a homophone sister-city, Croton, probably incited by vindictive exiles.

Hardly a lesser loss than the Archaic city is the natural beauty of its once fertile plain, ringed by forested mountains. Today the mountains are bare, and the plain, too, is dug over and bulldozed, even if it is once again extensively planted. The plain was still fertile in Roman times, as Varro attests. In the Middle Ages it became unsafe, and in modern times unhealthy, as malaria appeared – exacerbated, it would appear, by deforestation (deforestation increased the landslips, which increased the silt in the rivers, which increased their inclination to a meandering, shifting, shallow course, creating stagnant pools where the anopheles multiplied). Malaria was stopped by American DDT after the Second World War; even so it is only in the last thirty years that the plain has been reclaimed.

5

Calabria

Castrovillari

Having reached the top of the Val di Diano the *autostrada* climbs past Lagonegro and Mt Sirino to Lauria, a watershed between the Ionian and the Tyrrhenian slopes, into the deserted, mountainous Mercurio, the district of the river Mercure or (as it becomes) Lao, flowing down to Scalea on the Tyrrhenian. The motorway alternates between tunnels and long bridges, stretching, where it crosses the Lao just by Laino, into the longest, dizziest viaduct of its length, the 'Italia' (145m high, 1161m long). The name indicates a certain patriotic pride in the road's engineering achievement: Mussolini was not quite all bad and his heritage is not all lost. At Mormanno the road regains a valley, the so-called Campo Tenese, crossing into Calabria. Instead of following the older routes that cross the watershed at Morano Calabro, the motorway veers eastwards into remote mountains (passing beneath the 16th-century ruins of the isolated monastery of Colloreto), circling the basin in the valley of the Coscile occupied by Castrovillari.

On the Tyrrhenian side various panoramically situated hamlets and coastal resorts beckon, in particular Maratea, Scalea, Praia a Mare, Diamante. On the hillsides roads or mere tracks lead sometimes to dead-end villages or sanctuaries, entrancingly remote – Tortora, Orsomarso, and others – but except up the valleys of the Noce and the Lao the mountains are largely impenetrable. Formerly the area was largely Greek in population, and at Rivello, where the Greek rite was not suppressed until the 17th century, there are some architectural signs of a Byzantine culture. It was hermit country, and off a track on the way up to Orsomarso beside the river Lao an isolated pre-Norman Byzantine church, Santa Maria di Mercuri, still has the built-in benches on which the monks of the vanished community sat. In many places there are the ruins or the later conversions of castles, in or above their adjoining settlement. A fine ruin is that of Cirella Vecchia, above modern seaside Cirella: its centrepiece is a large Roman round tomb later incorporated into a medieval fort and a little town, abandoned at the end of the 18th century. From Belvedere, the next resort to the south, a long, tortuous but panoramic road leads up past Lungro, one of several Albanian settlements in Calabria dating from the late 15th century, and past Altomonte (see below) at last to Castrovillari.

Castrovillari is a genial and pullulating main street, via Roma, ending in a tree-lined avenue, corso Garibaldi, which leads to the castle and beyond it Santa Maria del Castello. In the *serata* it seems almost to be a seaside resort town, full of families in cars, litter on the pavements, a benign sun flitting through the plane trees in corso Garibaldi, much talk and endless greetings. But it is not by the sea and has no beach, nor anything else: it is a bubble, a grossly inflated village. I tried to buy a map: the old woman produced what she had, which was not what I wanted, from beneath other things I would not conceivably have wanted, either – but the reps circulate and sell, circulate and sell, always some new gadget or product (the inge- nuity and variety of down-market Italy have to be seen to be believed), which the shops store, piling one on top another in dusty glass cases or in heaps, but never seem to sell, because nobody buys any more than the little and limited they always buy, and so Calabria waits, as it has waited so long for commerce to happen, by osmosis, by contagion, by magic, by sympathy . . .

Cross the bridge at one end of corso Garibaldi, beside the castle, and the crowds and traffic vanish, shops and population melt away like a mirage, and here again is remote, backward, depressed Cal- abria, old Calabria, a few still streets in a torrid and ravined coun- tryside. The stern, square, round-towered castle is of the late 15th century; it is still used as a prison, as so many came to be used in Bourbon and still later times, for the incarceration in atrocious conditions of bandits. One road (via S. Maria del Castello) passes on through the old town, and after a mile or so reaches Santa Maria del Castello, an abbey founded in 1090: there are a few traces of Norman work at the west end, otherwise the church is 14th-century, redone in the 18th century. It has two highly Mannerist paintings by Pietro Negroni, signed and dated 1552 and 1560; one is a *sacra conver- sazione* and the other an *Assumption*, both excited in composition and preternatural in colouring; the link to central Italy was through Polidoro da Caravaggio working in Messina. Michelangelo da Cara- vaggio did *not* paint the dark and damaged *Pietà* in the church, despite what the highly present sacristan may say. The sanctuary is a popular focus of the ritual family expedition and is seldom empty.

In the less austere mountains around Castrovillari, smaller towns to visit include Altomonte, past Firmo off the road to Lungro: it was the fief of Filippo Sangineto (died 1352), who rebuilt the church (Santa Maria della Consolazione) and made the necessary arrangements for his tomb in the latest Neapolitan style. He would also have commissioned from Simone Martini the work from which there remains now a single fragment, a small standing figure of St Ladislas of Hungary. The figure has shimmering, shot, smouldering colours (the Italians call them 'quenched', *smorzato*) and a glowering regal frown; its quality is undoubtedly Simone's. The connection to Sangineto is demonstrated by the re-appearance of St Ladislas (and his attribute of an axe) among the saints of his tomb. As for the choice of saint, Sangineto served king Robert, whose cousin Carobert sat on the throne of Hungary. Perhaps the *Ladislas* was part of a portable diptych for the baron's use that he left to the church on his death; perhaps he commissioned it when he accompanied Charles duke of Calabria (who would predecease his father, king Robert) to Siena in 1327; but these are mere guesses. I would have said it belonged to a full altarpiece; I was told by the curator there were once two more such panels, but they were stolen. The museum beside the church seems to have been built solely in order to house the Simone, as it were the last Sibylline book; however, it also holds a Pietro Negroni and a variety of other paintings and treasures. Inside the church, Filippo Sangineto's anonymous tomb is splendid, newly restored in its original paint.

When first I went to Altomonte I succeeded in reaching it without a car, even though there was only one bus to it a day, which departed later than the one bus from it. I managed to leave only with the aid of the museum's curator who, after closing up, forced the parish priest to drive me to the Spezzano exit from the *autostrada*, and there to flag down a passing car. The whistling saloon screeched to an impressive halt as the priest's black-robed figure leapt out, and its banker driver delivered me with great solicitude to my further destination. He was on his way to Taranto: he hated Calabria, as so many Pugliese do, heaving a histrionic sigh of relief as we crossed the border. In the summer he did the journey by motorcycle.

Another excursion from Castrovillari is Cassano allo Ionio, settled probably by the ancient Greeks and a bishopric in the Middle Ages, when the Sibari plain became too exposed to attack. Its cathedral is now 18th-century and before that had been 15th-century, while its crypt, with frescos, is older still. Up above the town there are suggestive ruins, of the 12th-century castle and, towards Castro-villari past the Grotta di Sant'Angelo, more ruins presumed monas-tic; a more modern sanctuary, Santa Maria della Catena, is off the road to the town from the SS 105, with Baroque paintings by Nicolò Malinconico (also active at Gallipoli, see SOUTH OF LECCE).

Rossano

Rossano, '*città grecissima*' (most Greek city), has a metropolitan dignity belying a millennium of decline since its heyday as a seat of Byzantine power (substituting for Reggio when it fell to the Saracens) in the 9th, 10th and 11th centuries. This is no little *paese* or village clinging to its mountain-top above a jungle of concrete: the old town has ample streets, several squares, broad steps with balustrades linking its terraces, and is large enough to get confused in briefly.

Rossano's hegemony has been attributed to the migration into Calabria from the Levant of Iconodule monks fleeing Iconoclast persecutions during the 8th century. They are supposed to have brought with them the cathedral's two great treasures, the Madonna Acheropita (*acheiropoietos*, 'made by no hand') enclosed in an altar in the centre of the nave, and the Codex purpureus Rossaniensis in the Museo Diocesano. The codex is undoubtedly of the 6th century and of eastern provenance, whether from Syria or from Palestine, and must have been made originally for a very highly placed patron: its parchment is all of imperial purple, and its lettering is in silver throughout, except for the first three lines in gold. It was a Greek Evangeliary with canon tables and with the letters of St Eusebius of Caesarea, but much of it has been lost, seemingly in a fire: only 188 pages with the Gospel of St Matthew and a little of Mark and half of one of Eusebius's letters remain. It has superb miniatures, with an iconography sometimes without parallel offering tantalizing glimpses of lost ceremonial – and because it is all alone in this isolated place one can go and visit it, as one would not think of visiting the comparable manuscripts in the Vatican library in Rome or St Mark's in Venice, except as a specialist. St Mark sits on a fine wicker chair, writing at the finger of a personified female inspiration; Christ and the apostles recline to eat the Last Supper, Pontius Pilate delivers judgement between upheld painted imperial busts. The custodian of the Museo Diocesano is not too hard to find; the Codex is kept in a glass-plated safe so that only the one opening can be seen, but it is enough to make experiential contact with the sensible presence of the object's *Dasein* (otherwise known as 'doing' it), and there is a facsimile to hand for the others. There is no record of the Codex until the 19th century, but it may have been among the Greek picture-books which archbishop Adeodato was alleged to have buried beneath the sacristy floor in 1705, long after the Greek rite was meant to have been suppressed. Adeodato also refurbished the nave and aisles of the cathedral, though the east end remains as rebuilt with a donation from king Robert in 1330. Any quondam Byzantine cathedral is entirely lost; probably there was a Norman predecessor of the present basilica.

The Madonna Acheropita is a detached fresco, therefore not an import, but its style is said to place it in the 8th century. It is in the form of the Madonna Hodegetria, 'leading the way', except that the name derives from the archetype once in the monastery of Hodegoi in Constantinople rather than from any gesture of the Child or the Madonna. Its miraculous apparition (it appeared during the night in the chapel of a hermit called Ephrem) is mentioned in a sermon as early as 1140; in 1193 king Tancred made a donation so that a lamp should be kept burning perpetually before it. Now immersed in a pile of curvacious coloured marble, it is more for veneration than for inspection. Other frescos may be seen better in the Greek churches of San Marco and the Panaghia: in the Panaghia, a nave church built in the 10th or earlier 11th century, there is a contemporary, but retouched, fresco of St John Chrysostom, with another, very fragmentary, of St Basil, and in San Marco another Hodegetria, probably not as early. Architecturally the Panaghia is somewhat restored, but has tracts of original decorative brickwork. San Marco is of greater interest, a well preserved perhaps 10th-century five-domed cross-in-square brick church terminating in three apses, with an additional, later but harmonizing western part. A little larger than San Pietro at OTRANTO or the Cattolica at STILO, like the latter it was a monastic church, since the slope over which it presides has been found to have been full of hermits' caves. Both churches are usually shut, and one must enquire for the custodian: the message will be passed by the house-bound goodwives along the balconics in the very pronounced local dialect, in which 'rr' becomes 'rz' (*arziva* for *arriva*, arrive).

The native city of St Nilus (see THE SILA), Rossano and its vicinity nurtured a large number of anchorites and hermit communities, of which the greatest became the Patirion, or Santa Maria del Patire. Nowadays it is reached by a new extension (signposted) off a long climbing road lined with villas enjoying views over the city and gulf, but until this century it was reached only by difficult paths. It was founded by a second local St Bartholomew (of Simeri, not the disciple of St Nilus) about 1090 or 1095; in 1105 pope Paschal II confirmed its large privileges, and the church remains virtually unaltered, except that probably the nave originally terminated in a dome before the apse, although now the wooden roof continues the length of the church. It has, however, lost its fine furnishings and its books: St Bartholomew had visited Constantinople and had there received gifts for his monastery from the emperor and empress, and at home he had the support of the commander of the Norman fleet. The monastery had declined pitifully before its suppression at the beginning of the 19th century, and the cloisters beside it, of a late date (16th or 17th century), are ruined. It still enjoys a wonderful view over the Sibari plain.

The three apses of the east end of the church are richly decorated with a variety of different-coloured brick or tile and stone blind arches, in the heads of which are set coloured roundels – a hybrid, 'Greco-Norman' style merging Byzantine, local and Latin traditions, and anticipating the more celebrated and still more ornate late 12th-century east ends of Monreale and Palermo cathedrals. The elements of the Greco-Norman fusion are not easy to trace, but, for example, the roundels set in the heads of the arches distantly recall the lozenges and circlets set under the blind arches of SIPONTO and other churches like it – and later Pisa cathedral. The alternation of coloured materials recalls the brickwork patterns of Middle Byzantine churches. On the north door there is something very like Anglo-Norman chevron! Not so surprising: it is found again at Santa Maria d'Anglona and BITONTO, to name only two.

Inside, the nave arcade has no capitals – a plainness characteristic of Greco-Norman building in Calabria (compare GERACE) but established before the Normans (compare Santa Severina in THE MARCHESATO OF CROTONE or Santa Maria on the TREMITI ISLANDS). It aptly reflects the ascetic spirit of St Nilus's tradition. On the floor of the nave, by contrast, there are substantial remains of a mosaic floor, signed in mid-nave 'Venerable abbot Blaise ordered all this done'. The mosaic consists of roundels containing beasts – lions, a unicorn, a centaur, a griffin, a deer – adorable in the way of soft toys but correspondingly weak in draughtsmanship; the only modelling is highly stylized. Abbot Blaise existed in 1152, so these belong to a 'movement' of floor mosaic-setting 'sweeping' southern Italy in the third quarter of the 12th century – in style they recall those of TARANTO more closely than Pantaleone's OTRANTO workshop.

The Sila

The Sila is virtually a forgotten part of Calabria, which one tends to picture as a land of mountains, but is in fact a plateau of lakes, forests and farmland, which more closely resembles an alpine valley. Its area is bounded roughly by the towns of Rossano, Cosenza, Catanzaro and Crotone; to the east of Cosenza it is the Sila Grande, to the north of Catanzaro it is the Sila Piccola, and south of Rossano it is the Sila Greca. Parts of it are national parks, but these, oddly enough, are less pleasant than the undesignated country: they are both more monotonous, consisting mostly of pine forests (the Sila was de-forested without control in the 19th century; softwoods predomi-nated in the replanting, though hardwoods are included), and more populous with walkers and ramblers and others who come in groups and coaches to stay in condominium cabins like those in ski resorts. At Palumbo by lake Ampollino, unbeknownst to the rest of the world, there is a 'tourist village' of incredible proportions – it is more like a suburb, of perhaps 3000 houses – which is primarily a winter resort, boasting 12 miles of *piste* and a bobsleigh run, but is also frequented in the heat of the summer.

Driving through the Sila requires unchangingly low gear, both to go up and to come down. There is little traffic: lizards scurry away from the car; cows cross hazardously; the occasional snake will bask on the tarmac; a ponderous lorry carries timber. Pine-cones pop and crunch beneath the tyres as one circulates the lakes or winds through the forest; then the trees give way to cultivated land, ploughed reddish-brown or green with prairie grass or golden with corn. There are tractors, but also some fields are still hand-sown as it were from a Millet painting. However, it is never completely primi-tive, or wild or spectacular: the lakes are rather shallow and shrink from their edges unprepossessingly; the mountains are not high; settlement is never far. It is, after all, the playground of Cosenza and Catanzaro.

In the Sila there once dwelled – developing the land – many monks and hermits, among them St Nilus in the 10th century and Joachim of Fiore in the 13th. St Nilus, born of good family in Rossano, dying very old in 1004, was a figure of enormous prestige in his time, although, a typical ascetic, he refused responsible office and clung to his private spiritual exercise. However, he was always surrounded by followers, and insisted not only on singing but on working the land and on copying manuscripts as essential parts of the monkly discipline. Furthermore he intervened at Rossano with the Byzantine powers, and at Rome with the Holy Roman emperor on behalf of his friend and Rossanese compatriot anti-pope John XVI, ousted by the existing pope Gregory V and mutilated and imprisoned; though his appeal went unheard he probably helped to germinate at Rome the movement for reform that eventually made way with the papacy of Gregory VII. In the last year of his life he settled at Grottaferrata not far from Rome, in a monastery co-founded with his disciple St Bartholomew, also of Rossano; Bartholomew was on close terms with pope Benedict IX, and Benedict was closely connected with Hildebrandt, the future Gregory VII.

Earlier St Nilus had dwelt many years, from about 955 to 980, at Sant'Adriano in the remote mountains of present San Demetrio Corone (due east of Rossano), a town founded 500 years later as an Albanian colony: however, the church on the site dates from after the sanctuary's destruction by Saracens about 1000, to the late 11th or early 12th century. It has lost its east end and its western portico; only the nave survives, with frescos in the spandrels and round the arches representing saints, and various pieces of stonework, such as the carved fountain-head of the former monastery cloister, and four disparate pieces in mosaic (or rather the cruder *opus sectile*) of serpents or animals. The frescos have something of the more painterly quality of Byzantine art of the 13th century; the mosaics are earlier, and still more remote from naturalism than those of the Patirion above ROSSANO.

Joachim of Fiore (Gioacchino da Fiore) was born near Spezzano della Sila in Celico, a village with a pretty 15th-century church on an outcrop, now a mere episode on the *superstrada* SS 107 to Cosenza. Having professed as a Cistercian, he settled later in what was then nowhere and now is San Giovanni in Fiore, the largest town, such as it is, of the Sila. The 'Florensian' order he founded took over several earlier Greek monasteries in the tradition of St Nilus. His mystic writings, prophesying a third age due to arrive about 1260, were widely influential, especially on the more extreme Franciscans, since he supposed an age of contemplatives or spirituals succeeding on the ruder present age of mere clergy, which had succeeded the age of laity at the time of Christ. However, true to his Cistercian training, he kept his followers working the land, and, like St Francis, though his ideas verged on heresy he took care to keep within the Church.

The transition from medieval to modern can hardly be counted as progress in the Sila. When the monasteries died it became one of the most extreme examples of South Italian 'baronialism' or *latifondismo*, an economy of great estates both efficiently geared economically and rigidly backward culturally, under the absolute control of extremely few landowners – as few as five and always less than ten – over about 1,000 square miles. Though often called 'feudal', these estates emerged from the decay of the Bourbon state in the 18th and 19th century and were owned rather by descendants of the nobles' factors than by genealogical aristocrats; this was a more vicious system than feudalism, which is contractual. Instead, it was a regime of force, employing about ten per cent of the population to herd, control and exploit the migrant underclass of ninety per cent, whose tasks were deliberately restricted to the ignorantly physical – herding and harvesting. The only escape was banditry: the forests became the lair of bandits famed for their insensible brutality, matched only by the brutality of the attempts to flush them out (involving reprisal massacres many times worse, for instance, than the Gestapo's against the French Resistance).

'Were I sultan of San Giovanni, I would certainly begin by a general bombardment', wrote Norman Douglas in 1915. In a way that is exactly what has happened to 'old Calabria': the past was so irremediably degraded that the only hope has been to build absolutely new, literally and metaphorically. Literally, much has been achieved: the power of the 'barons' was at last broken, violently, after the fall of Mussolini's regime in 1943, and the signs of economic improvement over the last 50 years are unpicturesquely clear. Socially or spiritually – well, the likes of the tourist village of Palumbo will undoubtedly provide the infrastructure of a new civilization.

Cosenza

Though not the administrative capital, Cosenza is the largest and most important city of Calabria, and the only one that might be mistaken for a city anywhere else. It has expanded like a snake sloughing its skin northwards along the valley; the old town, with its castle, cathedral, grand theatre and prefecture wound around a steep hill, is a lifeless appendix, and even the older new town, just across the river Busento at the foot of the hill, is dying into decay and slum, while frenzy convulses the post-war streets around the anonymous piazza Fera. Cosenza station, which had first been set close beneath the old town, has been newly built further down the valley, in a smart new steel and glass construction around a circular taxi arena.

However, the roar of modern Cosenza subsides after the *serata*, and finding anything open becomes a difficult business. Alas, once found, the more interesting looking restaurant becomes one more variation on the standard pizza-house, serving indifferent food and indifferent wine (the local white Cirò – from the coast on the east side of the Sila – is rather too sweet) to very unsophisticated people. There is a university at Cosenza, founded after the Second World War, with a modernist campus out at Arcavacata, but in the town one would hardly know it; there are some of the better known high-fashion chain shops, but they do not appear to advantage; it is a mediocre place, even compared to BARI. In fact it is abnormally normal: almost uniquely in Calabria, Cosenza and its territory entered the 20th century as a society composed predominantly of small holders and artisans, more in the North Italian pattern, and in sharp contrast to THE SILA.

In the high Middle Ages Cosenza was, too, a Lombard and Latin outpost in Byzantine and Greek Calabria, defended from the sea by some distance to the west and high mountains to the east. On the summit of the hill the large castle was one of Frederick II's, later modified inside; from the outside, it has some fine passages of imposing masonry. It is now isolated by old stone walls and undergrowth and abandoned olive trees from the town beneath it. Entry requires application to the Soprintendenza per i Beni Artistici or, on the way up, to the Prefettura in piazza XV Marco, by the gardens of the *villa comunale*, opposite the theatre (Teatro Rendano) opened at the late date of 1909. Schools and other institutions also occupy this same area below the castle and above the cathedral, slightly eerie with its pre-First World War buildings and vacant streets, remote from the town's real life in the valley. One may apply again to the Soprintendenza to see, in custody in the former conventual buildings beside the church of San Francesco, a small 'national' collection of Calabrian paintings kept for the moment at the restoration laboratory, until a museum for them is opened. They include notably some *Labours of Hercules* by Mattia Preti.

Beneath piazza XV Marzo a once elegant curved street leads down to the cathedral. Almost all its shops are closed – even the cobbler who had hung on during the 1980s has gone now – and the Café Renzelli at the top, though still going at the time of writing, may not last long – a pity, since it is an old-fashioned *grand café de luxe* with panels and engraved glass. Its cake and ice cream were still quite good, but had waited too long for their customer. Up here it is unselfconsciously, indeed neglectedly, pre-war, but almost uninhabited and so bound to fall into decay. Down in the valley Cosenza is too busy boosting and busting with the 20th century to notice its loss.

The cathedral is still a fine building, though it suffered a face-lift in the 18th century; in the late 19th century and again in 1950 it was restored as far as possible to its original Gothic condition. That dates from between 1184, when the old church was damaged by earthquake, and 1222, when the new church was consecrated in the presence of Frederick II. The treasury of the bishop's palace still holds a reliquary given to the church by Frederick on that day, a golden crucifix with enamel roundels, made in Palermo. In the church, the body in an antique sarcophagus in the transept representing *Meleager hunting the boar* is supposed to have been emperor Frederick's eldest son Henry, elected king of the Romans (that is, his heir presumptive and deputy in Germany) in 1220, reprimanded by his father for his contrary policy in 1232, and in 1235 stripped of his power, publicly humiliated, imprisoned and ignored. In 1242 his father sent for him again, it is not known why, but while being taken to the court from his prison in Martirano (to the south, in the hills above Nocera; the ruins of the castle remain) he plunged, it was reported, to a deliberate death. Announcing the news, Frederick recalled the story of Absalom (II Samuel) – 'O my son Absalom, O Absalom, my son, my son', for whom his father David wept after defeating him in battle, when he had attempted to usurp the kingdom of Israel. Opposite, a more beautiful tomb commemorates another tragedy, the death by drowning in 1271 of the wife of king Philip III of France, Isabella of Aragon, returning from the

Crusade on which her husband's father, St Louis IX, had died; five years earlier her husband's uncle Charles had won the kingdom, defeating Frederick's son Manfred. The tomb's author was evidently French: king and queen are shown kneeling on either side of a standing Madonna in a restrained, economic Gothic style permeated with classicism – the Madonna has a gentle but firm *contrapposto* – slightly frigid but recalling the eloquent but serene statuary for Louis IX's Sainte Chapelle in Paris (now Musée Cluny).

Cosenza is set by the confluence of the Busento with the Crati, which, after circulating the Sila, finally exits in the plain of Sibari. A very high, sheer ridge separates Cosenza and its fertile valley from the nearer sea; even though it is not a bad road, it is an enormous toil up to Cosenza from Paola on the Tyrrhenian coast. Paola is the city of St Francis of Paola (1416–1507), an utterly Franciscan Franciscan who founded his own order of even more humble, even more poor, even more charitable, even more minor friars, the Minim friars. His widespread fame was further spread when he was summoned from his hermitage, as such holy men were, by the depressed and declining Louis XI of France. Apparently pilgrims still crowd the town on his feast-day, 4 May, and the convent above the town where he lived with his immediate followers has ample parking for buses. The church has 15th-century parts and bits of frescos, but has been transformed over the ages and is being transformed by living religion, which is not a pretty sight.

The Marchesato of Crotone

Emerging from the Sila to the south-east, past Cotronei or Petilia Policastro, on the way to Santa Severina, one may come to Roccabernarda, one of the most dismal habitations in modern Calabria. The higher hills and forests have given way to bare, eroded, sandy red rock; and though Roccabernarda dates back perhaps to the 12th century and has an old main square on a hill-top, it is all concrete constructions. Dust is everywhere. Along the roads little black widows populate the bare buildings; in the square at the top little old men sit on steps in a huddle – there is not even a café or a table for dominoes. For all the fairy-lights left on the trellises, there is nothing here except poverty. There is perhaps no longer malaria, and no longer economic imprisonment, but Roccabernarda remains a monument to old Calabria's misery.

Only a few miles along, Santa Severina is set in fairer countryside, and for its more lovely monuments, its castle, its cathedrals (old and new), its high medieval baptistery and its Middle Byzantine churches, it receives many visitors, who will find a bar normally equipped. The town seems to have been eponymous to the saint rather than the other way round: an older Siberene is mentioned and of any Severina there seems to be neither cult nor legend. Already sanctified, Santa Severina enters the records in the 9th century as a particularly obdurate Saracen fortress, finally flushed out by Nicephoros Phocas in 886. Its baptistery presumably dates from shortly afterwards; in the new dispensation it was raised to a bishopric of metropolitan status, the equal of Reggio, with jurisdiction extending even across the Gulf to Gallipoli. It again proved obdurate to the Norman conquest as a Byzantine strongpoint: Robert Guiscard could not take it until 1073, though his incursions into Calabria had begun in the 1050s and Bari itself had fallen in 1071. Its castle, perhaps, is the best preserved Byzantine fortress in Calabria – which is not to say that it has not been entirely rebuilt in its upper and internal parts, but that its plan remains, four-square with rounded angle turrets. There is no record or reason why it should have been laid out in the 13th century; it is not Norman; but it must have been to prototypes like this – rather than to similar Islamic examples cited – that Frederick II reverted when building his strictly geometric Sicilian defensive castles such as Catania. No wonder it resisted siege: it is very tall and sheer on its isolated rock, divided from the castle by a very deep ravine crossed on a very high bridge.

The baptistery is beside the west façade of the cathedral, from which it is now entered, though it has two external doors in arms that project from its central circle. Of these there are two and a bit; there were once four. The circular perimeter gives way above to an octagonal drum, which eight interior columns sustain, and the drum gives way to a shallow dome. Surviving fragments provided the basis for the restoration of the windows, slabs pierced with circular holes; there are four in the drum and four in the lower round wall between the arms. There is no great expertise shown in any part, but the capitals and dome are genuinely 9th-century; the surfaces must always have been plastered and were presumably painted, though only a fragment of a later fresco survives. The font is 16th-century, and the building was not necessarily built as a baptistery – it was perhaps simply a round church, like the larger contemporary Lombard church of Santa Sofia in BENEVENTO. The cathedral beside it is a building of the second half of the 13th century (of the same date as the external doors added to the baptistery), rebuilt in the early 18th.

Round behind the new cathedral the Addolorata is 17th-century, but the east end is much older. It is supposed to have been the former cathedral, and an inscription dates its completion to 1036, in the time of bishop Ambrose. It is important dated evidence of an absolutely plain Byzantine style of architecture in existence before the Norman conquest: the square piers are set on larger square bases but lack both mouldings and capitals; the only decoration is the variation between stone and stacked brick (so thin they could be called tiles). It is a longitudinal church with aisles, one main and two subsidiary apses, and a clerestory: the only decoration of the windows is a broad surround once more alternating brick and stone.

Further, in the rear of the modernized Chiesetta dell'Ospedale there survives some Byzantine brickwork, and, by the bottom of the ravine between town and castle, above and beside the former district of the Grecia (deserted after an earthquake in 1783 and recently built over) the intact church of Santa Filomena. The church is remarkable for its cupola, rising oddly sheer from a round drum set at the eastern extremity of the single nave. Entrance is at the side, as is quite common in such churches; inside, outjutting walls create a chancel beneath the dome on squinches. The drum is decorated with colonnettes forming blind arches, and has a conical top; the colonnettes are clearly Byzantine by the foliage of their capitals and also because they have bases instead of expiring into a cornice as the sloppy Latins did it. The foliage of the colonnette capitals is echoed in the foliage over one of the two side doors, but here the Greek seems to have been following a Norman idea, running a repeating motif round the two arch-heads. There is also an underchurch, provided undoubtedly by way of foundation or base on the steep slope.

Crotone is useful for such services as getting a tyre repaired, but for little else; it is a dull place on a flat headland, though it has an old town, a cathedral, a castle (16th-century), a beach and a port. There is also an archaeological museum, but little reminiscence of Pythagoras or indeed of Milo. These were the two most famous denizens of the ancient Greek city of Croton, Milo a wrestler who won six times at Olympia and whose strength was so great that once while Pythagoras was teaching, and the building collapsed, he held up a column while the master and his disciples escaped. He is better known for attempting to tear up a tree by the roots but being caught instead in the cleft of the trunk and there being consumed, helpless, by a lion. Historically he seems to have led the Crotonians when they were unsuccessfully attacked by Sybaris in 510 BC and then in victory utterly destroyed the rival city on the GULF OF TARANTO. Pythagoras, though best known for his theories of geometry and of metempsychosis, is said also to have been a wrestler, but later he claimed he preferred to be a spectator of the games and of life: he left Croton for the safer city of Metapontion before Sybaris attacked, dying there a couple of years later. Though Pythagoras seems to have been known as a philosopher before he left his native Samos, it was in this region that Pythagoreanism became a 'school' and a way of life, and well into the 4th century BC continued to produce eminent philosophers and leaders, such as Archytas of Taras (see TARANTO), who was Plato's informant of Pythagorean beliefs.

There is something more of a memorial of ancient Greek Croton at Capo Colonna a little to the south, the easternmost spur of Calabria. Here there was a celebrated temple of Hera, with bronze roof-tiles and, inside, Zeuxis's ideal portrait of Helen, the famous composite for which he selected the best features of five different models. One column still stands of the original 48 (in two lateral files) of the late 6th- or early 5th-century BC Doric building. More impressive now are the great tawny blocks of the walls of the sanctuary.

To the north of Crotone, Cirò should be mentioned, a medieval town now known for its rather sweet white table wine; so should Strongoli, for its imposing, modernized castle and the nearby, levelled site of Roman Petelia. Strongoli was the birthplace, in the early 1690s, of Leonardo Vinci, a leading composer of the generation following Alessandro Scarlatti, and even more perhaps than Scarlatti the father figure of the 'Neapolitan school' which dominated European opera for much of the 18th century – best known of them now is Cimarosa. Vinci died young, in 1730, after producing some 35 operas in eleven years. He was buried at the expense of a wealthy patroness, since he was, in the words of a contemporary, 'a man who would have gambled his eyes away'.

South of Crotone, round the coast past Capo Rizzuto, the isolated castle of Le Castella is almost ridiculously picturesque, an intact 15th- and 16th-century castle posing for a brochure on a virtual island reached from a beach across a causeway. It was built primarily against Turks and pirates; its 16th-century rebuilding was occasioned by its sack in 1536 by the corsair Barbarossa. Beside the beach are fish restaurants – surprisingly uncommon on the Ionian coast.

On and off the Autostrada: Catanzaro, Reggio and between

Catanzaro has a spectacular site, set high on hills over ravines: it is a city of balconies, terraces and viaducts, as it were a cross between the visions of the film *Metropolis* and the backgrounds of those Early Renaissance paintings in which onlookers peep over parapets and hang out carpets. It is full of zest and congestion, bureaucrats in cars and juveniles on motorbikes, stunning views and aspects grossly spoilt, fair vineyard terraces and waste-tips – a range of paradoxes rather like Sicily. Manners, too, are Sicilian: much squeezing of the cheeks (in which there seems implicit a constrained aggression); male dominance even among the young – for example, I observed almost neurotic self-correction and apology by girls in reaction to their companions' criticism; also heavy staring; and the same Sicilian duality of values, endorsing whatever is 'inside', within some network or family, and rejecting or denying everything, even its equivalent, if it is 'outside' – an attitude inevitably recalling the Mafia, even when harmless.

The city was a Byzantine foundation, and the cultivation of silk from which it derived wealth and fame in the Middle Ages may have been introduced from Syria. Unfortunately there is little to show for its erstwhile prowess: Europe's last great plague in the 1660s finished off the silk industry, and a succession of earthquakes its older monuments. It is admirably positioned at the point where the toe is narrowest, and is the administrative capital of Calabria (except for some functions which remain with Reggio). It has several modern hotels and some restaurants (one local speciality for the hardy is *morzello*, tripe in a peppery sauce, eaten with bread). Altogether it is a unique city, lively both in its genial people and in its topography: on its high platform it is shaped like a monkey nut, waisted at modern piazza Matteotti; one nut is the old town, the other the new town. Though sliced through in the 19th century by the corso Mazzini the old town still has many *viuzze* or winding alleys; but also the new town, climbing and grappling over inhospitable rock, is far from a grid. Avoiding the pompous, formal central hotels I found a boldly designed and well equipped one in the new town, reached by a labyrinthine route past piled mansion blocks; its superb view over a ravine was blocked by a hideous, half completed building which had been abandoned by government order because it was about to fall down the slope. Until it might do so the young hoteliers ignored its obvious eyesore; the general attitude might well be called blithe, to the point of myopia.

North of Catanzaro on the borders of the Sila Piccola lies Taverna, the birthplace of the painter Mattia Preti (1613–99). Preti belonged to the third generation of the Baroque era, taking over the frescos in Naples cathedral that Giovanni Lanfranco, the pupil of the Carracci, had started; he achieved a coherent but eclectic style, rather like Guercino's, combining certain Caravaggesque traits with Carraccesque Raphaelism and a bit of Titianism as well. He passed most of his career in Naples but thence sent numerous paintings to adorn the several Baroque churches of his native town, in particular San Domenico and Santa Barbara. Having long been absent for restoration in Cosenza, they have all now been returned except the enormous main altarpiece of the church of Santa Barbara.

West of Catanzaro, on the Tyrrhenian coast, the conurbation of Lamezia Terme occupies the plain of Sant'Eufemia, formed by several rivers. The historic core of Lamezia Terme is Nicastro, but that has been more than once devastated not only by earthquakes but also by floods. The *autostrada* down from Cosenza passes by Lamezia Terme (and there is a *raccordo* or 'expressway' linking across to Catanzaro); the railway passes through Lamezia Terme; there is also an airport to serve both Catanzaro and Cosenza. Not so long ago it was a village. Lamezia Terme is the sort of town one might expect from that.

South of Catanzaro, on the Ionian coast, one rejoins the SS 106 on its way from Taranto, now rather less busy, to visit SQUILLACE, STILO, GERACE and the Aspromonte (see below); the *autostrada* serves the Tyrrhenian side. It is piquant to learn that Maida, above the Sant' Eufemia plain, gave its name to Maida Vale in London: there was a skirmish there during the Napoleonic Wars, in 1806, that the British won. At Pizzo on its rock over the sea, Joachim Murat, Napoleonic king of Naples, met his end after having joined Napoleon on the road to Waterloo: he was shot in its 15th-century Aragonese castle. At Vibo Valentia the *autostrada* turns inland; the coast sweeps out in a broad headland of which the principal place is Tropea.

This headland has many good beaches, while both the cliffs and the interior offer fine views – notably around Zungri. They say tourism here is in the hands of the Mafia. It is impossible to tell from appearances; but the standard is quite high, and this is a comparatively cosmopolitan resort area of Calabria. At Capo Vaticano there is an enormous lighthouse and at Briatico more ruins. Tropea itself has an old town of labyrinthine streets and a not wholly rebuilt cathedral housing objects of some fame – but rather dubious quality – a wooden 'black crucifix' and a repainted Madonna 'of Romania' (the medieval term for Greece, because Byzantine – that is to say, Roman). Modern restoration has retrieved some 12th-century Greco-Norman patterning on the north flank, to be compared with those of the Patirion at ROSSANO or San Giovanni Vecchio at STILO or Monreale or Palermo cathedral, not now so very far away. On the south underhang of the headland, in the town of Nicotera, overlooking the gulf and the plain of Gioia Tauro, a local architect, Ermenegildo Sintes, was responsible for the castle and the cathedral in the 1760s and 1780s.

The ancient city of Vibo Valentia (Greek Hipponion; Roman Vibonia; medieval Monteleone) has several quite grand Baroque churches, among them the Rosario preserving a 14th-century baronial chapel; a 16th-century Renaissance church (following Tuscan models), San Michele; and a large cathedral of venerable foundation but 19th-century appearance. The cathedral contains one of the quite numerous works in Calabria by the Sicilian sculptor Antonello Gagini, who had served in 1505–6 as an assistant to Michelangelo, but seems to have found more demand (he died owning six houses) in following the style of his father Domenico, former collaborator of the more famous Francesco Laurana – very sweet, highly painted, porcelain-like figures, though his Madonnas have sturdy chins not unlike those of Giovanni Bellini. Vibo Valentia also has an archaeological museum and, on the site of the former acropolis of Hipponion and incorporating masonry quarried from ancient Greek temples, an imposing castle. Though it has been reduced by earthquakes the castle has an octagonal tower said to have been built by Robert Guiscard in 1070; the rest is 13th-century, by Frederick II and by Charles II. Of the Greek temples, off the road leading to the *autostrada* in the vicinity of the cemetery there remains one columnless foundation (stylobate), but stupendously sited; there is also a stretch of ancient wall in the vicinity that is architecturally more dramatic. It is isodome (regularly cut and bonded ashlars), of the 5th or 4th century BC, with four discernible towers and a postern gate; it had evidently been needed, for numerous arrowheads were found round about and even embedded in it. Off the road to Pizzo the little church of San Ruba preserves its cupola and apse, amid later superfetation.

Between Vibo Valentia and Mileto there is an exit east past Soriano to the forested Serra San Bruno. Mileto was abandoned after its destruction by earthquake of 1783, and the new town is remarkable for the number of its houses of only one storey. Off the road from the *autostrada*, the ruins of the old town and its abbey of La Trinità are discernible high up. Mileto was founded by Robert Guiscard's brother count Roger in 1057, in the early days of their conquest of Calabria before they could hope to take the leading Byzantine towns; but from such a place as Mileto they in their turn could not be winkled. In about 1070, when their grip had so tightened that only a few garrisons remained to the Byzantines, Robert Guiscard founded and richly endowed an abbey at Mileto dedicated, like that at VENOSA beneath Melfi, to the Trinity. It, too, was an Hauteville mausoleum like Venosa, since in it was buried count Roger on his death in 1101; it might well have resembled Venosa, but the remains and records are few and what is recorded and does remain cannot be dated (though a consecration is recorded in 1166).

Many other towns suffered a fate like Mileto's in the earthquake of 1783 – Rosarno, Polistena, Gioia Tauro, Taurianova, Cittanova, Terranova Sappo Minulio, Oppido Mamertina. The plain of Gioia Tauro was anyway by that time malaria-ridden and its population had been shrinking since the Middle Ages. So the Gioia Tauro plain is all modern. Gioia Tauro itself is the largest and least prepossessing town, resembling a film set for a Western transmogrified from shacks of wood to blocks of concrete; it is best known as a Mafia centre, especially after the trials of the 1970s exposing Mafia control of the construction of a state-financed industrial port. After Unification the town had greatly prospered and expanded, as the plain was at last profitably developed by the cultivation of vines, olives and citrus fruits; nevertheless it failed to evolve according to the usual modern European bourgeois norms. Its society remained fundamentally unstable and divided against itself, riddled with suspicions, prejudices and insecurities that only the artificial order and 'instrumental friendship' of the Mafia could regulate. Or so it is analysed. The 1970s trials frighteningly revealed how the Mafia *cosche* or 'societies' had evolved from a limited, local, economic parasitism – essentially, controlling justice and labour – to large-scale entrepreneurial capitalism, monopolizing and directing local businesses. The links which were forged as a result with business and government in the rest of Italy and the world have served both to legitimate them and to expand their potential sphere of operation.

By contrast to the hatefulness of Gioia Tauro itself, the plain of Gioia Tauro, as it gradually rises inland towards Taurianova, is planted fragrantly and enchantingly with olive trees renowned for their size. And in the smaller towns, for instance at Taurianova or Polistena during the *serata*, there is animation, gaiety, enjoyment and no visible travail or dissension. But the *serata* is the only entertainment, in a society that by all reports remains jealous and hidebound and in which the rules of a crude 'honour' smother individualism. Sometimes the Americans are blamed, because deliberately or not they turned in 1943 to Mafia leaders to maintain order in a context of hatred and violence exacerbated by the Fascist regime. But the Italian government itself was grossly deceived in the same way, and undoubtedly other factors have contributed to the resilience of a disease that in the 1960s had looked to be dying out.

Palmi, Seminara and Bagnara Calabra nestle on Monte Sant'Elia, closing off the south end of the Gioia Tauro plain. The mount takes its name from a saintly 9th-century Byzantine hermit who encouraged a population dismayed by Arab incursions. Over this coast, the Costa Viola, the *autostrada* is forced high on to spectacular and vertiginous viaducts. Like many of these towns rebuilt in a spacious grid plan following an earthquake, Palmi is reminiscent of Noto in Sicily (probably the fairest and most famous example of post-seismic urban renewal in South Italy), but here and at nearby Seminara as also at Bagnara Calabra the rebuilding dates from 1908 rather than from 1783 or 1693 (the earthquake that destroyed Noto). Palmi has a folklore museum.

At Seminara was born about 1290 the Greek scholar and theologian Barlaam, most famous for attempting to teach Petrarch Greek, but most remarkable for his command both of western and of eastern culture; he spent his life between Thessalonica, Constantinople, Naples, Rome and Avignon, and was conversant both with Greek Neoplatonism and with Aquinas's Latin Aristotelianism. Though his thinking was nominalist, he was more Greek than Latin, brought up in Calabria in the Greek Church, though later he converted to the Latin, after which he became, by Petrarch's influence, bishop of GERACE. In about 1331 he held a public dispute in Constantinople with the leading scholar there, Nicephoros Gregoras,

in which according to Nicephoros he was trounced, but only
Nicephoros's account of the argument survives. He was also
humiliated and forced to recant in the theological controversy over
hesychasm (an early-day movement asserting personal communication from the deity) and was fruitlessly employed in efforts to
reconcile the two churches, so that in 1341 he returned to Naples.
There he helped Paolo da Perugia in the mythological compilation
that Boccaccio soon used for his own *Genealogie Deorum*, which
remained the standard handbook of classical mythology throughout
most of the Renaissance. He died in Avignon in 1348, probably the
best instance that can be found of unrelinquished Byzantine culture
surviving the Middle Ages in Calabria; for all his Latin connections
Greek was his first language.

From earthquakes Scilla, too, has suffered, but its site remains
intact on the northern edge of the straits of Messina, with a view
across to the tip of Sicily, and it still has a castle, now a youth hostel.
It sits on the promontory known to the Romans as Scyllaeum and to
the Greeks as the lair of the horrible mate of Charybdis, Scylla,
whose clashing rocks and whirlpools Ulysses braved. In Ulysses's
sea there now teem swordfish, caught traditionally by boats that
on return would be moored beneath the fisherman's houses that
prettily encircle the Chianalea bay. Eaten in steaks like salmon or
tuna, their flesh is whiter and creamier and sweeter: fresh, they need
simply to be cooked in oil to be succulent.

With a car or by train, one crosses to or from Sicily at Villa San
Giovanni, one more reason for the decline of Reggio some way to its
south. Reggio is a dull town; there is virtually nothing of interest in it
except its National Museum. The National Museum houses the most
important archaeological collection south of Pompeii, and is worth
visiting even if only to see its now famous Riace bronzes (see
below). Though the ancient Greek city of Rhegion was powerful,
though the Roman city of Rhegium was significant, though Reggio
became the capital of Byzantine Calabria and a metropolitan arch-
bishopric, the town has been wasted by too many earthquakes,
recorded from 91 BC to AD 1908. Its castle survives in part but as
transformed in the 15th century. The nearby Chiesa degli Ottomati
contains pieces retrieved from the demolished Greco-Norman monastery church of Santa Maria at Terreti, a village just above Reggio.

One enters Reggio Museum by a *telamon* (male caryatid), retrieved from the top of Montescaglioso (see THE VALLEY OF THE
BASENTO), very like those of the temple of Zeus at Agrigento in Sicily

though a little smaller. One goes down the main stair to reach the great hall that houses the Riace bronzes and also the Porticello head of a philosopher. Ample is the hall, and sometimes needs to be, for after their eventual installation following a political struggle for their possession the Riace bronzes have transformed attendance at the museum. Found off Riace on the Ionian coast in the 1960s they underwent years of restoration, but on their emergence in 1980 these two more-than-life-size ancient Greek bronze male statues put all the textbooks out of date and have thrown into the shade the Delphi *Charioteer*, the Athens *Poseidon*, and every other surviving Archaic or Classical Greek bronze. Only the Elgin marbles from the Parthenon are superior, and the case is strong that they are by the same author. Nothing of course is certain, but the consensus of their date in the middle of the 5th century BC seems unshakable (though one scholar has placed them in the Roman imperial period, where Richard Payne Knight in the early 19th century placed the Elgin marbles). If the world is small, then they may be associated with Pausanias's report of the Athenian monument to the victory of Marathon at Delphi, which had many bronze figures by Pheidias. The case is grounded on stylistic comparison but can be supported by a few other straws: a decree documents the existence of a bronze foundry in Athens in the middle 5th century, and the use in it of materials found in the Riace bronzes (but also no doubt in many others); it is not recorded who ran it but before he received the Parthenon commission (that is, *c*.450, exactly when these monuments belong by style) Pheidias was known in the first instance for his bronze statuary. Only two other sites from which they may have come are known, and they are less likely – although of the second of these, an unattributed monument in the Athenian *agora*, very little is known, and they may come from an unrecorded site. In favour of a Delphi origin may be the fact that one of the Riace bronzes has been damaged and repaired, which might have happened after the 4th-century BC earthquake at Delphi. Rather more telling, a Roman herm in Ravenna figuring Miltiades, hero of Marathon, closely resembles the head of the helmeted Riace statue and so might derive from the same monument.

So, the Riace bronzes are warriors, always nude, but who have now lost their arms; in particular one has lost his helmet so he has a grossly elongated head. The unhelmeted one especially stands more in repose after the battle than ready for action in it, but the torsion of both their bodies is nevertheless powerful, a palpable spiral convin-

cingly binding the exactingly portrayed musculature into an animate unity: they are paradigms of classical *contrapposto*. Obviously
they are idealized, but neither bland nor abstract, thanks to the
density, depth and detail of the modelling, especially of the beards,
which impart great force to the heads. They are more than life-size,
so that one gawps up at them (and in antiquity they would have
stood on a base); today as they must always have done they will
deliver a positive electric charge even to the most negative be-
holder.

In the same room is the detached bronze head of an intellectual,
only a few years later in date, also found in the 1960s in a shipwreck
that took place about 400 BC in the straits of Messina at Porticello
just south of Scilla. The rope-like strands of his long beard are
admirable, and the distant gaze under the bony forehead, although
idealized again no doubt, has an irreproachable naturalism. Further
fragments found in the wreck suggest that he, too, formed part of a
bronze group; it is conjectured that he might be the good centaur
Cheiron surrounded by his young charges, one of them Achilles.
Nearby displays give further, less spectacular but in some ways still
more tantalizing tokens of what has been found and may yet be
found as marine archaeology continues.

On the museum's ground floor the very considerable finds from
LOCRI are displayed in several rooms – including numerous offerings
from the sanctuary of Persephone there, among them painted tablets
retailing rare chthonic mythology; from the temple of Zeus the
bronze-tablet archive and a terracotta statue of a youth on a horse
(not closely modelled, because once painted); from another temple
at Locri there are Archaic statues of the Dioscuri also in terracotta.
The finds of other sites are displayed on the first floor: from Croton
there is some good-quality armour, including a belt with applied
figures; from Caulonia a fine mosaic with a marine monster, of a date
nearer the Roman period; from Cirò pieces from the site of the 5th-
century BC temple of Apollo.

On the second, top floor is the picture gallery, opening off the
stairs with two small fragmentary pieces of *Abraham visited by the
three angels* and *St Jerome*, attributed with perhaps too little caution
to Antonello da Messina. They show a meticulous technique profoundly and directly influenced by Netherlandish example; but if
they are by the youthful Antonello, it is strange they do not have
more in common with Colantonio, Antonello's supposed master in
Naples, or with some *Crucifixions* elsewhere also attributed to the

early Antonello. One may suspect the authorities' enthusiasm to
have works in their museum by this most important master of the
South Italian Renaissance, who was so very influential on Venetian
painting during his brief visit north in the mid 1470s. There follow
some 17th-century paintings, and then all too rapidly the Risorgimento period.

Squillace

The concrete despoilment typical of Gioia Taura spills over on to
the Ionian coast at the homonymous Gioiosa Ionica, across to which
a new *superstrada* will provide a fast link, tunnelling through by
Polistena. The Ionian coast is definitely inferior to the Tyrrhenian, as
seaside and in quality of resorts, but even so the SS 106 running
beside the shore ploughs frequently to a crawl in an almost ceaseless
succession of ribbon-development high streets strung from Catanzaro to Brancaleone (at the southernmost inside tip of the toe).
The old settlements are inland up the deeply cut valleys – for
example, Squillace, STILO, Mammola, GERACE.

However, just by Catanzaro itself, flanking the *lido* of Squillace,
the large archaeological zone or virtual park of Greek Skelletion,
Roman Scolacium, has become an oasis of olive groves and pasture.
In the middle of the zone the archeological headquarters has an
antiquarium that provides orientation as well as housing finds. Most
notable among these are a head of Augustus's son Germanicus
(found in 1984) and statues retrieved from the sizeable Roman
theatre (Hadrianic period), the most considerable surviving monument of ancient Scolacium. It had an amphitheatre, discernible but
not yet excavated. In addition part of the centre of both the Greek
and Roman cities has been exposed close by the antiquarium. At
various other points in the 'park' further detritus can be found, for
instance a group of mausolea. The charting of the ancient city has
been fairly recent, and it has not long been accepted that the
Roccelletta of Squillace, the largest monument in its midst, is not
ancient or high medieval, but was built among the ruins.

La Roccelletta or the abbey of Santa Maria della Roccella still
remains rather mysterious. It was founded before 1094, when it was
subtitled '*apud Palaepolim*, by Oldtown', that is, by what was left of
Scolacium, probably abandoned at the end of the 6th century. It is
recorded once more in 1287, and thereafter as a ruin. It is the largest

church in Calabria after GERACE, but not a single name, of abbot, bishop, saint, baron or king, can be associated with it. It has a long, broad but aisleless nave of six bays; the crossing has collapsed but the foundations of the protruding transepts remain; the main apse and choir and one side apse rise to their full, towering height, but the other side apse has gone; though it is blocked by rubble, there is a crypt. The church is all of brick, decorated with double blind arches over the windows and over niches – the niches an unusual and advanced motif, but one which has precedent, amid brickwork patterning of a different kind, in the remote 12th-century Santa Maria di Tridetti near Staiti. The Roccelletta has also been compared to Monreale and to Palermo cathedrals, and it is most unlikely that the church was yet built or started in 1094; it does not look even 12th-century, and is perhaps entirely of the 13th century, nearing completion by 1287 – for it seems it never was quite completed. Its missing crossing seems to have been influenced by the French plan that appeared in the 12th century at VENOSA – or possibly nearer by at Mileto – and then again, in the late 13th century, at ACERENZA. Here, however, there were no radiating chapels, only a deeper main apse and side-apses, but there were protruding transepts, not found in earlier Greco-Norman monastic churches, and in them probably stair-turrets, as at Venosa. Since the nave, an aiseless box, does not continue the lines of the eastern end, and since the crossing has no neat geometric shape, the logic of the original French design has vanished. It was not adopted but instead fused, rather unsynthetically, with the older plan of San Giovanni Vecchio at STILO and the other Greco-Norman abbeys of the region. The high, aisleless nave also recalls the late 13th-century Santa Maria del Casale at BRINDISI.

Utterly deserted, the enormous ruin of La Roccelletta or Santa Maria di Roccella rises almost unbelievably before the unprepared visitor. My sense of the bizarre was heightened when I discerned nearby a man up a tree, who turned out to be eating its fruit, loganberries. We discussed the contrast between the paradisiacal beauty and plenty of the landscape and the misery of its human occupants, an old saw of South Italy. He was not idle or a truant: he was a herdsman, and his animals were not far away. Although it turned out that he not only watched but owned his animals, he complained of the lack of economic opportunity and of what he called 'the corridor of labour' – he felt he had never had any choice about the way he gained his livelihood. It is true that in Calabria

La Roccelletta, Squillace

there is virtually no industry, let alone services. Why, I do not know.
It seems a paradox that so much emigration – to America a hundred
years ago or to northern Italy since the Second World War – should
have produced so little feedback, especially since such a high
proportion of emigrants return. But it has been recognized that
emigration in fact enabled a backward economy and conservative
society to remain unchanged, by ridding it of its dissidents and
adventurers, and by supplying it with money.

A little further south, by Copanello on the small headland of the
Punta di Staletti, the excavated outline of a 6th-century church
marks the site of the monastery of Vivarium founded by Flavius
Magnus Aurelius Cassiodorus, *quaestor* to the Ostrogothic king
Theodoric. Cassiodorus has not unfairly been described as the last
ancient and the first humanist in the Renaissance sense. Born in
Scolacium, he came home in old age and just before the time of the
Lombard invasions, about 555, founded a monastery, Vivarium,

which he endowed with a library and a scriptorium. He intended it
should preserve civilization and letters (he himself was author of a
short treatise on the copyist's art, besides his history, his sacred
commentaries, his compendia, and the *Variae*, the official letters he
wrote at the Ostrogoth court). Up the hill he founded a second
monastery, Castellense, with which the more vulnerable Vivarium
was forced not long after to amalgamate – but here the monastery
survived, despite Lombards, Saracens and Normans, and in a bull of
1219 pope Honorius III recalled the deemed existence within it of
Cassiodorus's Vivarium. Castellense's church has survived in a state
datable to about the time of Honorius's bull, a single-naved much
botched church including bits and pieces of a 6th-century original;
it is now known as Santa Maria del Mare. There is a fountain nearby
known as Cassiodorus's, and back in the church of Vivarium a
sarcophagus known as his tomb. By Vivarium steps have been found
cut in the rock, apparently leading down to the marine stewponds
Cassiodorus describes, where the fish might flit about 'in free
captivity', as he described it with a rhetorical flourish in the best
tradition. The church itself had a triconch east end, and a western
porch or narthex; if illustrations of the church (and its stewponds)
in manuscripts of Cassiodorus were reliable – but they are not – it
might be reckoned to have had two towers over the narthex.

With troubled times, Scolacium migrated to present Squillace on
a hill inland; the town retains its castle and olden aspect, thanks not
least to an edict of the mayor that all roofs should have tiles of
traditional and conforming colour. I met the mayor: I had thought I
should like to see the castle, and so was led to the mayory, and there
the mayor himself, on his last day of office as it turned out, enter-
tained me. He told me he would have liked to order all the town's
buildings to be faced in stone; he hated concrete. He showed me his
watercolours and brimmed with enthusiasm. But not much remains
to match the town's comparatively well documented medieval
history: the castle is greatly altered and anyway is overgrown (the
mayor, frustrated with the Soprintendenza's inactivity, had begun
excavating himself, but had no funds or expertise). The churches
are Baroque, except for the little Gothic building of Santa Maria della
Pietà. Formerly the castle was the residence of the Arab 'emirs'
established here from 904 until about 965, when the Byzantines
drove them out again; the Normans took it in 1059; possibly it took
rectangular shape around a courtyard in the time of Frederick II.
From 1493, when Alfonso II's daughter married Jofré Borgia, bastard

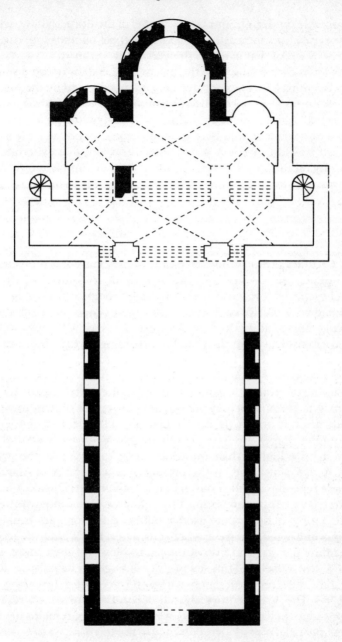

Cassiodorus's Vivarium, Squillace

of pope Alexander VI, Squillace was a fief of the Borgia family, whose arms remain on the castle gate. One of their number founded the nearby town of that name in the early 16th century.

As I was conversing with the mayor on the steps of the mayory a man swept past in an expensive car and was greeted by the mayor's aide. Scenting the reek of Mafia corruption, I enquired who he might be; he was a government clerk but could own such a car for no more sinister reason than that his father and brother were well off and he himself was not married. It did seem, however, that everyone not working on the land worked for the state or the municipality. From the mayory, the mayor was returning to his job in the post office.

Stilo

The Cattolica at Stilo enjoys an extraordinary fame: it is reproduced, for instance, on the cover of the *Blue Guide* to Southern Italy, and coaches pay it ceaseless visits. It looks remote in photographs, clinging to a cliff over a wide valley, and no doubt it once was, serving monks rather than parishioners (so its name is false), but the photographs leave out the railed path leading up to it, the souvenir stall and bar-shack a hundred yards away, the car-park. This little cross-in-square Greek church, like so many in Greece or other Byzantine provinces, is generally dated to the 10th century, though there is no certainty it may not be later; the frescos of standing saints inside are not obviously earlier than the 11th century, either. Its quintuplet domes are its most remarkable feature: the central one rises a little higher than the four lateral to give just the profile repeated, for instance, in the mosaic over a portal of St Mark's in Venice reproducing the church in the 13th century. Inside, the tiny church is rather disappointing: one column is club-footed, its length made up by an old capital used as a base; the domes are timid, the floor is unflagged, the frescos lack character. But it is a little icon of Byzantine history, and I do not mean to blow out the candle.

The town itself of Stilo sits prettily enough on its hillside site; it has some old streets but much of it was terraced after the earthquake of 1783. The 17th-century church of San Domenico, where Tommaso Campanella (1568–1639) spent some years, remains in ruins. His statue nearby marks the entrance to the town: he was a Calabrian for Calabrians, ardent and bizarre, combining science and theology, a visionary at odds with the world in which he lived. He is commemorated, however, primarily as a political theorist and critic, and as a precursor of the Risorgimento patriots for whom Calabria is well known. Another church, San Giovanni Teresti, is dedicated to a local hermit saint of the 11th century, St John Therestes, whose monastery, San Giovanni Vecchio, lies across the valley (see below). High above the town, and above the Cattolica as well, the Norman castle haunts the hill: it still has substantial remains of the towers and walls of the bailey, and the round towers flanking the entrance to the inner courtyard are largely intact, still menacing an arrival through raking slits. It is all overgrown. Inside there is later building, so it must have been long inhabited, but the castle is a typical bandit's or robber baron's lair, unassailable but as remote as an eagle's nest and incompatible – unlike a Byzantine fortress – with civilized life.

San Giovanni Vecchio or Giovanni Teresti is reached from the road that continues beyond Bivongi on the other side of the river Stilaro. Rediscovered only in the first years of this century, it is a ruined Greco-Norman monastery to be grouped with the Roccelletta below SQUILLACE, the Patirion at ROSSANO and, least well known, Santa Maria di Tridetti (see below) and the destroyed Santa Maria di Terreti above REGGIO. San Giovanni was consecrated in 1122; in theory, it should have been built after the Patirion and before Santa Maria di Tridetti and the Roccelletta, because its external decoration and its plan are intermediary: entirely of brick, the building is decorated externally with double blind arches which, at the ends of the transepts, are varied into two outward-facing half arches flanking a single central arch. The motif is developed still further in the apses, where the blind arches overlap to create an interlace as they do on the east end of the later Monreale and Palermo cathedrals, or, of course, on the earlier Durham cathedral. In plan San Giovanni has advanced over the Patirion by lengthening the choir, which protrudes one bay beyond the domical crossing; the extension also gave greater support to the more ambitious dome, which rises on a square base to a circular drum garlanded by arches or colonnettes. In the same way the main apse protrudes beyond the side-apses at the Roccelletta, but that has an additional transept before the nave begins. Both have an aisleless nave, broader than the choir but narrower than the transept. Inside, the overlapping corner arches or squinches under the dome are Sicilian in kind, recalling San Giovanni degli Eremiti or other churches in Palermo.

Further inland from Stilo the road leads eventually to Serra San

Bruno and a kind of miniature repeat of the Sila – from its narrowest point by Catanzaro the sock of the peninsula has widened again. Serra San Bruno is another broad, grand, post-seismic town, originally servicing the large nearby Charterhouse, later a great Cistercian abbey, and then again a Charterhouse. It was originally founded by the founder of the Carthusians himself, St Bruno. From Cologne, Bruno taught at the cathedral school in Reims, where his pupils included the future pope Urban II, the reformist Gregory VII's successor. After founding La Chartreuse, he left his own community to advise the newly elected Urban before moving on in 1091 to create, with the blessing of count Roger, a new community at Santa Maria del Bosco, where there is a mock-up of his cave, a few miles from the present Charterhouse. In the midst of a forest, the Charterhouse is inevitably a popular spot for a family day-excursion; but the late Renaissance church and cloister were ruined by the 1783 earthquake and the present Charterhouse beside them is 20th-century.

Near the mouth of the valley of the Stilaro, Monasterace is an evocative name, but no more. The archaeological site nearby has been identified as ancient Greek Caulonia, wrongfooting modern Caulonia (Castel Vetere) in the valley of the Allaro; the name was changed in 1863, while the site was discovered in 1912. In between the two is Riace, now famous for the two over-lifesize 5th-century BC bronzes found off its coast (installed in the museum in REGGIO). Roccella Ionica has a ruined castle, built against 16th-century corsairs; somewhere in the morass of Gioiosa Ionica there is meant to be a Roman theatre, and up beyond the old town it has a fine castle. Further inland Mammola and Grotteria are two picturesque historic settlements set high over their valleys. Past Mammola will run the fast road cutting through Monte Limina to the Autostrada del Sole; till then, the route from Locri past Gerace over the Mercante pass is the better.

Locri, Gerace

Modern Locri used not to exist before the railway came; the ruins of ancient Locri are some way to the south, beside the SS 106. It perished about the 7th century AD and was replaced by Gerace (the name is a corruption of Hagia Kyriake, St Cyriaca) on a better defensible site inland. Ancient Locri Epizephyrii or western Locri, so called to distinguish it from its mother-city Locri on the Corinthian Gulf, was an interloper on an Achaean coast, and was attacked about the middle of the 6th century BC by the more powerful Croton. However, aided by an apparition of the Dioscuri, Locri won the battle by the nearby river Sagras: the victory was so unexpected that 'truer than at Sagras' became a Greek way of saying 'too good to be true'. It is reported that Locri was the first Greek city to codify its laws on stone. Its shrine of Persephone was a goal of international pilgrimage – attracting even Carthaginians.

Beside the entrance to the archaeological zone, an antiquarium houses the lesser finds; the greater finds, for instance the equestrian Dioscuri statues from the 6th-century Ionic temple just across from the museum, are in REGGIO. The site is a large one and not so easy to find one's way around. Locri had not only an Archaic but a Hellenistic and Roman history. Beside the Ionic temple is a considerable stretch of ancient Greek wall (4th-century BC?), including one tower; further inland there is more such wall, in particular off the second turning inland south of the antiquarium (to Portigliola), which leads eventually to the so called Torre di Castellace (more ancient wall) and then on to the once famous sanctuary of Persephone, whence came the remarkable painted tablets now in Reggio. The road that leads inland past the museum leads towards another 5th-century Doric temple and to a Hellenistic or Roman theatre.

South of Locri, various marine establishments punctuate the SS 106 as it makes its increasingly lonely way round the Aspromonte towards Reggio, past resorts such as Bovalino, Brancaleone, Melito di Porto Salvo. Inland, there is little population: the 6000 ft Aspromonte is a hard mountain, true to its name. From Melito there is a scenic road that penetrates inland, past Bagaladi (from the Arabic for 'God's beauty') to Gambarie, headquarters of the recreation park Aspromonte (skiing, rambling, etc). Almost by the straits of Messina, Motta San Giovanni has the remains of a Norman castle; Motta is the same word as in English 'motte and bailey'. In this countryside there are several tiny ruined rural churches, among them San Nicola in contrada Zurgonà, datable to the 10th century. Otherwise the Aspromonte is remarkable for its bergamot, a citrus fruit used in perfume; 80 per cent of the world's production comes through Reggio.

At Brancaleone, on the furthest far side of the Aspromonte, off the road that ends at Staiti, there is a track to Santa Maria di Tridetti, another ruined Greco-Norman monastery rediscovered by the passionate archaeologist Paolo Orsi just before the First World War. In plan it is a standard nave-and-apse church, though the chancel is distinct from the nave and is flanked by deacons' chambers (pastophories). Its dome, constructed on squinches in Sicilian fashion (compare San Giovanni at STILO), once rose over two staggered square drums decorated with one more variation of blind arch: the flanking arches each are bisected and inverted to create a swallowtail shape, and the central one houses a niche – anticipating the niches of the Roccelletta near SQUILLACE. In the nave walls, in which the windows alternate with niches, the arches run the full height of the wall (as they do not at the Roccelletta, but do in Palermitan churches). Its pointed arches again have close Sicilian parallels. The ruin is usually dated perhaps too early: it might be placed beside rather than before Monreale and Palermo cathedrals, and antecedent only to the Roccelletta – therefore to the middle or later 12th century.

Poet of the Aspromonte – of all Calabria, but particularly the bare, remote Aspromonte – was Corrado Alvaro (1895–1956). He is best known for his short stories, vignettes of traditional, local life impinged upon by the rest of modern Italy but not absorbed by it. Or, to translate a blurb, 'In his tales Alvaro sings the simple and painful reality of his land . . . the world of Calabria seen through his eyes becomes something almost mythical, remote, archaic and perhaps doomed, like a remembered infancy . . . '. He was also an acute journalist, but his stories, while spare and truthful, enhance and magnify Calabria's sun, sea, rock, people and white houses, rather as if one were seeing them superbly photographed on location. His sometimes surreal, sometimes naturalistic cameos are written in Hemingwayesque prose with a Hopper-like intensity of description.

Gerace is a fitting climax to any tour and to this book. The town is still contained within its medieval walls; up the hill beyond the west end of the colossal cathedral one can walk the ramparts of the castle and take the view. North of the cathedral and the town's main café (Bar Cattedrale) rise the rude stone walls of the single-nave 12th-century San Giovanello, isolated in a piazza; nearby are the similar, but much more restored La Nunziatella and the Gothic church of San Francesco, with the intact tomb of Nicola Ruffo (died 1372). (The Ruffo were a prominent Calabrian baronial clan; one Folco Ruffo had been rhymester of the pre-Dantesque so called 'Sicilian' school of vernacular poetry.)

Almost incredibly, Gerace cathedral is one of the very grandest and most beautiful in Europe – and so little known! It can be dated to not later than the early 12th century by the report of a mosaic now lost figuring king Roger II – a parallel to the enamel above the ciborium in San Nicola in Bari (showing him with St Nicholas) and to the mosaic in the Martorana in Palermo (showing him crowned by Christ). When exactly it may have been begun is not clear: though little documented, Gerace had become a significant Byzantine civil centre and bishopric, and retained its importance at least for a time under the Normans. However, it remained strongly Greek – therefore an appropriate see for Barlaam of Seminara (see ON AND OFF THE AUTOSTRADA) – retaining a Greek rite until the late 15th century.

Norman is the scale, for the church is nearly 250 ft long. Greek is the utter simplicity and absence of mouldings: all that adorns the church is its series of antique columns, stolen no doubt from ancient Locri. It seems that something not too small antedated the extremely tall and spacious crypt, since there was a consecration recorded in 1045; but it need not have had the same plan, or the same two rows of columns running laterally across the transepts at right angles to the two rows underpinning the projecting choir. Certainly nothing like the present nave was then in place or even envisaged; instead the first Norman bishop would have initiated a new church perhaps in the 1080s, transforming into Latin form and scale what had been there before. So high is the crypt at Gerace that it might rather be called an underchurch, and it may be entered on the level at the east end; behind it the ground rises steeply, and it must have been made lofty in order to raise the upper choir and transept level with the nave. Whether and how the earlier building determined the shape of the choir and transept above is indeterminable; but such a deep choir between wide transepts had precedent already at CANOSA, and there is no reason to suppose French influence. There is nothing French in the nave arcades, each of two sets of five antique columns between massive piers. Instead the crypt, the long nave and even the atrium in front of its western façade place Gerace among churches of the Gregorian reform such as Salerno, TARANTO or OTRANTO.

Unlike Greco-Norman monastic churches, which are of brick, Gerace is of stone, in great blocks of clean ashlar. A restoration concluded in 1971 stripped out later superfetation, though not such structural changes as the chapel added in the 15th century, creating a second apse beside the main apse. Fortunately the dome on its sturdy squinches seems to have been restored after the earthquake of 1783 to just the way it was. Barrel vaults over the chancel and transepts support it; the original window embrasures illuminate it, flooding the open spaces but with a generally quiet and diffused light, hardening into spots and shadows towards the end of the day. A plain wooden roof covers the nave and aisles; the nave is untrammelled, the archivolts and piers in bare stone and the walls rendered. Though the columns bear antique capitals, there is no moulding at all at the imposts: the piers run up round into the arches without a mark. Of course it was once painted. Ink has been spilt on the question of why the colonnade should have been broken into two sets by a central pier, but it was the usual practice at that time to range columns between piers (one might compare BOVINO cathedral, the first church visited in this book): no doubt too long a row of those frail, delicate marble columns would have looked unsafe. As it is, the middle piers support diaphragm arches over the aisles. Shallow blind arches buttress the walls externally. Gerace cathedral is a stately and majestic building, exquisitely austere, without parallel in the world.

Afterword

I confess that when I drove through Basilicata and Calabria in the late spring of 1990 forming the impressions I have conveyed in this book, I failed to visit Aliano, the village in LATINIANUM to which Carlo Levi was exiled and about which he wrote *Christ stopped at Eboli*. In his book he calls it Gagliano, which, unfortunately, is the real name of another place, near Catanzaro, to which I drove instead. When I saw I had it wrong I was not prepared to drive back, but I did not look forward to covering up the fact that I had never been there. Fortunately, just before the book went to press, I had another chance to reach Aliano, because I was in Ancona and had a day free.

The point of this glimpse behind the mantle of the writer's authority is not to imply irritation at Carlo Levi, though changing Aliano's name was unnecessary and I have increasingly come to suspect that his book contains artificial colouring – purple tinged by Red. Instead I want to emphasize just how easy it is to get to South Italy. Ancona is on almost the same latitude as Florence, which is a long way north of Rome, but I was in Aliano by lunchtime despite not denying myself another attempt at getting into the castle of Lagopesole (still being restored) on the way. Admittedly I got up early. I hired (quite cheaply) a brand new fast car in which I flashed down the motorways and *superstrade* until I reached the VALLEY OF THE BASENTO; there I had to turn off on to narrow roads that went up mountains and down vales, but that was quite fun in itself while it lasted (although extensive reforestation obscures many of the views).

Then, having visited Aliano, I was in Rome by the evening. Once again the going was exceedingly easy, at least until I reached the approaches to Rome, where the volume of traffic became too great for comfort. I had zipped along yet another *superstrada* along the valley of the Agri and then past BRIENZA to join the Naples-Reggio *autostrada*, which carried me uninterruptedly northwards. A slight impediment to my progress were two road checks in Basilicata, but on both occasions the police were extremely polite, even gracious, and no mention was made of my speed. On the second occasion they were a little long about the documentation and one policeman was a most unprepossessing figure so that I began to recall Norman Douglas's description (which I have quoted under VENOSA) of cretinously malicious officialdom of the kind that prevailed in the days of Bourbon rule; but as he gave me back the documents his potato face widened in a cracking smile.

It would have been equally easy to continue down into Calabria; in fact it was rather less far down to Sicily on the *autostrada* than it was up to Rome. Though I have never done it, crossing over from the island for an excursion into mainland South Italy is an excellent option. There are numerous nice places to stay on the Tyrrhenian coast, which make a welcome change from too touristic Taormina but are not out in the sticks. Even leaving it a little late, it is seldom difficult to find places to stay overnight – except perhaps by the sea in August. It is perhaps a pity I have not written more about beaches and resorts: they are not all the same, and a little more *Holiday Which?* might have been useful. However, preferences are personal and conditions are ephemeral. Also, resorts are special holiday worlds *sui generis*, to which either one belongs – because you have booked it beforehand or because you light on it and like it – or one does not. They are not the sphere of a Traveller's Guide.

Though the sea is a constant complement to the landscape, it seldom invited me to sit by it – not when there was something else round the headland. However, in more than one book I have read on this country the author, having traversed the landscape, has ended staring out to sea. Thereby he has struck a suitably elegiac mood of contemplation, appropriate not only to departure but also to the odd fact that here it seems natural to be solitary and a stranger. Certainly for me South Italy is still a foreign country, in a way that the north of Italy, full of cities and sophisticated and responsive people, is not. One hears of foreigners living in certain spots only – for instance, around LECCE: it is not easy to integrate either economically or socially into what is still fundamentally a village outlook and way of life. Everybody here was born here, and everybody as they grow up acquires a certain mentality peculiar to the south. They can be rid of it only by leaving permanently.

What this mentality may be is not easy to sum up in a few words. But it is closed rather than open, and to a northerner's way of thinking ultimately dishonest, because it prefers an egotistically determined system of values to the facts. One might call it a metaphysical nepotism, a spiritual extension of the literal nepotism so common in South Italian society (less so in Puglia). Not everyone is a *mafioso*, but southerners themselves speak of *mafiosità*, a general state of mind. Not many belong literally to a *cosca* or Mafia band, but everyone belongs mentally to a family or *cosca* even if it is not criminal. Society consists of a mesh of autonomous, rival *cosche* which, even if they do not murder one another, still range against other 'families' atavistically disposed to civil war. It is a community both internecine and xenophobic.

In this book I have not greatly dwelt on the people of the south. Others who travel here may gush about their qualities and what a nice time they had but their rosy impression is based probably on superficials and unfamiliarity. It is the medieval monuments which catch my breath and fascinate my curiosity: they are unique in the world and very indequately known outside Italy.

If I had to choose one favourite place to which to return, it would be Canosa. (It is, besides, very easy to reach – just off the junction of the Naples-Bari and the Ancona-Bari *superstrade*.) The town had an imperturbable sleepiness, utterly remote from the 20th century. The plain, cool, dusty domes of the cathedral had a palpable antiquity, and the lustrous grey marble of which Acceptus's severe, august pulpit is made remains in the memory almost like a sensation on the tastebuds. Through a door from the south transept, enclosed in a kind of pit, Bohemund's tomb resounds with its miniscule challenge to the mighty: *Boamundus boat mundus*, it puns – the world shouts the world's shout. In such a silent place!

GENEALOGIES

The Hauteville and Hohenstaufen

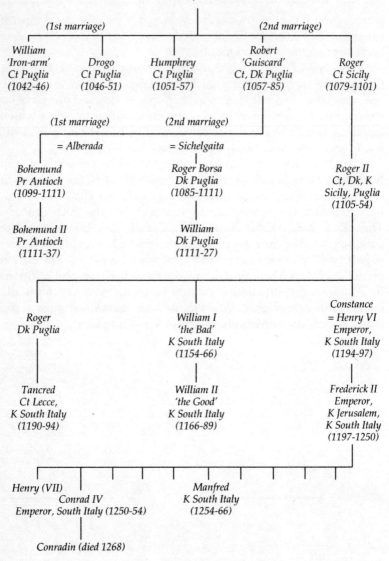

The Angevins

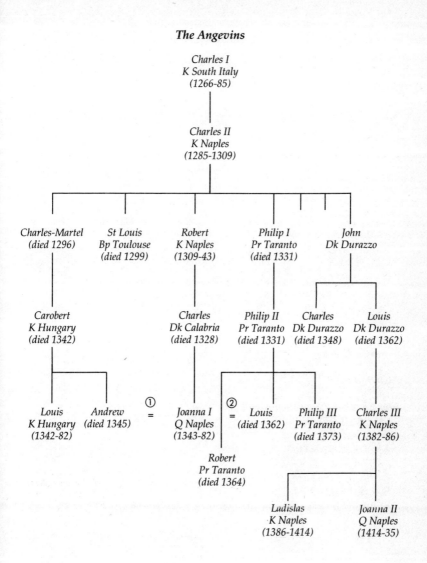

The Aragonese

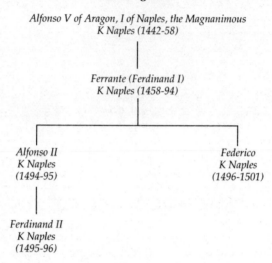

Alfonso V of Aragon, I of Naples, the Magnanimous
K Naples (1442-58)

Ferrante (Ferdinand I)
K Naples (1458-94)

Alfonso II
K Naples
(1494-95)

Federico
K Naples
(1496-1501)

Ferdinand II
K Naples
(1495-96)

Spanish Viceroyalty : 1504-1713

Austrian rule : 1713-34

Bourbons (and Napoleonic rulers)
   Charles III (1734-59)
   Ferdinand I (1759-99)
   Joseph Bonaparte (1805-08)
   Joachim Murat (1808-15)
   Ferdinand I (restored; 1815-25)
   Francis I (1825-30)
   Ferdinand II (1830-59)

Calendar of festivals

In the south of Italy quaint customs and folklore have tended to retreat in the face of modern uniformity – they lasted perhaps a little longer here than in the north but most have now disappeared just as finally. This is particularly regrettable in the case of those rituals which were very ancient – sometimes going right back to pagan times, not merely Roman but even Greek – and yet still claimed a place in the local calendar. However, it is not easy to maintain a faltering tradition, especially with no better motive than antiquarianism. A considerable effort was made in the late 19th century to record and document threatened popular culture of all kinds – from folk songs and proverbs to funeral rites, marriage ceremonies and seasonal festivities – particularly in Calabria, where the Greek and Albanian immigration had rendered it especially rich.

Nowadays virtually all that survive, at least that a visitor is likely to witness, are the annual and seasonal feasts: Christmas, Carnival, Easter, the feasts of the Virgin Mary, and local saints' days. In many cases the south has been less active than North Italy in reviving defunct antics, for example the Scoppio del Carro on Easter Day or the football match in historicizing costume of 24 June in Florence. Probably the most genuine are the religious festivals that attract great numbers of pilgrims, but they are, of course, more narrowly religious. Probably the most enjoyable are the wedding parties which one may happen upon and be sucked into. Not everybody likes boisterous crowds, and especially the fringes of fairs and festivals seem to become all the same, but the following list can be a guide to what to avoid as well as what to catch. Especially during the larger festivals it will be important to arrange somewhere to stay well beforehand.

At **Christmas**, the crib is popular throughout Italy, but particularly in the south villages vie with one another to create the most elaborate Nativity tableaux. Some of these are even preserved in chapels and museums. At Castro in the Salento a crib is set up in the Zinzulusa grotto, and at Nardò not far away a Nativity play is performed on **Christmas Eve** in another grotto; also another in another grotto at Grottaglie near Taranto.

The **Epiphany (6 January)** is celebrated at Lizzano in the same region with a Coming of the Magi play.

On **16 January**, Novoli near Lecce celebrates its patron saint's day (St Anthony) with a procession and a bonfire.

On **12 February**, at Palo del Colle near Bari there is a bumpkins' tournament, in which youths astride donkeys attempt to spear a suspended pig's bladder. (Carnival happens in one way or another everywhere, but especially around Catanzaro and Cosenza, where a rich Carnival tradition is recorded, featuring for example a notary who reads the dying Carnevale's last testament.)

Easter is again a universal feast. Often processions or plays re-enacting the way to Calvary are organized, for instance processions in Taranto on Maundy Thursday and Good Friday; a Passion play on Good Friday in the *gravina* at nearby Ginosa; a torchlight procession on Good Friday at Nemoli in Basilicata; more processions in Gioia Tauro and the surrounding region on Good Friday; a procession so slow it is known as 'the snail' (*caracolo*) on Holy Saturday at Caulonia on the Aspromonte; and real flagellations at Nocera in the same region.

May 4 is the feast-day of St Francis of Paola, which produces an enormous influx of pilgrims to Paola and various entertainments for them. Also on **4 and 5 May**, there is the first of two festivals of St Nicholas held at Bari; the other is on **6 December**. A procession in historicizing costume re-enacts the translation of the saint's relics to the church of San Nicola, and the following day his effigy is borne by a flotilla of boats. On **8–10 May** it is the turn of Taranto to celebrate the feast of St Cathal (San Cataldo). On the second Sunday in May, Crotone celebrates the efficacy of the image of the Madonna di Capo Colonna. And on **28 May** in Potenza St Gerald (San Gerardo) is honoured with a parade in supposedly Saracen costume.

On **2 June** the feast of Corpus Domini, commemorating the miracle of a bleeding host, is celebrated in Brindisi, where a white horse bears the host in a procession. This also occurs in Nemoli in Basilicata.

On **2 July** at Matera the float of the Madonna della Bruna is ripped apart after a parade: it is good luck to have a piece. At the end of July/begining of August there is a music festival at Martina Franca.

On **3 August** at Trani the town's patron saint, St Nicholas the Pilgrim, occasions the activity along the waterfront. The feast of St

Tripho (San Trifone) gives rise on **10 August** to a horseback procession at Adelfia outside Bari. On **14 August** Monopoli near Bari holds a festival for its icon, the Madonna della Madia, a feast that merges into the celebration for *ferragosto*, the **Assumption of Our Lady (15 August)**, a major holiday kept throughout Italy.

September and **early October** are full of local harvest and vintage festivals, or rather fairs, set up in fields and advertised by the wayside. It is also the season of mushrooms, about which a fuss is often made, and there are fairs of caged birds.

All Saints (1 November) is another important feast throughout Italy, centred on visits to the cemetery. On **16 November** St Roch (San Rocco) is celebrated at Roccanova in Basilicata.

On **6 December** Bari celebrates St Nicholas for the second time in the year, on his feast-day.

Sources and Bibliography

One reason for writing this book has been the comparative dearth of guides to the heel and toe of Italy. In guide-book series, Puglia, Basilicata and Calabria are merely an appendix to Naples and Campania or even the whole mainland south of Rome. However, there are more adequate guides in Italian and German. In what is designated 'travel literature' there are in English from this century only H. V. Morton, who is tedious (*A Traveller in Southern Italy*, 1969), Norman Douglas with his *Old Calabria* of 1915, not one of his best, and George Gissing's *By the Ionian Sea* of 1901, notable for its descriptions of some horrific conditions in Calabria. There is a somewhat larger literature of traveller's tales and impressions from the 19th and the later 18th century.

The bias of this book has been towards the medieval monuments, about which the current literature is mostly Italian, otherwise German or French. French historians have provided some fundamental works, among them Gay (*L'Italie méridionale et l'Empire Byzantin depuis l'avènement de Basile Ier jusqu'à la prise de Bari par les Normands*, 1904), Chalandon (*Histoire de la Domination Normande en Italie et en Sicile*, 1907) and Léonard (*Les Angevins de Naples*, 1954). In *The Normans in the South, 1013–1130* and *The Kingdom in the Sun, 1130–1194* (1967 and 1970), J. J. Norwich acknowledges Chalandon.

Naturally Germans have studied the Hohenstaufen. The best known book on Frederick II is Kantorowicz's *Kaiser Friedrich der Zweite* (1927; English translation 1931). The modern German authority is C. A. Willemsen, who has written a guide specifically to Puglia's medieval monuments (1971), but his work is unsatisfying. More interesting is H. Götze's book on Castel del Monte, first published in 1986. Though written in a bad style, there is now a good modern book on Frederick in English by D. Abulafia (1988).

For the history of medieval art and architecture, Bertaux's three-volume *L'Art dans l'Italie méridionale* of 1904 will not be supplanted, especially since it has been supplemented by a modern commentary of another three volumes, edited by A. Prandi (1978). On the sculpture, Wackernagel's *Die Plastik des XI. und XII Jahrhunderts in Apulian* of 1911 is fundamental. For Orsi's *Le chiese basiliane della Calabria* (1929) there is no substitute, either. Modern works unfortunately seldom consider Puglia and Calabria together, although by the same token it is a defect of this one not to include Campania.

In the last twenty years P. Belli d'Elia, currently director of the museum at Bari, has made lasting contributions to the history of Pugliese art, above all with the exhibition catalogue *Puglia XI Secolo* (2nd edition Bari 1987). With this and with the 1978 edition of the Puglia volume of the *Guida d'Italia del Touring Club Italiano*, which also bears her stamp, I learnt my way round the monuments. While the Puglia volume is one of the best of the whole series, the TCI guide to Basilicata and Calabria (1980 edition) rambles by comparison.

I have seldom entered into the *storia minuta* of the outer provinces of the Kingdom after 1500: such history as happens has to do overwhelmingly with Naples, and a work such as Acton's on *The Bourbons of Naples* (1956) is more or less irrelevant to the heel and toe. But Benedetto Croce's *Storia del regno di Napoli* of 1925 (translated as *History of the Kingdom of Naples*, 1970) is essential, though it requires prior knowledge of the facts. For the Risorgimento I have antipathy, and whether Garibaldi was black or white I do not care. Instead, the sociological work by P. Arlacchi on the context of the Mafia, in English as *Mafia, peasants and great estates* (1983) and as *Mafia Business* (1988), is extremely illuminating.

I am not fond of caves, though Puglia, if anywhere, might have led me to geology. I have also avoided all mention or discussion in the text of folklore, pageants, marriage parties and religious processions. For these shortcomings I apologize only stiffly. I apologize more penitently for the lack of archaeological descriptions of any technical standard. Although the ancient monuments of Puglia and Calabria do not compare either with Sicily for the Greeks or with Campania for the Romans, they are very considerable and there is a considerable literature, which I have not mastered. Too often A. R. Burn, *The Lyric Age of Greece* (2nd edition, 1967), told me just what I wanted to know.

This is a guide essentially for first-time visitors; obviously I could have put more in, but I would have had to leave more out. The nature of the region is such that there are advantages in joining a

210 SOURCES AND BIBLIOGRAPHY

tour, in particular the art tours run by Martin Randall (now Martin Randall Ltd, London). I have myself 'led' some of his tours to South Italy and used them to expand my own knowledge of the place. I have made grateful use of the Warburg Institute Library, which has many books formerly belonging to Evelyn Jamison, the outstanding Girton scholar on the Normans in Italy. I am glad to have written this book for John Murray (Publishers). Everything in the following bibliography is worth reading, but it is not comprehensive nor even a deeply informed selection.

H. Acton, *The Bourbons of Naples (1734–1825)*, London 1956

G. Alvisi, *La viabilità romana della Daunia*, Bari 1970

A. Ambrosi, *Architettura dei crociati in Puglia: il San Sepolcro di Barletta*, Bari 1976

P. Arlacchi, *Mafia, peasants and great estates. Society in traditional Calabria*, translated by J. Steinberg, Cambridge 1983

P. Arlacchi, *Mafia Business*, translated by Martin Ryle, Oxford 1988

P. Belli d'Elia, 'La cattedra dell'abate Elia', *Bollettino d'Arte* lix, January-June 1974, p.1

P. Belli d'Elia, 'L'officina barese: scultori in Bari nella seconda metà del XII secolo', *Bollettino d'Arte* xxvii, Sept-Oct 1984, p.13

P. Belli d'Elia, *La basilica di San Nicola a Bari*, Lecce 1986

P. Belli d'Elia, *Puglia XI Secolo*, 2nd ed. Bari 1987

H. Belting, 'Byzantine Art among Greeks and Latins in southern Italy', in *Dumbarton Oaks Papers* no. 28, 1974

E. Bertaux, *L'Art dans l'Italie méridionale*, Paris 1904, 3 vols; *Aggiornamento*, ed. A. Prandi, Rome 1978, 3 vols

G. Bertelli and M. Falla Castelfranchi, *Canosa di Puglia fra tardo-antico e medioevo*, Rome 1981

C. Bozzoni, *Calabria Normanna: Ricerche sull'architettura dei secoli undicesimo e dodicesimo*, Rome 1974

C. Bozzoni, *Saggi di architettura medievale: La Trinità di Venosa. Il Duomo di Atri*, Rome 1979

A. R. Burn, *The Lyric Age of Greece*, 2nd edn. London 1967

M. S. Calò Mariani, *L'arte del Duecento in Puglia*, Turin 1984

F. Carabellese, *L'Apulia ed il suo comune nell'alto medio evo*, Bari 1905

F. Chalandon, *Histoire de la Domination Normande en Italie et en Sicile*, Paris 1907, reprinted New York 1969

B. Croce, *Storia del regno di Napoli*, Bari 1925, etc; English translation *History of the Kingdom of Naples*, Chicago 1970

C. Di Taranto, *La Capitanata al tempo dei Normanni e degli Svevi*, Matera 1925

Ed. G. Dotoli, *Puglia Europea* (selected, translated accounts by 18th-and 19th-century travellers to Puglia), Bari 1985, etc.

C. J. Eiseman and B. S. Ridgeway, *The Porticello Shipwreck*, University of Texas 1987

V. von Falkenhausen, *Untersuchungen über die byzantinische Herrschaft in Süditalien vom 9. bis ins 11. Jahrhundert*, Wiesbaden 1967; Italian translation *La dominazione bizantina nell'Italia meridionale dal IX all'XI secolo*, Bari 1978

Federico II e l'arte del '200 italiano. Atti della 3a settimana di studi di storia dell'arte medievale dell'Università di Roma, ed. A. M. Romanin, Galatina 1980, 2 vols.

W. Fuchs, 'Zu den Grossbronzen von Riace', in *Praestant Interna. Festschrift für Ulrich Hausmann*, Tübingen 1982

T. Garton, *Early Romanesque Sculpture in Apulia*, Ph.D. thesis, Courtauld Institute of Art, London, 1975; published New York and London 1984

C. Garzya Romano, *Calabre et Basilicate Romanes*, Ste-Marie de la Pierre-Qui-Vire 1988

G. Gay, *L'Italie méridionale et l'Empire Byzantin depuis l'avènement de Basile Ier jusqu'à la prise de Bari par les Normands*, Paris 1904; Italian translation Florence 1917

G. Gissing, *By the Ionian Sea. Notes of a Ramble in Southern Italy*, London 1901

A. Giuliano, 'I grandi bronzi di Riace: Fidia e la sua officina', in *Bollettino d'Arte*, special number no. 3, II, 'Due bronzi di Riace', 1984

A. Giullou, *Studies on Byzantine Italy*, London 1970

H. Götze, *Castel del Monte. Gestalt und Symbol der Architektur Friedrichs II*, 3rd edition Munich 1991

F. Jacobs, *Die Kathedrale S. Maria Icona Vetere in Foggia: Studien zur Architektur und Plastik des 11.-13. Jh. in Süditalien*, Ph.D. dissertation, Hamburg 1968

E. M. Jamison, *The Norman Administration of Apulia and Capua* (1913), edd. D. Clementi and T. Kölzer, Aalen 1987

E. G. Léonard, *Les Angevins de'Naples*, Paris 1954

I Longobardi, exhibition catalogue, Cividale di Friuli and elsewhere, ed. G. C. Menis, Milan 1990

Mostra dell'arte in Puglia dal tardo antico al Rococò, ed. M. D'Elia, exhibition catalogue, Pinacoteca di Bari, Rome 1964

D. Minuto and S. Venoso, *Chiesette medievali calabresi a navata unica*, Cosenza 1985

P. Orsi, *Le chiese basiliane della Calabria*, Florence 1929

M. Paone, *Chiese di Lecce*, Lecce 1979, 2 vols

M. Petrignani and F. Porsia, *Bari*, Bari 1982

E. Piceno and M. Monteverdi, *I De Nittis di Barletta*, Barletta 1971

La Puglia fra Bisanzio e l'Occidente, Milan 1980

La Puglia tra Barocco e Rococo, Milan 1982

L. Renzo, *Archidiocesi di Rossano-Cariati*, Rossano 1990

Roberto Guiscardo e il suo tempo. Relazioni e communicazioni nelle prime giornate normanno-svevo (Bari, maggio 1973), Rome 1975

H. W. Schwartz, 'Die Baukunst Kalabriens und Siziliens im Zeitalter der Normannen', *Römisches Jahrbuch* vi, 1942–44, p.1

C. Shearer, *The Renaissance of Architecture in Southern Italy: A Study of Frederick II of Hohenstaufen and the Capua Triumphator Archway and Towers*, Cambridge 1935

S. Schwedhelm, *Die Kathedrale S. Nicola Pellegrino in Trani und ihre Vorgängerkirchen*, Ph.D. thesis, Tübingen 1972

C. Settis Frugoni, 'Il mosaico di Otranto: modelli culturali e scelte iconografiche', *Bullettino dell'Istituto Storico Italiano per il Medio Evo e Archivo Muratoriano* lxxxii, 1970

M. Wackernagel, *Die Plastik des XI. und XII Jahrhunderts in Apulien*, Leipzig 1911

C. A. Willemsen, *Apulien, Kathedrale und Kastelle: ein Kunstführer durch das normannisch-staufische Apulien*, Cologne 1971

C. A. Willemsen, *Castel del Monte*, Italian translation Bari 1984

R. B. Yewdale, *Bohemond I, Prince of Antioch*, Princeton 1924, repr. Amsterdam 1970

Die Zeit der Staufer. Geschichte, Kunst, Kultur, exhibition catalogue, Württembergisches Landesmuseum, Stuttgart 1977–79

Index of places

Index of places

This is an index to places in southern Italy mentioned or discussed in the book. Bold figures indicate a more extended discussion and the main mention. Accents indicate the stress. Objects and individual buildings are listed under the village or city in which or near which they stand, but some isolated abbeys, etc., appear under their own name. Battles (for example, of Benevento) and Councils (for example, of Bari) are indexed in the Index of people and terms. Places outside South Italy to which reference is made (for example, Paris, Palermo) also appear there.

Canosa, 4, 21–2, **51–9**, 201;
bishopric, 51, 65, 104;
bishop's throne, 55–6, 95,
142; cathedral, **52–6**, 97, 197;
pulpit (cathedral), 43, 54–5,
103, 142; San Leúcio, 52–3
Canusium (modern Canosa), 4,
21–2, 73, 105
Capitanata, 23, 29, 32, 36, 147
Capo Bianco, 124
Capo Colonna, 178
Capo d'Ótranto, 136
Capo Rizzuto, 178
Capo Santa Maria di Léuca, 134
Capo San Vito, 122
Capo Spúlico, 162
Capo Vaticano, 181
Capua, 3, 4, 91; cathedral, 26;
duchy, 4; Gate, 3, 4, 6, 7;
museum, 7
Capurso, 107
Carapelle river, 4, 13, 22, 23, 51
Carovigno, 109
Carpignano, 134, 138, 143
Carpino, 42
Casamassima, 110
Casareno, 137
Casaranello, 121, **137–8**
Cassano allo Ionio, 166–7
Castel del Monte, xiv, 5, 17, 31,
41, 44, **81–6**
Castel Fiorentino, 31, 33, 35
Castellana, 110; caves, 109, 110,
111
Castellaneta, 89
Le Castella, 178
Castelpagáno, 41
Castel Vétere (modern
Caulonia), 194
Castro, 136, 205
Castrovíllari, 164, **165–6**
Catánia castle, 30, 84, 176
Catanzáro, xiii, xvi, 156, 170,
179–80, 206

Caulonia, 186, 194
Caulónia, 194, 206
Céglie Messápico, 105, 109, 120
Célico, 171
Cerignóla, 23, 51
Cerváro river, 4, 11, 51
Cesano, 76
Chianaléa bay, 184
Chianca, dolmen, 70
Chieuti, 35
Cilento, 148, 149
Cirella, 164
Cirella Vecchia, 164
Cirignano, 70
Cirò, 178, 186
Cittanova, 182
Civitate, 35
Colloreto, 164
Colobraro, 154
Conversano, 69, 71, 81, **107–8**,
110
Copanello, 189
Copertino, 134, 136
Copia Thurii, 163
Corato, 73, 74; San Vito, 70,
74–5
Corigliano, 134
Coscíle river, 162, 164
Cosenza, xiii, xvi, 58, 87, 156,
170, **172–5**, 180, 206
Costa Viola, 183
Cotronei, 175
Craco, 153
Crati river, 162, 163, 175
Croton (modern Crotone), 161,
162, 163, 186, 194
Crotone, 170, **177–8**, 206
Cupersanum (modern
Conversano), 107

Daunia (modern Tavoliere), 20,
23
Deliceto, 13
Diamante, 164

Peter's, 95, 97; Vatican library, 167
Rosarno, 182
Roseto, 162
Rossano, 6, 8, 167–8, 170, 171; Patirion, 39, 108, 169–70, 171, 181, 193
Rubi (modern Ruvo), 4, 105
Rutigliano, 107
Ruvo di Puglia, 4, 13, 73, 74–6; cathedral, 62, 75–6, 95

Sagras river, 195
Salandra, 157
Salapia, 50
Salénto peninsula, 70, 119, 128, 149
Salerno, 6, 87, 90; cathedral, 95, 97, 141, 197
Salénto peninsula, 123
Salpi, 50
Samarra, 59
Sammichele di Bari, 110
Samnium, 149
San Basílio (near Terlizzi), 76
San Chírico Rapáro, 153
San Demétrio Coróne, 171
San Dómino (Tremiti islands), 37
San Felíce, 40–1
San Ferdinando di Puglia, 50
San Giovanni in Fiore, 171
San Giovanni in Lamis, 41
San Giovanni Rotondo, 41, 44
San Marco Argentano, 163
San Marco in Lamis, 41
San Mattéo in Lamis, 41
San Menaio, 42
San Michele, 15
Sannicandro Gargánico, 41
San Nicóla (Tremiti islands), 37
San Nicóla di Varáno, 41
San Nicóla in contrada Zurgonà, 195
San Pietro di Balsignano, 79

San Pietro Vernótico, 121
San Ruba, 182
San Sevéro, 34
Sant' Ágata di Puglia, 13
Santa Maria d'Anglona, 154, 169
Santa Maria del Bagno, 136
Santa Maria del Bosco, 194
Santa Maria della Catena, 167
Santa Maria della Lizza, 137
Santa Maria dell'Alto, 122
Santa Maria delle Cerrate, 123
Santa Maria di Calena, 41
Santa Maria di Cesano, 76
Santa Maria di Crepacore, 121
Santa Maria di Gallana, 121
Santa Maria di Léuca, 134, 137
Santa Maria di Pierno, 16
Santa Maria di Terreti, 184, 193
Santa Maria di Tridetti, 46, 188, 193, 195
Sant'Ángelo abbey, 153
Santa Severina, 85, 158, 169, 175, 176–7
Santéramo in Colle, 88
Sant'Eufémia plain, 180
Sant'Eustachio (near Terlizzi), 76
San Vito (near Polignano), 107
San Vito dei Normanni, 109
Sauro river, 153
Scaléa, 164
Scanzani, lido, 162
Scilla, 184
Scolacium (modern Squillace), 187, 189
Scyllaeum (modern Scilla), 184
Seminara, 183
Seppanníbale, 6, 108, 109, 121
Serracaprióli, 35
Serra San Bruno, 182, 194
Síbari, 163
Síbari plain, 162, 169, 175
Siberene (modern Santa Severina), 176
Sila, xvi, 170–2, 194

Index of people and terms

Index of people and terms

Bold figures indicate a page where a definition or explanation can be found.

Calabria, duke, 119
calanchi, 151
Calixtus II, pope, 24
Campanella, Tommaso, 192–3
Cancho, Alvise, 101
Cannae, battle (216 BC), xv, 20, 60, 153
Cannae, battle (AD 1018), 24, 60
Caravaggio, Michelangelo da, 165
Carducci, Achille, 133
Carmelites, 133
Carobert, king, 8, 166, 203
Carthaginians, 195; *see also* Hannibal
Carthusians, 194
casali, 70
Cassiodorus, Flavius Magnus Aurelius, 189–90
castrati, 133
catepan, 23, 91
Cathal (Cataldo), saint, 117, 118, 206
cave-churches, *see* Index of places: Ginosa, Gravina di Puglia, Grottaglie, Laterza, Monte Sant'Angelo, Massafra, Mottola, Poggiardo, Rapolla, San Vito dei Normanni
cave-dwelling, *see* troglodytism
Cefalù, 14
Celestines, 131
ceramics, 73, 75–6, 119
Charlemagne, 5, 37, 42; chesspieces 'of', 56
Charles, duke Calabria, 9, 166, 203
Charles, duke Durazzo, 9, 203
Charles V, emperor, 9; castles, 64, 124, 130
Charles I, king Naples, xv, 8, 29, 31, 44, 149, 175, 203
Charles II, king England, 132
Charles II, king Naples, 8, 9, 28, 29, 31, 127, 181, 203
Charles III, king Naples, 9, 203

Charles-Martel, 8, 203
La Chartreuse, 194
Charybdis, 184
Cheiron, 186
chesspieces, 56
chiancarelle, 74, 81, 109, 111
Chrysolea, wife Leo, 134
church forms: ambulatory, 18, 65; cave, 15, 45; *see also* cave-churches; chevet, 18, 64, 84; contracted cross, 70, 71, **74–5**, 76, 79; cross-in-square, 120, 140, 143, 159, 168, 192; crutch capitals, 77, **126**; crypt, 18, 33, 48, 54, 66, 77, 92, 100–1, 140, 141–2, 156; domical nave, 5–6, 41, 47, 68–9, 71, 73, **79–80**, 107, 109, 110, 121; doubled columns, 65, 66; Greco-Norman, 39, 46, 73, 127, 153, 154, **169**, 188, 193, 195, 197; 'Gregorian', 95, 117, 197; hybrid, 15, 71, 130; *matronea*, 66, 71, 77, 97, 98, 102; nave with east dome, 138, 153, 177; north Puglia type, 13, 26, 33, 35, 46, 48; pastophory, 12, 196; pattern of San Nicola, Bari, 66, 70, 72, 73, 77, 79, 88, 102, 108; porches, 63, 67, 81, 98; *porticus*, 12; quadrant vaults, 41, 47, 69, 107, 109, 126; Romanesque, 126; rose-windows, 98; square, 48, 68; squinches, 196; T-shaped (boxed T), 12, 66, 77, **95–7**; tetraconch, 52; triconch, 190; Venetian Gothic, 121
Cicero, Marcus Tullius, 161
Cicolella family, 32
Cima da Conegliano, 158
Cimarosa, Domenico, 178